Please remember that this is a library book,
and that it belongs only temporarily to each
person who uses it. Be considerate. Do
not write in this, or any, library book.

Empowering Older Adults

**Elinor B. Waters
Jane Goodman**

EMPOWERING OLDER ADULTS

Practical Strategies for Counselors

Jossey-Bass Publishers

San Francisco • Oxford • 1990

EMPOWERING OLDER ADULTS
Practical Strategies for Counselors
by Elinor B. Waters and Jane Goodman

Copyright © 1990 by: Jossey-Bass Inc., Publishers
                     350 Sansome Street
                     San Francisco, California 94104
                                &
                     Jossey-Bass Limited
                     Headington Hill Hall
                     Oxford OX3 0BW

Library of Congress Cataloging-in-Publication Data

Waters, Elinor B.
    Empowering older adults : practical strategies for counselors /
Elinor B. Waters, Jane Goodman. — 1st ed.
        p.   cm. — (The Jossey-Bass social and behavioral science
series)
    Includes bibliographical references and index.
    ISBN 1-55542-286-1
    1. Aged — Counseling of — United States.   2. Aged — United States —
Psychology.   I. Goodman, Jane, date.   II. Title.   III. Series.
HV1461.W36   1990
362.6'6 — dc20   90-37167
                                                                      CIP

Manufactured in the United States of America

The paper in this book meets the guidelines for
permanence and durability of the Committee on
Production Guidelines for Book Longevity of the
Council on Library Resources.

JACKET DESIGN BY WILLI BAUM

For information about our audio products, write us at:
Newbridge Book Clubs, 3000 Cindel Drive, Delran, NJ 08370

FIRST EDITION

Code 9088

**The Jossey-Bass
Social and Behavioral Science Series**

We dedicate this book, with love,
to our husbands and to our parents and children
— the generation that came before
and the one that follows.

Contents

Preface   xi

The Authors   xv

**Part One: Identifying and Meeting the Needs
of Older Adults**   **1**

1. Empowerment: A Framework for Counseling   3

2. Understanding Why Clients Seek Help   26

3. Assessing Older Clients   47

4. Getting Started: Techniques for Working with
Older People   65

Part Two: Major Issues Affecting Older Adults   **81**

5. Developing and Maintaining Self-Esteem   83

6. Planning for Work and Leisure   97

7. Relationships with Family Members   113

8. Adjusting to Loss and Grief   134

Part Three: Action Strategies for Counselors   157

9. Employing Special Techniques   159

10. Developing Programs and Workshops   180

11. Advocating for Individuals and Groups   199

    Resources: Selected Organizations in the
    Aging Network   215

    References   219

    Index   235

Preface

The graying of America is much more than a catchy phrase. At present, approximately 12 percent of the U.S. population is over sixty-five. Within the next twenty to thirty years, as the baby boomers grow old, this percentage is expected to increase dramatically, perhaps reaching twenty-one percent by 2030. The need for a book such as this one stems from more than mere statistics, however. With the greatly increased numbers of older people comes a corresponding increase in the need for mental health services for older people and their families.

This book suggests counseling strategies for the 95 percent of older persons who live in the community and wish to remain independent as long as possible. Despite their independence, most of these older people experience (or fear experiencing) many losses, which constitute a threat to their self-esteem and sense of power. Our goal here is to provide counselors with information and techniques that will assist them in empowering these older people. That goal is represented by the empowerment model that is the theme of the book. It suggests that older adults can *learn, change,* and *take control* of their lives. Counselors and other mental health professionals trained to assist people in coping with normal developmental crises and transitions can be extremely helpful in this empowerment process. However, most of today's practicing counselors were trained in programs that stressed counseling of younger people. Older adults thus are a new client population, and many counselors need to adapt their skills to working with this new group.

In learning to serve a new population, counselors clearly do not have to start from scratch. There are many more similarities than differences in counseling older and younger people. Regardless of the age of their clients, counselors need to listen actively, respond to thoughts and feelings, ask effective questions, and assist people in making decisions and solving problems. However, some modifications in basic skills may be called for. For example, confrontation may need to be done more gently, although avoiding it altogether would be patronizing. Planning is necessary, but long-range plans may be inappropriate. Assessment of client interests and abilities is essential, but traditional measures may be of questionable value with an older population.

Another challenge is that many of today's older people, who grew up in an era when independence was revered, may be leery of counseling or uninformed about its availability and benefits. It seems likely, however, that this orientation will change. Coming generations of older people will be better educated and more familiar with the idea of emotional problems than older adults now are and will probably be more willing to utilize mental health services. Again, adaptation may be called for. Older adults who resist asking for therapeutic help may be receptive to "consulting" or to attending a class on personal growth. Counselors need to understand the importance of "by-the-way" counseling and know how to create "by-the-way" opportunities.

Audience

Empowering Older Adults is practitioner-oriented. Its joint emphasis on describing counseling skills and providing information about aging is designed to round out the training of a variety of helping professionals. Just as many practicing counselors and therapists have limited knowledge of aging, many people working in the field of aging have little or no training in counseling. Nevertheless, staff members in senior centers, congregate living facilities, and adult day-care centers are frequently called on to perform counseling functions. The book will be useful to these professionals as well as to students who wish to prepare for careers in counseling and would like to have older adults and/or their families as part of their clientele.

Throughout the book, we have intertwined theory and practice. The goal is to help readers know what to do with what they know. We also want readers to understand the major issues that surface in counseling older people so they can effectively address them. For example, counselors need to be able both to provide older people with information about the normality of their reactions to transitions and losses and to help them cope with the feelings engendered. Counselors need to understand intergenerational conflicts about values or life-styles so they can help family members talk about and negotiate these differences. They need to be aware of the typical concerns of older adults so they can help clients cope with problems ranging from the discovery of gray hair to the loss of a spouse. They need enough information to be able to assist clients in making decisions as diverse as whether and where to retire and whether and when to drive. Our hope is that the information and strategies we present will empower counselors as well as older people, and that this book will help counselors see gerontological counseling as an exciting field in its own right.

Overview of the Contents

The book is divided into three major parts. Part One includes theoretical and demographic background information. It provides a conceptual framework, looks at the needs of the older population from the viewpoint of both clients and counselors, and discusses similarities and differences in counseling younger and older people. Part Two examines four major areas of life in which older adults may seek counseling help. In chapters on self-esteem, family relationships, work and leisure, and loss, readers will find information on the relevance of each topic to older adults, along with recommendations for counseling interventions. Part Three emphasizes the multiple levels on which counselors work. One chapter is devoted to special techniques

for helping older adults, individually or in groups; one deals
with the role of counselors as program developers; and the last
chapter challenges counselors to function as advocates for older
people. Details about the contents of each chapter are provided
in the part introductions.

Acknowledgments

We would like to thank our editor, Gracia A. Alkema,
who approached us with the idea for the book and believed we
could do it; our colleagues at the Continuum Center and at Oakland University who supported us during our work; and Nancy
K. Schlossberg, who encouraged us personally and helped sustain our interest in adult development and aging.

Rochester, Michigan   Elinor B. Waters
August 1990   Jane Goodman

The Authors

ELINOR B. WATERS is director of the Continuum Center and adjunct associate professor of education at Oakland University in Rochester, Michigan. She received her B.A. degree in sociology from Antioch College, her M.A. degree in sociology from the University of Chicago, and her Ed.D. degree in guidance and counseling from Wayne State University. She is a nationally certified counselor.

In 1988–1989 Waters was president of the Association for Adult Development and Aging, a division of the American Association for Counseling and Development. She has held a variety of positions in the organization and its branches over the years. She and the Continuum Center under her directorship have been honored for work in adult counseling and aging by the National University Extension Association, the Michigan legislature, and the Michigan Association for Specialists in Group Work.

She has published widely in the field of aging as well as on topics related to sex-role stereotyping, careers, and group-leadership training. In previous careers she has worked as a researcher for human-development institutes in Michigan, Ohio, and Jamaica, West Indies, and as a representative for the Michigan Civil Rights Commission.

JANE GOODMAN is associate director of the Continuum Center at Oakland University. She received her B.A. degree in sociology from the University of Chicago and her M.A. and Ph.D. degrees in guidance and counseling from Wayne State University. She is a nationally certified counselor and career counselor.

Goodman has been actively involved in professional associations for many years; she has served as president of the Michigan Association for Counseling and Development, as editor of that association's journal, and as secretary of the National Career Development Association. She has received awards from the Michigan and National Career Development Associations, the Michigan Association for Specialists in Group Work, and the National University Extension Association. She has published and presented workshops for professionals in the areas of aging, career development, leadership training, and group process. Her past professional careers have included teaching at the elementary and university levels, technical writing, research, and running an art gallery.

Empowering Older Adults

PART ONE

Identifying and Meeting the Needs of Older Adults

The four chapters in this part set the stage for the rest of the book. Chapter One explores such basic questions as why counseling helps older adults and where and how counselors work with this population. We consider the similarities and the differences in counseling older and younger people. In our view, similarities outnumber differences, but the differences must nevertheless be heeded. The section on demographics enables readers to survey the older population in order to identify current and future needs. It looks at this population both as a whole and in subgroups based on sex, age, education, race, ethnicity, and socioeconomic status. Above all, this chapter exhorts readers to be alert for ways in which they can help older adults gain and maintain control over their lives.

Chapter Two begins with a theoretical section that presents various approaches to adult development and informs readers of our orientation so that they have a basis for interpreting our views. The chapter considers reasons why older adults seek counseling. It examines the differences in meaning between temporary crises and long-term problems and between normal transitions and abnormal ones, and considers the implications of these differences for the kinds of help needed. For example, older people react differently to short-term hospitalizations than to long-term disabilities, to needing bifocals than

1

to becoming blind, to voluntarily retiring at sixty-five than to being forced to retire at fifty-two.

Chapter Three defines assessment in broad terms, discusses special considerations in assessing older people, and underlines the crucial role of assessment in determining the services older people need. It suggests how to evaluate an older person's physical functioning and ability for self-care as well as emotional and cognitive abilities. The chapter presents a scheme for using Maslow's hierarchy of needs in assessing older adults. Several case studies suggest possible ways to determine the needs of older people.

Chapter Four is designed to help counselors think about basic interactions with older clients and actions they can take on behalf of these clients. It covers such down-to-earth issues as how to establish a relationship and help clients solve problems. It presents suggestions for making the counseling office or other work site meet the needs of older clients and for arranging contact with the aging network. It helps counselors think about how they can adapt their basic skills for an older clientele.

1

Empowerment:
A Framework for Counseling

Clara Jones, a seventy-two-year-old widow, was released about two months ago from the hospital after having a minor stroke. Her doctors have assured her that she has made a full recovery and that she has little reason to fear a recurrence. However, she has been having trouble sleeping, is not eating well, and has not resumed her formerly active social life. When her friends call, she finds an excuse not to see them. Susan Walker, her married daughter, received a call from one of Mrs. Jones's friends expressing her concerns. Susan has spoken to her brothers, and they have all been calling their mother to say they are worried. The family has persuaded Mrs. Jones to see a counselor, and the intake worker at your agency has assigned her to you. She comes in and says that she is here because her children wanted her to come and that she is fine; she just does not feel like doing much. "I'm an old woman; why can't they let me be in peace? I'm happy being by myself."

Why Counseling Works with Older Adults

Mrs. Jones and her family have turned to a counselor for help. For the kinds of issues that concern them, counseling should prove to be an appropriate and useful service. Mrs. Jones can benefit from learning about herself and her current situa-

3

tion, changing some of her self-defeating behaviors, and regaining control over her life—goals that fit well with counseling's philosophy and approach. Most counselors want to help clients identify their strengths, to assist them in bringing these strengths to bear on new problems as they arise, and thus to empower them. Our approach to counseling older people presumes that older adults can *learn,* can *change,* and can *take charge of their lives.* This belief system is graphically presented in Figure 1. This framework countermands the old saw "You can't teach an old dog new tricks" and creates a new one: "That depends on the dog, the tricks, and most of all on the teaching strategy!"

If we look again at Mrs. Jones, it seems likely that counseling may help her to *learn* about herself, to *develop and use some new behaviors,* and *to discover ways of taking charge* of her life rather than withdrawing. With appropriate help she may find some new ways to handle her reduced energy and develop a social life that fits her current needs. She may decide to experiment with new behaviors, perhaps trying several activities until she

Figure 1. A Paradigm for Empowering Older Adults.

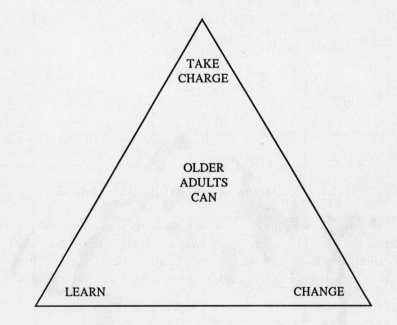

finds some that satisfy her. With proper support and encouragement, Mrs. Jones can stop reacting against her former, no longer
functional, way of life, and start acting to find new ways of living.

The first step for the counselor is probably to help Mrs.
Jones disentangle her needs from the wishes of her friends and
children. Clearly, their worry is appropriate; Mrs. Jones is not
happy and is possibly depressed. But the solutions must be Mrs.
Jones's, and they may be quite different from her children's apparent wish that she resume her previous life-style. Mrs. Jones,
for example, may want and need more quiet time and more
time alone for rest and reflection than she did before. She may
need to set limits on her social life but not abandon it entirely.
She may wish to be selective in what she does, whom she sees,
when and where she sees them. The counselor may find it useful to help Mrs. Jones prioritize her daily activities and learn
and rehearse some assertive ways of telling her children and
friends about her needs and desires. If Mrs. Jones and the counselor both deem it advisable, the counselor may meet with the
family.

In addition to helping people learn and change, counselors
typically support the goal that most adults strive for — to take
or maintain control over their lives. Egan (1986) talks of client
self-responsibility as a principal value. As people reach advanced
ages, this basic goal of maintaining independence and control
often becomes increasingly difficult to meet. Counselors can help
older people develop strategies for maintaining as much control as possible. In practical terms, they may encourage families to accept that older people are entitled to make their own
decisions about where to live, despite some risk. They may encourage new retirees to seek volunteer work in an area of interest rather than automatically responding to any organization's
request for help. Or they may encourage extremely frail older
people to decide for themselves where they want to sit on a given
day or whom they want to visit them.

Often when older people seek help, they want assistance
in solving particular problems. They may be concerned about
their own health. They may want to know about alternatives
to nursing homes or to talk about their feelings of guilt for considering nursing-home placement for a loved one. Alternatively,

they may be looking for a new job or new career. From the clients' point of view, the basic job of the counselor may be to help them make appropriate decisions about such problems. Kottler and Brown (1985) list twenty-six ways in which counseling helps "relatively normal individuals" to function effectively. Included in this list are such action-oriented steps as developing alternatives to self-defeating behavior, formulating a plan of action, and rehearsing and practicing new behaviors (p. 7).

When older people discuss the past, they generally want to learn from it, not to uncover hidden meanings—an orientation shared by many counselors, who generally have a present-oriented, problem-solving approach to helping people. Although counseling and psychotherapy are often distinguished theoretically along such lines as present versus past orientation, or normal versus pathological personality, these distinctions often blur as real helpers work with real individuals. This book focuses on the counseling end of the continuum, but we borrow freely from psychotherapeutic literature and encourage readers to consider the full range of helping activities.

Effective counselors function at many different levels. In addition to providing emotional support and assisting clients in the problem-solving process, they act as advocates for their clients, presenting their needs to appropriate social and governmental agencies as well as occasionally to family members. As a part of their advocacy function, counselors also assist agencies in developing programs suited to the needs of older adults.

To explain further the fit between counselors and older adults, it may be helpful to review the basic components of a counselor's job, delineating some of the ways in which counselors work with older adults. Counselors are trained to "help people of all ages, cultures, and physical capabilities reach their maximum potential in their personal lives, their education and their careers" (American Association for Counseling and Development, undated, n.p.). In Schlossberg's (1984) view, the basic goals of the helping process are to assist clients in exploring, understanding, and coping with their life situations and transitions (p. 113). A basic step is to help people be aware of, understand, and express their feelings. (This step is part of the

learning process in our model.) For some older adults, expressing feelings is in itself a new and rewarding experience. During
a discussion of the joys and problems of being old, one woman
talked of her surprise when she was first asked by a staff member how she felt about something. Her first response was "I've
been so busy raising seven children I never had time to think
about what I felt." Subsequently she realized that understanding and labeling her feelings provided a solid base for making
both large and small decisions as she considered what she wanted
to do with the rest of her life.

Two additional and interrelated counselor functions are
the provision of emotional support and education. A major need
of those in crisis or transition is to know that there are people
who understand and care. They also need to be reassured about
the normalcy of their behavior and reactions.

To fulfill their education function, counselors often provide practical information about community resources. Such
resources may run the gamut from older-worker employment
programs to adult day-care centers; from volunteer centers to
Meals on Wheels; from information on how to get your leaves
raked to suggestions about where to rent a hospital bed. Sometimes educational efforts take the form of classes or workshops
in which older adults are taught assertiveness, stress-management, or job-seeking skills (see Chapter Ten). The ability to
conduct such workshops is part of the repertoire of many counselors, who may need only to tailor their presentation to the needs
of an older clientele.

Overcoming the Reluctance of
Older People to Seek Counseling

Mrs. Jones was seen in a community mental health center.
Older adults may also be counseled at senior centers, lunch programs, congregate living facilities, doctor's offices, hospitals,
funeral parlors, and private nonprofit social agencies, as well
as in the offices of counselors in private practice. The reluctance
of older adults to see counselors in the traditional "fifty-minute
hour" may be changing as today's middle-aged adults grow older.

Newer cohorts of older people are more likely to be amenable to this treatment modality than are earlier cohorts, as are better educated, more economically advantaged people. Knight (1986) also postulates that when older adults do seek counseling, "increased interiority ought to make the therapist's job easier in that introspection and a search for meaning in one's life are important ingredients in psychotherapy" (p. 33). Although Knight speaks of psychotherapy, the same principle applies to counseling.

However, the current reluctance of many older people to seek traditional counseling means that counselors in private practice must consider the marketing of their services. Speeches at senior centers, churches, and public meetings provide opportunities to discuss problems encountered by older people and to explain them in psychological terms. Connections with the "aging network," outreach efforts with the medical community, and similar activities also increase gerontological counselors' visibility and may lead to referrals.

Counselors working in other settings need to consider other approaches. In a special issue of *Generations* (Waters, 1990), counselors from a variety of settings emphasize the importance of providing concrete services for clients (for example, arranging for a home-care aide, making a referral to a respite service, assisting in preparing a resumé) as a way of building trust in the counseling process. In the same issue, several writers stress the importance of an informal approach — talking with people over a cup of tea, meeting in the cafeteria — rather than scheduling a formal session.

B. White (personal communication, 1977) coined the term *by-the-way counseling* to reflect this casual manner of initiating counseling contacts. Because older adults are so often seen in nontraditional settings and time blocks, this informal approach is encouraged. An older person will call or stop by a staff member's office with a routine request for information about the time of a meeting or about Social Security benefits, and, with a "while you're up" approach, ask for help with a personal problem. Such by-the-way counseling is often provided by people who are not trained as counselors. Van drivers, dining-room hostesses, and activities directors may be sought out at least as often as counselors or social workers. People in these capacities who are trusted by older people can provide support and help and serve as referral sources, sometimes linking older people and counselors. Counselors can capitalize on this propensity to approach personal problems indirectly by having informal drop-in time available and by allowing older adults to be casual in their approach, not pushing them to formal appointments before they are ready.

Counselors can also use an "anticipatory-socialization" strategy. Originally developed for people not educated about the ways and whys of counseling (M. T. Orne and P. H. Wender, cited in Knight, 1986), this strategy can be used to prepare older adults for counseling by educating them about the counseling process and debunking myths. These goals can be accomplished by the demonstration, through on-the-spot assistance, that help can be useful. The counselor who takes a presenting problem (whether it is a concern about transportation, about dealing with bureaucrats, or about an ailing pet) at face value and helps the client solve it is showing that help is available and accessible. The client may then be predisposed to seek assistance on other matters as well as to begin developing trust, which is central to the helping process. Or the person may tell friends about the help received. Advertisers know that word of mouth is the most effective technique for getting people to buy. Similarly, in the helping field clients seek out counselors whom their friends talk about as having been helpful. Educating older adults themselves is only part of this strategy. Referral sources must also be sensitized to the idea of suggesting counseling. "In several instances, once the senior service worker became confident enough to refer an older person, that potential client has been pleased, if not actually relieved, to have someone to talk to about his or her problems" (Knight, 1986, p. 51).

Counselors of older people need not only to be alert to indirect requests for assistance but also to give careful consideration to the titles attached to counseling services. Many older people prefer to attend discussions, workshops, or meetings rather than to come for counseling. As long as counselors are clear about what will happen in these sessions, such title adaptations may be helpful and appropriate.

Family members who are caregivers may also be beneficiaries of by-the-way counseling. Ganote (1990, p. 33) states that, in her adult day-care center, "a common phrase is, 'Have you got a few minutes? Perhaps we can talk.' . . . Typically caregivers are open to discussing their loss and also the frustration and despair associated with the 24 hour/day job. After several visits with the counselor, the caregiver may begin talking about the past relationship with the older adult." Once again, a by-the-way beginning is an entrée to further and perhaps more in-depth counseling. Lazarus (1988), in discussing methods for overcoming barriers to counseling—all directed toward what he terms "forming an alliance"—points out that although it is important for gerontological counselors to work with the families of their clients, one must interview the older person first, then interview families to obtain additional information and determine who requires help.

Overcoming Counselors' Reluctance to Work with Older People

Most practicing counselors have little or no experience or training in working with older persons. Some see it as a challenge, others as a threat. Counselors' views are undoubtedly affected by stereotypes about aging. Some may romanticize and imagine "dear old souls" pouring out their hearts and regaling them with wonderful stories of the good old days. Others may picture the experience as boring, if not downright depressing, and assume that nursing homes and hospitals are the major work sites for gerontological counseling.

A number of writers have discussed the resistance of many counselors to work with the aged. Kastenbaum coined the term *reluctant therapist* in 1964. A decade later, Garfinkel (1975) found that therapists at a New York mental health clinic had generally open attitudes toward the elderly but agreed on the "fact" that old people usually do not talk much. To the extent that counselors hold such a belief, whether or not it is true (and our experience certainly calls it into question), it can serve as a convenient justification for concentrating on the needs of younger people. Cohen (1984, p. 97) states that the low utilization of counseling-related services by older, as compared with younger, adults "is less an issue of the level of their interest . . . than [of] the behavior of the delivery system in making the services available and accessible." Myers and Salmon (1984) identify a number of attitudes that may serve as internal barriers for counselors, including counselors' own fears of aging, unresolved conflicts with parents, feelings that older persons cannot change, or fears that the older person may die while in counseling. Regardless of whether such fears are conscious or rational, they may well deter counselors from working with an older population.

When considering gerontological counseling, some counselors fear that working with older people will be totally different from counseling younger people and assume that they have to start from scratch in preparing for the field. Other counselors may deny any differences and assume that their knowledge and skills will be sufficient regardless of the age of the client. In our view neither assumption is correct. We believe that although basic counseling skills apply across the life span, counselors must acquire new knowledge and be aware that older people may bring special needs to a counseling situation. As discussed later, counselors also need to be particularly aware of transference and countertransference issues.

In order to present a realistic picture of gerontological counseling, we discuss below how counseling older people is both similar to and different from counseling younger people. The similarities section includes suggestions on special challenges and modifications in basic approaches that may be necessary in working with older adults.

Basic Similarities. Counselees of all ages need both support and challenge from their counselors. They need to know that their counselors respect them and expect them to grow. To meet these needs, regardless of the age of the client, counselors need to communicate clearly, respond to both thoughts and feelings, ask effective questions, and confront when appropriate. We believe that it is patronizing for a counselor to fail to confront an older person who is acting in a self-defeating manner and that this failure prevents clients from learning about themselves and may deny them the challenge to change behaviors. For example, if an older counselee does not follow through on commitments made to investigate housing alternatives or to talk with a daughter about pent-up resentments, the counselor needs to discuss the procrastination or resistance with the counselee. Given the socialization messages such as "respect your elders" that most of us have received, confronting an older person in this manner may be difficult.

Humor is another important tool for counselors to use with people of all ages. Appropriate humor establishes bonds between counselor and client and also helps clients put their problems in perspective. For many people, maintaining a sense of humor is an important survival skill. If counselors consistently view the lives of older people as grim, they may fail to tap into this important coping skill. A poem written by Louis Bloch, father of author Elinor Waters, on the occasion of his seventy-fifth birthday provides a good example of this skill.

It isn't bad to be alive
To reach the age of seventy-five.
But if, my friends, the truth be told,
I flatly state, "I don't feel old."

Primarily, that thought's addressed
To ladies who would be caressed.
And if they ask, "Sir, what comes next?"
I say politely, "How 'bout sex?"

You youngsters ask, "Is that all bluff
Or will we not have had enough
Of wooing when we first arrive
At the grand age of seventy-five?"

I'll never tell—you'll have to get
The answer from some other vet
Or learn, yourselves, as you arrive
At the young age of seventy-five.

Counselors working with a man like this would miss the boat if they failed to tap into the client's humor.

A first step in establishing any counseling relationship is the development of trust. Younger counselors working with older people may find this step takes longer than it would if they were working with someone their own age. They may want to think carefully about what they wear and the kind of language they use. They may also need to overcome real or imagined client concerns about age differences. Middle-aged and older counselors do not find developing trust in older clients as much of a problem. And many of the counselors developing an interest in the field do fall in those categories. Workshop participants often report that their interest in counseling older people increased markedly when they reached forty, fifty, or sixty years of age. Gerontological counseling may indeed be one field where gray hair is an asset!

Another basic goal of counselors is to help counselees clarify their values and their goals as a prelude to making decisions and developing action plans. Counselors accustomed to working with people who have most of their lives ahead of them may find it difficult to think of older people as having much future to plan for. Such planning is essential, however, if older people are to retain control of their lives as long as possible. As we saw with Mrs. Jones, the lack of a plan can lead to depression and perceived helplessness.

Major Differences. This section needs a disclaimer, as many of the differences to be discussed are generalizations that do not fit all older people. "Older people" are a heterogeneous group and "old age" may easily encompass a span of more than thirty years. Responding to that heterogeneity is itself one of the differences in counseling older people. When we consider experience, knowledge, health, and many other such dimensions, the diversity among older people may be greater than that of any other age group. The usual distinction between "young-old" and "old-old" by chronological age (fifty-five to seventy and seventy and over, respectively) is called into question by Schlossberg (1990, p. 7). She suggests that Neugarten (1979), who created the distinction, referred not to age but to level of functioning, with the young-old being "vigorous, active, and independent" and the old-old having "physical or mental problems that lead to impaired functioning."

With either group, a major, and obvious, difference between younger and older people is that older people have lived longer. One of our jobs as counselors is to help clients identify and appreciate the advantages of their longevity. Encouraging clients to see themselves as having a track record of coping skills rather than as being stuck in their ways is an excellent example of how counselors can help people reframe their views. For example, Mrs. Jones's counselor might want her to think about how she had identified her interests and prioritized her time in the past and suggest that she use a similar procedure in the new situation.

A related difference in working with older people is that you may find flatter affect and more difficulty in talking about feelings than with younger people. Feelings of anger and fear in particular are difficult, as many of today's older people were socialized with messages such as "If you can't say anything nice, don't say anything" or "Laugh and the world laughs with you, cry and you cry alone." Given this kind of socialization, it is especially important for counselors to help people identify, label, and accept their feelings without using mental health jargon.

Counselors also need to be aware of the normal physiological changes that occur with aging, particularly the sensory losses. To accommodate these changes, they should give special attention to the physical settings in which they work with older people, as discussed in Chapter Four. In addition, they need to realize that not infrequently the emotional and behavioral concerns that bring older people to counseling have a physiological or medical base. Memory loss or anxiety, for example, can be triggered by a number of physical problems as well as by drug interactions. Therefore, cooperation between counselors and physicians may be more often necessary when dealing with older clients than with younger ones.

To assess differences in working with younger and older adults from the practitioner's point of view, Tobin and Gustafson (1987) conducted a survey of subscribers to the *Journal of*

Gerontological Social Work. Respondents perceived themselves to be more active in working with older people, more likely to touch older people, and more likely to use reminiscence to validate the present. The increased activity included "more coordination of services, more concrete assistance, more reaching out to families, and more talking by the worker in sessions" (p. 116). The need for the increased activity stemmed from the fact that older people had more concrete problems that were less amenable to change and required assistance beyond the counseling session itself.

In working with clients of all ages, counselors often need to provide information or to make appropriate referrals. Although the function is the same in counseling older adults, the content is likely to differ. Thinking back to Mrs. Jones, we can see that her counselor might need information about volunteer opportunities or support groups for recovering stroke patients or for adult children of aging parents. In general, gerontological counselors need to know more about Social Security and Medicare regulations than about child-care services. Career counselors to the elderly may need to focus more on retirement planning than on helping clients prepare for their first job interview. However, some people, particularly widows, seek their first paid employment at an age when most others are retiring. Counselors working with older people who are entering or reentering the job market need not only to provide them with the usual job-seeking skills but also to prepare them to cope with ageist hiring practices.

Substance abuse can be a problem for people of all ages. However, counselors who work with older adults are more likely to encounter problems stemming from alcohol use or drug interactions than from the use of marijuana or crack. Gerontological counselors may therefore need to consult with pharmacists or physicians as well as to suggest to their clients that they discuss with their primary-care physician all the medications, both prescribed and over-the-counter, that they are taking.

Another area in which counselors may need special information to work with older adults is that of assessment. As discussed in Chapter Three, many traditional measures of intellectual and emotional functioning are inappropriate for some older adults because of the content of the instruments, the timed nature of the tests, or the attitudes of many older people toward test taking. Assessment, typically not of a test-taking nature, is nevertheless essential in working with older adults in order to identify potential problems and determine appropriate interventions. In the absence of appropriate assessment, for example, symptoms may be attributed to the aging process or emotional problems instead of to treatable physical conditions.

Regardless of the age of their clients, counselors encounter ethical issues in their work. In this area, as with referrals, the content may differ with the age of the client. Thus, counselors who work with adolescents may be faced with such decisions as whether to talk to parents or school administrators about a student's problem. Gerontological counselors are more likely to face dilemmas about whether to talk to adult children and grandchildren about their clients' problems. In dealing with a frail population, counselors may be asked to express their views about a client's ability to live alone or to continue to drive. Counselors may also be consulted by older people or their families on such questions as the right to die and the use of life-sustaining methods — issues that are poignantly explored in a publication of the Older Women's League (1986) entitled *Death and Dying: Staying in Control to the End of Our Lives.*

Any counseling relationship, indeed any relationship, includes some transference and countertransference. Older adults may see the counselor, particularly a younger counselor, as a "good child." They may also endow the counselor with more authority than do younger clients, perhaps because of age-cohort conditioning to respect health care figures and authority figures in general (Tobin & Gustafson, 1987). For counselors, older adults may stir up unresolved issues with their own parents. Countertransference may also include the arousal (or the lack) of sexual feelings, attempts to be the "good child" desired by the client, and a tendency to recommend physical treatment to avoid complex psychological issues. Poggi and Berland (1985) sum up their views on this topic: "We believe that much of what has been done badly with the old is done . . . on the basis of countertransference responses conditioned by cultural biases and by the unique and important relationship between the young and old. We think, too, that these difficulties are part of larger, inadequately understood existential issues; the demand that the young validate the importance and value of the very old; and profound physical and psychological differences between the old and young" (p. 512). Being aware of these issues will help the counselor avoid this trap. In other words, the counselor must make an implicit, or explicit, agreement with the older client: "I'll keep my parents out of this if you'll keep your children out of it."

To end this section on a positive note, we want to point out that people new to the field of gerontological counseling are often pleasantly surprised by the appreciation and demonstrativeness displayed by many older counselees. We know several counselors who experienced considerable trepidation before participating in their first group-counseling program for older adults. They left the program heartened by the growth of the participants and touched by the hugs, cookies, and other expressions of appreciation they received. They were able to see for themselves the reality of the concept that older adults can indeed learn, change, and take control of their lives.

An important requirement for gerontological counselors is to try to see things from the older person's point of view. This need can be illustrated through a story. An insurance salesperson was most enthusiastic about a new policy his company had introduced. In extolling its virtues to a woman of eighty, he explained that the policy got more valuable with each passing year. She looked at the salesperson and said tersely, "Young man, I don't even buy green bananas." The balance of this book is designed, in part, to help readers avoid trying to sell green bananas.

What Does the Older Adult Population Look Like?

In order to understand the counseling needs of older adults, we need to consider the demographics. Although in-

dividuals need individualized service, knowledge of the big picture lays a foundation for predicting counseling needs and for
planning programs and services. Furthermore, outdated information or myths can lead to ill-conceived services and to frustration on the part of both the older adult and the service de-
liverer. Counselors need to stay abreast of current information
and avoid making judgments based on impressions rather than
data. In addition to the current demographics of the older adult
population, it is important to consider the effects of living through
a certain period of time. What does it mean that today's older
adults may have lived through two world wars and a depression? What does it mean that future older adults will have
healthier, better-educated, longer-lived role models than current older adults do? These issues should be kept in mind as
you read the following.

Consideration of demographics is complicated by differences in race, ethnicity, and gender. For example, the subgroup
of older Americans of Chinese origin, unlike the majority group,
contains more men than women. The reason is not that their
life expectancy is different from the life expectancy of other
Americans but that Chinese men came to the United States in
greater numbers than did Chinese women.

Intergenerational relationships are also influenced by ethnic origin and such factors as the time of emigration. Older
adults with strong cultural beliefs in family cohesiveness may
feel doubly betrayed by their children's or grandchildren's assimilation into the mainstream culture. The demographic data
that follow must, therefore, be seen as presenting a necessarily
oversimplified portrayal of current American society.

Population Data. Media hype about the increasing proportion
of older people has led to a growing uneasiness on the part of
younger adults about their anticipated support of the older population and about the anticipated lack of resources when they become old. Increasing Social Security taxes and the increasing
visibility of gray power have created an adversarial climate that
can have a negative impact on the relationships of older and
younger adults. Such prognostications make headlines but do
not provide much useful information to counselors.

What are the facts? Older adults constitute about 12 percent of the U.S. population. (All data are from *A Profile of Older Americans* [1988], published by the American Association of Retired Persons and the Administration on Aging.) Predictions about the future are based on a number of assumptions about birthrate, immigration, and mortality. Clearly any of these assumptions may turn out to be erroneous. Between 2010 and 2030, when the baby boomers become old, the proportion of older adults in society will grow to about 22 percent. In the year 2000, however, the proportion of older people, 13 percent, will be much as it is today.

The actual numbers of older adults, however, are also important to scrutinize. Between 1987, when there were 29.8 million older adults, and 2000, when we anticipate there being 34.9 million, the increase is impressive. The estimate for 2030 is 65.6 million — more than double today's figure. Although the anticipated growth in the total population accounts for much of this change, the actual numbers have implications for services such as health care and housing.

Another factor to consider is the aging of the older population itself. The over-eighty-five segment is the fastest growing subgroup of this population. The increase raises many ethical questions for counselors and clients. This segment of the older population is most likely to need long-term care. Another problem is weighing the autonomy and self-determination of these very old adults against their safety and their adult children's peace of mind. Issues around the cost of prolonging life also become relevant. In addition, the increase in this subgroup means that many older adults have an even older living parent. Hagestad (1988) studied five-generation families in Germany with three layers of widows on top — some of whom had been widows since World War I! Ninety percent of the oldest were living with a family member, usually a daughter who was herself quite old.

The Census Bureau predicts that by 2050 one-third of all Americans over sixty-five will have a living parent, primarily because people are living longer. Average life expectancy increases are strongly influenced by declines in infant and child mortality, but more pertinent data are derived from life expectancy at age sixty-five. Men at sixty-five can expect to live 14.8 more years, women 18.6. These figures have increased by 2.6 years since 1960, with an earlier increase of 2.4 years between 1900 and 1960.

Women outnumber men in all segments of the population except the period right after birth. The ratios stay close to 50:50 however until late-middle and old age. By the time women are in the over-sixty-five group, they outnumber men 3 to 2 (17.7 million older women and 12.1 million older men in 1987). These summary data again blur important distinctions. For people sixty-five to sixty-nine, there were 120 women to 100 men; for people over eighty-five, the proportion increases to 256 to 100. Men and women spend the last phase of their lives in different social worlds — men married, women single. Half of all women over sixty-five in 1987 were widows, five times as many as there were widowers. In addition to the practical problems faced by both men and women, widow(er)hood presents its own set of emotional issues. The implications for counselors are important to consider. In addition, women often have less money than men, are less likely to have Social Security or pension benefits, and are therefore more likely to be poor. Indeed the poverty rate for older women is more than half again that of men (15 percent to 9 percent). Men, however, are less likely to have experience in creating a social life for themselves or in the nitty-gritty of home care, meal preparation, and so forth. Men often do not know their own children's phone numbers or even birthdays!

Income Data. Statistics on income and poverty levels of older adults lend themselves to a variety of interpretations. Older adults have greater net worth than younger adults. This figure, $60,300, is well above the U.S. average of $32,700 (1984 data). Even excluding home equity, the elderly had a median household net worth of $18,790 compared with $7,783 for the general population (England, 1987). Net worth, however, can be a misleading indicator. Younger adults anticipate continuing to earn money to meet obligations. Older adults usually feel the need to save money to meet future obligations — specifically, the costs of catastrophic illness and long-term care.

The median income in 1987 for older adults was $11,854 for men and $6,734 for women. This amount clearly does not allow one to live in luxury but is above the official poverty line. The poverty rate for persons over sixty-five in 1987 was 12.2 percent, compared with 10.8 percent for persons age eighteen to sixty-four. Median data, however, can obscure the real poverty faced by a substantial segment of older adults. When Samuelson (1988, p. 68) wrote that the elderly's poverty rate was lower than that of the nonelderly, he received a rash of letters protesting his assertion. Rita Ricardo-Campbell (cited in England, 1987) found that those over eighty-five are still the poorest in society. In addition, if we add those in "near poverty" (125 percent of the poverty line), 20.2 percent of older adults are poor compared with 18.7 percent for the nation as a whole. An astounding 44 percent of black aged persons live in or near poverty. Blacks and Hispanic Americans are also overrepresented below the official poverty line. While 10 percent of older whites fall below this mark, 27 percent of older Hispanic Americans and 34 percent of older blacks do. Clearly many older adults live in marginal circumstances, vulnerable to inflation or to sudden increases in health care or other costs. Counselors must be aware that fear of poverty or destitution is often a constant in the lives of older adults, whether or not they are presently poor. Today's older adults lived through the Great Depression; their fears are based on past experience.

Furthermore, longitudinal studies demonstrate that older adults stay poor longer than their younger counterparts. Although at any one time the percentage of older adults who are poor is about the same as the percentage of younger adults who are poor (11 percent), older adults account for between 25 and 33 percent of the group experiencing long-term poverty (Policy Research Associates, 1988). This group is likely to feel apathetic or even hopeless. From the counselor's point of view, they may be hard to motivate.

Counselors need to be alert to the special concerns of the poor elderly. A lifetime of pride in independence ill equips one for taking advantage of safety nets and other services to the poor. The 35 percent of the elderly who rely on Social Security as their major source of income usually feel entitled to this support, as they have paid into the fund for much of their working life. They often have difficulty, however, accepting other assistance, which they define as charity. Some elderly people eat pet food and are undernourished when help is available because they do not know of its availability or their pride precludes them from asking for it. Sensitive counselors may be able to help them redefine the situation.

The fact remains, however, that although many elderly are needy, many are not. Society's challenge is to meet genuine needs without burdening the young. The counselor's challenge is to help older adults receive, with dignity, the services to which they are entitled, to encourage self-sufficiency when possible, and to work with family members in following both these courses. The challenge may also be to help those who do have some disposable income to enjoy it. Perhaps we need to see more bumper stickers saying, "I'm spending my grandchildren's inheritance."

Living Arrangements. Although the number of noninstitutionalized older persons who live alone is increasing—16 percent of men and 41 percent of women in 1988—the majority live in family settings. The composition of these families varies widely with the gender of the older person. Of men over sixty-five, 72 percent live with their spouses compared with 37 percent of older women. Seven percent of men live with other relatives; 18 percent of women do so. Again we see evidence that old age is a different experience for men and women.

Isolated, abandoned elderly people clearly present a tragic situation. They are, however, a minority. Two-thirds of older persons with living children live within thirty minutes of a child. Three-fourths talk on the phone at least once a week with a child, and 62 percent have at least weekly visits with a child. Counselors must help the alone elderly develop alternate support systems. They must help those enmeshed in families to negotiate or renegotiate those relationships.

Region of Residence. Because the Golden Girls live in Florida, it is easy to think that everybody retires and moves to a warm climate. The fact is that the elderly are less likely to change residence than are those in other age groups. In 1985 only 16 percent of persons over sixty-five had moved in the previous five years, compared with 45 percent of persons under sixty-five. And the vast majority of these had moved to another home in the same state. Those elderly who do move are somewhat more likely to head for good weather than are younger persons. Of the 880,000 older persons who moved in 1985, 35 percent moved from the Northeast or Midwest to the South or West, compared with 26 percent of younger persons who moved.

Older people are well represented in virtually all states. Nationally, older people were 12.3 percent of the population in 1987. Alaska's 3.6 percent and Utah's and Wyoming's 8.2 and 8.9 percent, respectively, as well as Florida's 17.8 percent were minor deviations. The older population in the rest of the states ranged from 9 percent to 14.6 percent. The elderly are, however, more likely to be poor in the South than in other regions. Poverty rates of over 25 percent are found among older people in Alabama, Arkansas, Georgia, Louisiana, Mississippi, South Carolina, and Tennessee. This rate, however, mirrors that for all people in the South.

Education, Health, and Work. One of the areas most affected by the age cohort issue is that of education. In 1970 the median education level of the older population was 8.7 years; in 1987 it was 12.0 years! In the same time the proportion who had completed high school rose from 28 percent to 51 percent. (The speed of this change is exemplified by the fact that in 1986 it was 49 percent!) Education varies by race and ethnic background but not by gender. In 1987 whites over age sixty-five had 12.1 median years of education, blacks 8.4, and Hispanic Americans 7.4. Assumptions about the educational background of elderly clients must therefore be continually revised and may well be different at the ends of the elderly age spectrum.

Technological sophistication is related to education. Older adults born in the days of horses and buggies are withdrawing money from their banks via computer; those born before radio was a household item are programming their VCRs to tape their

favorite television shows. For the many older adults who left
school in the early grades, these changes can be frightening.
If the only way to reach a counselor is to leave a message on
an electronic answering machine with voice-mail capabilities,
they may not overcome the discomfort barrier.

Older persons use a disproportionate percentage of the
U.S. health dollar, and the amount will probably increase as
older people live longer. In 1987 the sixty-five-and-over group
accounted for 31 percent of health care costs while constituting
only 12 percent of the population. Most older persons have at
least one chronic illness and many have multiple health problems.

Although older workers have fewer days of absence from
work than younger workers do, older people have a greater number of days in which usual activities are restricted because of
illness or injury. Here again, racial differences occur. Older
whites spend an average of fourteen of these days in bed; older
blacks spend twenty-one days. About 23 percent of community-
living older adults have health-related difficulties with one or
more personal-care activities. They account for 31 percent of
all hospital stays and remain in the hospital 8.6 days on the average as compared with 5.4 days for people under sixty-five.

Medicare, Medicaid, and other government programs
spent $81 billion in 1984 on health care benefits for older adults.
This amount covered about two-thirds of their health care ex-
penditures. (Similar figures for younger adults show such government programs paying 31 percent of health care costs.)

Counselors need to be alert to both the physical health
care needs of their older clients and the emotional concomitants
of these needs. Hospital stays make most of us uneasy and often
feeling out of control and at the mercy of others. When we see
the stay as perhaps the beginning of continuing deteriorating
health, the emotional impact is intensified.

Working older Americans are the subject of Chapter Six.
What is important here as we look at demographic statistics is
that about 11 percent (3.1 million) of older Americans were in
the labor force in 1987. Half of these worked part-time (47 percent of the men, and 60 percent of the women.) The statisti-
cally normal age of retirement in 1988 was sixty-two. Labor-

force participation by older men has been declining steadily, from two out of three in 1900 to one out of six in the early 1980s. Older women are even less represented in the labor force — one out of fourteen. Older workers are much more likely to be self-employed than younger: 25 percent versus 8 percent. Presently most of these are men, 75 percent, but the increasing number of women entrepreneurs may well change these percentages in the future.

Older adults who work generally do so for the same reason as younger workers do — to earn money with which to support themselves or their families. Counselors must be aware that the need to be productive does not disappear at age sixty-two or sixty-five, nor does the need for a decent standard of living.

Implications for Counselors. The increasing numbers of older adults, particularly the old-old, will require increases in an array of services, including such disparate offerings as low-impact aerobics, adult day-care programs, continuum-of-care nursing homes, Meals on Wheels programs, and hospices. The limited financial resources of many older adults will require that these programs be externally funded, at least in part. The variability of needs within the older adult population should invite locally designed programs that take into account differing needs of racial or ethnic minorities or of people living in particular geographical areas.

Counselors must keep up-to-date on this ever-increasing range of services; maintaining an accurate referral file becomes important. Effective counselors balance these support possibilities with the belief in assisting clients to achieve or maintain maximum autonomy. They also always remember that data are accurate only for groups; each individual has a unique set of characteristics.

2

Understanding
Why Clients Seek Help

Chapter One described a conceptual framework for counseling and indicated what counselors, in general, bring to working with older adults. It also painted a broad picture of the older adult population. In this chapter we look further into the counselor/ client relationship, considering first the role of theory in helping counselors understand their clients and interpret their behavior. The second part of the chapter explores what is happening to the client in this relationship. It suggests a variety of factors that may bring older adults to counseling and thus introduces an array of issues that counselors may encounter as they work with older adults and their families.

Theoretical Background

In this section we briefly review some of the major theories of adult development that can affect counseling relationships. Schlossberg (1984) categorizes adult-development theories into three major groups based on their emphasis on (1) age and life stage, (2) life events and transitions, and (3) individual timing and variability. We use these categories as the basis for the following discussion, which suggests ways in which various theories can be helpful in understanding the situations and perspectives of clients.

In our view it is not necessary to choose one theory or to align oneself with a particular school. An awareness of the various theories enables practitioners to know what to look for and to formulate some hunches or possible explanations for their clients' behavior. To bring these theories to life, we will return to Mrs. Jones and suggest ways in which proponents of various theories might approach her situation.

In Chapter One, the intake worker referred Clara Jones, a seventy-two-year-old widow, to you. During your first interview with Mrs. Jones, she tells you that she has not regained her former energy and that she does not feel like doing things the way she did. "My heart just isn't in it. I don't want to sit around and be a downer for my friends. They'll have a better time without me." She also confides that she does not want to drive, fearing that she will have another stroke that might cause an accident in which she could seriously hurt someone else. "I'm sorry my children are worried," she says, "but I can't live my life for them."

When encouraged to discuss her feelings about her stroke, she tells you that it was terrifying at first but that after a while she came to terms with her expected death. "When I didn't die, it was kind of a surprise. I'm ready to go. My children are all settled. My husband is gone. I have no grandchildren. No one really needs me." When queried about her sleeping and eating patterns, she replies, "I'm just not as hungry as I was. It's too much trouble to fix a real meal. I don't sleep as much as I used to. I generally fall asleep pretty easily, but then I wake up in the middle of the night. I do a lot of thinking and reading at night these days. Since there's no one else in the room, I can turn the light on whenever I want. [Awkward laugh.] That's about the only good thing about being alone I can think of."

After talking a little about her loneliness as a widow and gently pointing out that fatigue and eating and sleeping problems are often associated with depression, you ask Mrs. Jones to describe her relationship with her children. She tells you that it is warm and loving, that they really care about her, but that "they have their own lives to live. They don't need to be bothered with me. I always said I would never be a burden to them. I'm not going to start now."

This beginning exchange would be likely to occur regardless of the theoretical orientation of the counselor. It illustrates the
basic role of counselors in helping to provide emotional support
and information to clients as they encourage them to explore,
understand, and cope with their life situations. Once a counselor has established rapport with Mrs. Jones and learned some
basic information about her, the direction of the counseling interviews might change, depending on the orientation of the counselor.
**We begin by describing how the interview might un-
fold with a counselor who has an age-and-stage perspective.**

Counselor: Mrs. Jones, you seem to feel very strongly about
not wanting to be a burden on your friends and family. And
from what you have told me about your life, I can really understand that. At this time, what do you see as your main role in life?

Mrs. Jones: Why I don't have one I guess. [She hesitates for
a while.] I'm an old woman. I guess my role is to take care of
myself and not be a burden to others.

Counselor: Are you happy in that role?

Mrs. Jones: [Slight laugh.] Well hardly. But where does it say
I should be happy? I'm an old woman. It's time for me to go
and let others take over the work of the world.

Counselor: Did you work very hard when you were younger?

Mrs. Jones: You bet I did. I raised four children, helped my
husband in his business, helped out at my kids' schools and my
church. Before this stroke I volunteered at the hospital, but they
tell me I'm not strong enough anymore for the work I did.

Counselor: What were those busy days like?

Mrs. Jones: Those really were the good old days. I was often
tired, but I felt so alive. I don't want to brag, but I really was
important to many people. They needed me, and I liked that.

Counselor: Clearly this is a different period in your life and your
responsibilities are not as clear-cut as they once were. You're right.
It's not possible to go back, but let's think about what you can do
to make your life now as satisfying and worthwhile as possible.

In this interchange, the counselor asks a series of questions that encourage Mrs. Jones to think about her major roles at different stages of life. As the interview progresses, Mrs. Jones defines herself as an old and somewhat feeble woman and believes that it is appropriate for her to disengage or pull away from active involvement at this time. The counselor has an opportunity to help Mrs. Jones look further into her roles and relationships, and figure out where she fits in the developmental tasks sequence. It may also be appropriate for the counselor to point out that a woman of seventy-two has an average life expectancy of over fourteen more years!

Proponents of age-and-stage theories assume that most people's lives have a predictable sequence; they typically pass through similar experiences at similar ages or at least in the same order. For example, Havighurst (1952), an early representative of this school, identified a number of tasks that he deemed appropriate for people of different ages. He thought it imperative for people in middle age to have adult civic and social responsibilities, to establish and maintain a viable standard of living, to assist teenage children in becoming responsible, and to adjust to the physiological changes of middle age and to aging parents. He saw the major tasks of people in old age as adjusting to decreasing strength and health, retirement, reduced income, and often the death of a spouse, while continuing to meet social and civic obligations.

Havighurst's theories are somewhat middle class in their approach and imply an inevitability and a reactivity on the part of people as they age. Nevertheless, they do provide a framework that counselors can use to help clients examine issues that may be troubling them at different life stages. In addition, some of the tasks identified by Havighurst are those that many clients consider age appropriate. (For example, Mrs. Jones's interview suggests that she may be more willing to adjust to losses than is necessary in view of her situation. Although she may not know about the theory of disengagement or the research that indicates that people who stay active tend to be happier, she seems to be choosing disengagement.) Counselors who are alert to the stages and the possibility of their clients' being hemmed in by beliefs of what is and is not age-appropriate behavior may be able to help their clients sort out those tasks and expectations that fit them and those that do not.

One of the most useful of the age-and-stage theories is that of Erikson (1950), who sees developmental tasks as a series of eight conflicts that need to be resolved during one's lifetime: trust versus mistrust, autonomy versus shame and doubt, initiative versus guilt, industry versus inferiority, ego identity versus role diffusion, intimacy versus isolation, generativity versus stagnation, and integrity versus despair. Although these conflicts, or themes, do follow a progression from infancy to old age, many of the issues surface—and resurface—at every stage of life.

Troll (1976, pp. 6-7) indicates how successful or unsuccessful resolution of "earlier" tasks may affect an adult in midlife or old age. For example, an adult who never successfully resolved the infant's basic conflict of trust versus mistrust may as an adult be a loner who is reluctant to confide in others. People who have successfully resolved the trust issue are likely to be optimistic and have confidence in themselves. Similarly, the adult who has not resolved the young-adult conflict of intimacy versus isolation may avoid intimate contact with others, may have relations with others that are stereotyped or formalized. In old age this person may be unable to form new relationships or to deepen relationships with family. The inability to maintain meaningful relationships may emerge as a problem when retirement or lessened involvement with community organizations leads spouses or families to spend an increased amount of time together. Older adults who have resolved this conflict are likely to have close relationships with family and friends and to be able to reach out to new friends and groups.

Although Erikson's formulation may be extremely useful in helping counselors to understand their clients, it is essential that unresolved conflicts be viewed as challenges to be addressed not as immutable past failures. Recall our framework for counseling from Chapter One: Adults can learn, change, and take control of their lives. For example, although it may be easier to learn to develop intimacy as a young person than as an older person, adults who have had trouble expressing their feelings can, with proper support and help, develop intimacy at a later

age. The teenage years are typically the time when people struggle to establish some independence from parents. Although it
may be harder, and less traditional, to develop autonomy later
in life, it is certainly possible to do so. In helping clients deal
with unresolved conflicts, intensive psychotherapy may sometimes be in order. Often, however, counselors can take a present-
oriented approach and help people analyze their current behavior, thoughts, and feelings, and look at alternative ways of
acting.

**Now let us consider how a transition theorist might
have proceeded with Mrs. Jones.**

Counselor: Mrs. Jones, you've told me that your life has really
changed since your stroke, that you no longer maintain the same
social life, and that your eating and sleeping are very different
also. What do you think has happened?

Mrs. Jones: When I had the stroke, I thought I was going to
die. It made me realize that I really am old. I think I had been
fooling myself before. I really shouldn't be doing so much. You
never know when another stroke might hit. There's nothing to
do but wait and see.

Counselor: It sounds like you feel out of control, that your stroke
changed everything about your life.

Mrs. Jones: Well, it did. I used to be healthy. Now I'm not.

Counselor: Clearly, that is an enormous change and must make
you very apprehensive. What have your doctors told you about
what you can do, what you can expect?

Mrs. Jones: Oh, them. They always want to make me feel better. But I know the truth.

Counselor: It sounds as if you think the stroke was more serious than they say it was and that you don't fully trust them. That
must be very difficult, not to trust your doctors. What have you
considered doing to deal with that?

Mrs. Jones: I don't think there's a darn thing I can do.

Counselor: I'm aware of what a big change in your life the stroke has made. I'm concerned, though, that you are putting your life on hold, considering your stroke to be almost a death sentence for you, and that doesn't have to be. What other major changes have you had to cope with during your life?

   After encouraging Mrs. Jones to talk more about the meaning of the stroke to her, a counselor operating from a transition perspective might encourage Mrs. Jones to look back on previous transitions she has weathered. This discussion should help Mrs. Jones identify some of her personal resources, sources of support, and coping strategies. Proponents of this approach look at adult development from the viewpoint of marker moments that give "shape and direction to the various aspects of each person's life" (Schlossberg, 1984, p. 11). These theorists reject the inevitability assumed by the age-and-stage theorists. They focus instead on the impact on individuals of life events and transitions, regardless of when they occur. For example, newly married or newly divorced people face many of the same challenges regardless of their age at the time of the marriage or divorce. More broadly, they believe that an understanding of adult development requires knowledge of more than age or stage; it requires an understanding of circumstances, the life event or transition currently being experienced, as well as past experiences and coping strategies.

   Schlossberg (1984) looks closely at life-event and transition perspectives. She believes that because human lives are complex, the model must take into account a complex set of variables. Some examples of the applications of her model can be found later in this chapter. Schlossberg defines a transition (p. 68) as an "event or nonevent resulting in change." The success of the individual in coping with the transition depends on the characteristics of the transition, the environment, and the individual. The major characteristics of the transition are the kind or type, the context in which it occurs, the impact that it has on the individual, and the kind of role change involved. For example, the transition may represent a role loss (losing a job) or a role gain (becoming a grandparent).

   An individual's ability to cope with a transition is influenced by such factors as the cause of the transition, whether it is on or off time (for example, being widowed at thirty is different from being widowed at sixty), whether the individual views the change as permanent or temporary, whether the individual has previously gone through a similar transition, and other stresses the individual is experiencing at the time. In planning an intervention with someone in transition, the counselor should assess each of these variables. For example, clients who have weathered similar storms may need to be reminded of that fact and encouraged to remember what coping strategies they used at that time. Clients who may have no control over current transitions may be able to control some of the other stresses in their lives or may need to learn some stress-management techniques.

A counselor who emphasizes variability may have the following interview with Mrs. Jones.

Counselor: Mrs. Jones, it sounds as though you put a real premium on being independent. Has that always been true of you?

Mrs. Jones: Yes, it certainly has. I grew up being told you had to pull your own load. My mother always said things like "Don't count on other people and you won't be disappointed." I've lived my whole life that way.

Counselor: I hear a lot of pride in your voice as you say that. What else are you proud of?

Mrs. Jones: I think I passed those values along to my children, along with my views about the value of money.

Counselor: It sounds as though you are a product of the Depression?

Mrs. Jones: [Laughs.] You sound just like my daughter! She says I never got over that. But I do feel good that we never had to go on welfare, even when my Dad lost his job.

Counselor: That was clearly a triumph for you. Tell me about some of the other events in your life that have been especially important to you.

In this exchange, the counselor is trying to learn about Mrs. Jones's values and life experiences. Although theorists who emphasize individual variability do not discount age as relevant to understanding adults, they see other aspects of life as equally or more salient. They contend that variability increases with age and that, as Neugarten (1979) says, ten-year-olds are more alike than seventy-year-olds. Proponents of this school consider historical time (for example, surviving the Depression as Mrs. Jones did), social class, religious and ethnic background, and societal expectations as being as important as simple chronological age in determining the counseling needs of individual older adults.

Although theorists who stress the importance of individual variability do not see chronological age as a primary determinant of behavior, social expectations of age — that is, age bias — may be. When age bias exists in older adults, their families, or their counselors, they may see some options as inappropriate or fore-chosen because of age. Age bias is so pervasive in our society that many older adults have developed a group self-hatred. Reluctance to participate in senior-center activities or live in a retirement community may reflect the feeling of many older people that "I'm not one of them."

Why have we presented these theories of counseling? As you progress through the rest of this book, you will read about older adults and the typical issues they face. You will look at assessment and program-development techniques and learn about the helping process and how it must be varied to meet the needs of older adults from different backgrounds. In all these areas it is important to have a thought-out perspective on aging and the role of counselors in helping older adults maximize life satisfaction and control over their lives. We believe that an Eriksonian unfolding framework, coupled with Schlossberg's insights into the transition process, provides a good basis for this perspective. The knowledge and views of other theorists continue to enlighten and challenge us to add their observations to our approach.

In practice, counselors can draw on the range of theories described above. Knowing about typical challenges of various stages of life can be helpful, but such information tells only part of the story. Individuals' experiences are mediated by their unique life histories, their present situation, and their attitudes toward events. Attitudinal differences often detemine both whether an older adult seeks counseling and the outcome of that counseling.

What Prompts Clients to Seek Counseling?

We now delineate certain factors that might lead older adults to seek counseling: temporary crises, long-term problems, normal and abnormal transitions. After giving examples of each category, we turn to a discussion of internal needs and the effects of one's point of view about aging.

Temporary Crises. Although temporary crises can have long-term implications and carry over, their onset tends to be somewhat sudden and their salience to diminish with time. The client seeking help at this point usually wants short-term assistance in dealing with the present crisis. In the following example, Schlossberg's (1984) transition model is used to understand the impact of hospitalization.

Illness or hospitalization often propels older adults into crisis even after the immediate health problem has passed. Often hospitalization brings the first major awareness of present or future frailty or of one's mortality. The sense that this is the beginning of the end may induce an older adult to seek counseling. Let us use this common crisis as a sample event to which we can apply Schlossberg's diagnostic questions (1984, pp. 54, 70, 72). She suggests that in order to understand a transition and the influences on an individual's coping process, we must look at several characteristics of the transition. These characteristics are type, context, impact, and the kind of role change involved, as we mentioned above, and also trigger, timing, source, duration, the person's previous experience with similar transitions, and concurrent stress.

The *type* of transition in this case is hospitalization. The *context* in which it occurred is the first question for the counselor to investigate. Was the client living well and comfortably, happy in her or his life? Or was that life on the edge, ready for any small push to fall off into crisis? Might the illness be a relief, for example, from oppressive caregiving? And what is the *impact* on the individual? Is the hospitalization being taken in stride, or is it being seen as a devastating blow? Will it force life-style changes?

What has *triggered* this transition from health to illness? Was it an accident? Could it have been avoided? Was it caused by an enjoyed activity like skiing? Was it caused by failure to accept limitations like impaired vision? Perhaps the illness was caused by poor health habits (for example, smoking) or perhaps by genetics. These and many other possible triggers have an influence on the client's perceptions of the crisis and therefore on the counselor's reactions to the client. For example, many people, particularly older women, may be blamed by others or may blame themselves for tripping or falling and breaking a hip when in fact they may have fallen because of a spontaneous hip fracture.

What is the *timing* of this event? To the extent that many older people expect to have health problems, the timing may not have a negative impact. If one is retired, one does not need to be concerned about lost work days or using up sick leave. However, older people may perceive the illness as the first step in invalidism. The illness or hospitalization of a spouse or other significant person can also confront an older adult with feelings and decisions with which they may require assistance. Here timing may be an issue. A young-old person, for example, may be faced suddenly with caring for a disabled spouse just when she or he felt it finally time for freedom and fun.

What is the *source* of the crisis? In most traditional formulations, the source of illness is seen to lie outside the person — that is, out of the person's control. Counselors can help clients distinguish what they can control from what they cannot? Lowenthal (1984) describes her experiences when totally paralyzed with Guillain-Barré's syndrome. She says that she obsessed terribly over the straight edges of her covers because this was the only aspect of her life she could control. New medical research is focusing on how we can work with our bodies to help effect our own cures. Helping clients walk the line between doing what they can to enhance health yet not feeling responsible or guilty about the illness may be a new challenge for counselors arising out of this research (see Pearsall, 1987).

Another of Schlossberg's transition characteristics is *role change*. In our example there does not appear to have been any major gain or loss of role. *Duration* is the next characteristic for us to consider. In the example we are using, we are assuming that the duration is temporary. Clients' *previous experiences* with similar events provide additional clues for the counselor looking for ways to be of assistance. Helping clients draw on past coping strategies is one of the strongest tools in the gerontological counselor's box. Finally, Schlossberg suggests that we examine the *concurrent stresses* in our clients' lives. Is the ill person leaving others at home about whom she or he is worried, be they spouse, friend, or pets? Is this event coming on top of several other crises or does it stand alone? Sometimes a counselor can be most useful in helping clients resolve other compounding problems, even if the presenting event does not lend itself to major interventions.

In addition to characteristics of the transition, characteristics of the individual and of the environment require analysis. Counselors need to look at the personal and demographic characteristics of the individual, the individual's psychological resources, and the coping responses available. Strength in any or all of these areas bodes well for successful resolution. Many theorists see self-esteem, in particular, as integral. Counselors can help by finding or creating these strengths. Environmental characteristics may call into play the counselor's role as advocate (see Chapter Eleven), as program-development specialist (see Chapter Ten), or as assistant in support-system analysis and development (see Chapter Nine). In our example, the counselor may need to help the client lobby for choices about medical treatment and perhaps work with the hospital administration to develop flexible health care programs for older adults. Counselors may also develop support groups for people with specific disabilities or may create transportation options for those whose mobility has been decreased as a result of their illness or accident.

This discussion of how to apply a conceptual approach to a particular problem is meant to suggest a pattern for reading the rest of this section. As other examples are presented, the reader is encouraged to follow a similar process of analysis.

Sometimes the event that impels an older adult to seek counseling forces recognition of old age. Having to get false teeth, looking at oneself in the mirror and seeing an old man or old woman, being offered a seat on the bus, being asked whether one wants the senior citizen discount, all can induce a redefinition of self. The death of a friend or acquaintance, an increasingly common experience as one ages, in additon to inducing grief, leads to a shrinking of one's support system, an anticipation of future losses, and an awareness of one's own vulnerability. In addition, as we discuss in Chapter Eight, the cumulative effect of losses often exacerbates their impact.

Another major crisis in the life of an older adult, as of any adult, is divorce. Once rare among older adults, divorce is becoming increasingly frequent, although far from commonplace. In addition to coping with the losses experienced by anyone during a divorce, the older adult may also be dealing with shame (remember the age-cohort effect) as well as facing the restructuring of a lifetime of connections—family, friends, church, community. Furthermore, the older woman is facing the extreme unlikelihood of remarriage. She has, in effect, acquired the trappings of widowhood without the status or life insurance benefits.

The disruption created by voluntary or forced relocation can lead to a crisis. Cleaning out an attic with a lifetime of memories can occasion a positive life review (see Chapter Nine) or extreme grief for the past. For some, the number of decisions that need to be made can be paralyzing, although, for others, this process can be freeing. We know one woman who sold everything, down to the last dishtowel, and started anew with a small number of things that actually matched! When the relocation is forced, as when a freeway or factory takes over one's neighborhood, the potential for distress is great. Anger can be directed inward — "Why am I so upset about a house? It's not as if someone died" — and can lead to depression, loss of energy, and other psychological effects. As with many of the crises discussed here, the client may not be aware of the precipitating event. Counselors need additionally to be aware of cultural differences in facing many of these events. Relocation may be disruptive to one whose identity is closely tied to the community, whose grandparents tilled that land or worshipped at that church. It may be taken somewhat casually by one who has moved frequently or who does not put down roots.

On a lighter note, inheriting a large sum of money is another event that can create a need for decision-making assistance. Frugal habits of a lifetime may be called into question. Past privations may be regretted, or new possibilities and horizons may be gratefully embraced. That trip around the world may be possible after all!

A sadder event, but one whose incidence is growing, is being robbed, mugged, or in some other way being a crime victim. In addition to the actual crisis engendered by the crime, the sense of vulnerability creates a crisis of its own. Even when the crime has happened to a friend or neighbor, has happened in the immediate vicinity to a person not known, or simply has appeared in the newspaper, perceived vulnerability rises. This phenomenon has been called "vicarious victimization" (Sunderland, cited in Norton & Courlander, 1982, p. 388). When the crime has been committed against an older adult, the fear increases. Many older adults "collect" incidents of crime to feed their fear. The unhappy outcome can be reduced social activity, reluctance to go out after dark or when teenagers are on their way home from school, or, at the extreme, refusal to go out at all. Increased care and caution may be necessary; but timidity and terror may create serious psychological problems. Several community-based programs have been instituted to help deal with such fear and isolation. Those who have participated report that they "feel less alone, better informed, and increasingly willing to venture back into the community" (Hayes & Burke, 1987). Clearly, perceived options are increased.

Long-Term Problems. Unlike the situations discussed above, the problems discussed below are likely to last for the rest of the older adult's life or at least for the foreseeable future. They may, therefore, call for a different set of responses.

The incidence of chronic illness increases with age. Reduced reserve power in the older adult can lead to any organ's functioning below par. In particular, arthritis, emphysema, and heart disease are often the lot of an older adult and always require some adjustments in life-style. Similarly, the chronic illness of a spouse, parent, child, or anyone else for whom one is the caregiver can create disturbances in one's life. These disturbances can then lead to emotional turmoil or simply to the need for assistance in finding resources, making decisions, or both. Counselors need to be particularly attuned to anger and guilt, sometimes found in disguise as depression or somatic symptoms.

Another physical problem is the reduced night vision that often accompanies the aging process and that may lead to an inability to drive at night. Although the problem itself is minor, the consequences are often far-reaching. Particularly in the winter, when daylight hours are short, the older adult may have to curtail activities sharply. Social life tends to take place in the evening. Parties even on weekends begin after dark; plays and concerts are almost always evening events — matinées are increasingly rare; movies rarely have daytime performances unless they are geared to children. With the exception of occasional baseball and football games, most sporting events also take place in the evening. Even something as simple as a trip to visit relatives or dinner with a friend may necessitate arranging for a ride or spending the night. Often pride forecloses some of these options, leaving older adults to make up excuses for withdrawing from social activity, a withdrawal that tends to be self-perpetuating. Others drive anyway, risking accident to themselves and others, unwilling to pay the price of reduced mobility. The poor or nonexistent public transportation systems in most of our towns and cities deprive older adults of one possible remedy to this problem. As will be discussed in Chapter Eleven, here is one arena in which the counselor can take an activist stance.

One of the challenges for counselors who work with the elderly is that the isolation that often causes or exaggerates their problems may keep them from seeking or seeing the help that is available. Loneliness both causes many of the problems outlined above and is the result of them. If the deaths of friends lead to a diminished support system or if being widowed results in being cut off fom previous activities and social networks, these events can lead to increased loneliness. The death of a spouse obviously has further-reaching effects than social isolation, but social isolation is not to be ignored.

Although most older adults remain in their homes or at least in their neighborhoods, many do move. Even carefully chosen, looked-forward-to moves may create distress. Furthermore, any move disrupts a support system that may consist of people as diverse as one's best friend, the next door neighbor who notices when the paper has not been taken in, and the local dry cleaner who also replaces buttons. Relocation experts say that it takes one to two years to feel at home in a new house. That is a long time for anyone. For an older adult who may have few resources for coping with change and may envision a short future, it can seem like an eternity. In addition, a move to a nursing home or to the home of a family member is almost always accompanied by serious physical or mental health problems. (Thus the need for the move.) These same problems reduce the ability to cope with the change, often further exacerbating both the problems and the adjustment difficulties.

In addition to their inherent problems, the situations described above may also constitute an attack on an older person's independence. For all humans, this sense of independence is critical. The fear of and actual loss of independence threaten our basic core. To a lesser extent, the normal transitions described in the next section may also threaten that core. Counselors need to be alert to this issue as they work with their older clients.

Normal Transitions. Certain age-related changes are almost guaranteed to occur in each of us, although their time of onset, severity, and extent vary widely. This section illustrates the varying arenas in which normal transitions occur.

It is by now well known that the desire for sex and the
ability to perform sexually do not disappear with age. There
are, however, normal changes in frequency of desire for or ability
to have orgasms, duration and intensity of erection for men,
lubrication for women, and sensitivity to touch. These changes,
coupled with many older persons' belief that "I'm too old for
all that," can lead to an unnecessary abandonment of sexual activity. Even when sexual intercourse is not wished for or available, needs for physical intimacy continue. Counselors can help
people consider alternative methods for meeting this need, for
getting touching back into their lives—by initiating more hugs,
getting a weekly massage, acquiring a cat or a dog to pet and
cuddle, joining a dance club, masturbating or engaging in other
activities that fit within their value system. In a situation where
women greatly outnumber men, for some women same-sex intimacy may be a new option to explore or resume after years
of heterosexual activity. Counselors can help older adults recognize that these needs are normal, and that there are ways of
at least partially gratifying them.

Retirement is an event that has long-term implications.
Depending on the individual, retirement may result in a gain
or a loss of self-esteem. It can deprive older persons of goals
to strive for. The need to be productive, to contribute to the
society in which one lives—sometimes called the need to be
needed—is lifelong; it does not terminate with retirement. Counseling may be helpful in assisting the older adult to plan for a
meaningful use of time and handle the identity issues that arise
when one is no longer an engineer, a carpenter, mechanic, or
nurse. Counseling may also help older people adjust to new relationships with their spouses or feel comfortable with diminished
income or perceived diminished social status.

Another normal transition that begins in middle age and
intensifies or speeds up with older age is reduction in energy
and the need for an increaingly longer time to bounce back.
Most older adults find that they cannot quite do all that they
used to do. However, among older people, as among all people, the range of energy is enormous. Many older people still
have more energy than many younger people—that is, the dis-

tribution curves overlap. For each individual, however, the loss is real and requires adaptations in life-style, in planning, and in time for recuperation from high energy use.

In the usual course of existence, people age, retire, and die. Like William Saroyan, however, who is reputed to have said on his deathbed, "I knew everyone had to die, but somehow never thought it would happen to me," we spend much of our youth and middle age blissfully denying this reality. The psychological awareness of its truth, therefore, can be quite a blow. For many this awareness leads to a determination to live life fully, to appreciate existence, to, in the words of the old cliché, pick more daisies. For others, this awareness can lead to depression or panic, occasioned by a sense of urgency to "do it now!"

Another normal transition many older adults experience is increased psychological distance from younger people. "What's the matter with the younger generation?" has been a cry since Socrates. The rapidity of change in today's world only exaggerates that normal tendency. Today's older adults have seen more technological change than all that took place in previous history. Along with this technological change has come enormous social change, some of which tends to distance older adults from their children and may create even more distance from their grandchildren. (In some cases, however, grandparents may be more accepting of different behavior on the part of their grandchildren than are the parents. With a longer life and a deeper perspective, grandparents may see the differences as typical generation-gap issues.)

People raised in an era when bobbed hair and knee-length skirts were considered shocking are seeing even the U.S. Census Bureau accede to change. The newly created category POSSLQ—persons of opposite sex sharing living quarters—attests to how many unmarried people are living together. Distancing life-styles may include remaining single or deciding not to have children. Or they may be life-styles that are in opposition to the moral or ethical values of the older adult, such as homosexuality or communal living. The book *Mother I Have Something To Tell You* (Brans, 1987) discusses this issue at length.

Generational change is a normal transition; nonetheless, it can create a sense of loneliness or even anger. Sometimes the distance created is so great that it can cut older persons off from a critical part of their support system, their family.

Many transitions in the lives of older adults relate to the social, economic, and political circumstances of today's world. Not only does the counselor need an understanding of these conditions, but older adults themselves will profit from this kind of understanding. An appreciation of the context of one's life, sometimes called contextual awareness, can ameliorate the impact of change.

Abnormal Transitions/Off-Time Events. Off-time events are those that happen at a different time or in a different order than usual. For example, retirement is a normal transition; forced early retirement is an off-time event. The death of a parent is a sad event; the death of a child is traumatic. The care of an older parent by a middle-aged adult may be a problem; the care of an even older parent by an older adult can be a devastating responsibility. Other abnormal transitions include diabetic or other medical problems such as amputation of a limb, blindness, or loss of hearing.

Another type of abnormal transition is what Schlossberg (1987, p. 74) calls a nonevent. These are "the expected events that fail to occur" such as not having grandchildren or living longer than expected. These nonevents create a different kind of counseling need. Sometimes all that is necessary is a recognition of their existence. Sometimes one must mourn the nonhappening. Sometimes one must find alternative ways to meet the need. In the case of not having grandchildren, for example, one might find other ways of nurturing another generation.

Internal Needs. Some counseling needs are not created by events or transitions but arise instead out of the internal needs of the individual. These may be looked at from a Maslovian (Maslow, 1954) perspective—that is, after basic needs for security, shelter, and so forth, have been met, the need for self-actualization is able to emerge. Self-actualization may include the

desire to make sense of one's life, to have new challenges, to
plan or set goals, and to maintain one's independence. For example, for older adults, the need to maintain control over their
lives often takes on increased importance, commensurate with
its difficulty. Overprotective friends and children, no matter how
well meaning, may cause distress. Maclay (1977) expresses this
feeling eloquently in a poem:

> My children are coming today. They mean well.
>   But they worry.
> They think I should have a railing in the hall. A tele-
>   phone in the kitchen. They want someone to
>   come in when I take a bath.
> They really don't like my living alone.
> Help me to be grateful for their concern. And help
>   them to understand that I have to do what I can
>   as long as I can.
> They're right when they say there are risks. I might
>   fall. I might leave the stove on. But there is no
>   real challenge, no possibility of triumph, no real
>   aliveness without risk.
> When they were young and climbed trees and rode
>   bicycles and went away to camp, I was terrified.
>   But I let them go.
> Because to hold them would have hurt them.
> Now our roles are reversed. Help them see.
> Keep me from being grim or stubborn about it. But
>   don't let them smother me.

If the woman who voices the above concerns seeks counseling,
she may require help in sorting out her own needs and desires
and practicing ways of expressing them to her children. The
Eriksonian (1950) conflict, mentioned previously in this chapter, between integrity and despair seems relevant here. A counselor could help the individual with the thinking and remembering necessary to resolve this conflict in an affirming manner.

   To take another example, the need for mastery does not
disappear with retirement or old age. When work does not pre-

sent challenges, older people must find new ones, sometimes through discovering new parts of themselves. Grandfathers perform child-care functions — even changing diapers — that they never performed when their own children were young. Grandmothers who would never travel across town alone fly across the country to visit children. Widows who would not go to a restaurant without their husbands travel to Alaska with the senior citizens' group. The move to androgyny that accompanies such changes typically begins in middle age but reaches a height in old age.

Point of View. A final factor that can cause older adults to seek counseling is their own views about aging. Do they celebrate gray hairs as badges of honor? Or do they deplore them as signs of lost youth? Are they thrilled to save money with their senior citizen discount? Or are they upset that clerks think they look old enough to suggest it? Do they share the prevailing view that youth is in and age is out? Or do they, like the Chinese, venerate age? We know a man who couldn't wait until he was fifty-five so he could play tennis with the older men and increase his chances of winning tournaments. We also know a widow who was suddenly faced with decisions about what to do with her husband's business. She had access to technical advice from an attorney and from people who knew about the product and sales techniques. However, none of that advice worked until a counselor helped her to reframe her need to manage the business and see it as a challenge rather than a burden. Sometimes whether the glass is half empty or half full depends on your angle of vision. An important counselor role is to affect that angle of vision.

3

Assessing Older Clients

Samuel Cohen is an eighty-seven-year-old, Russian-born, former accountant. He was widowed twenty-five years ago and has been living with his oldest daughter since then. He has a bedroom and a small kitchen of his own on the second floor of the house and until quite recently was able to make his breakfast and lunch as well as dress himself and handle his financial affairs. According to the daughter, who contacted you, he has always been a demanding man, and recently his demands have been increasing. He calls her to come upstairs twenty times a day, and she is exhausted and impatient with him. She also reports that her father has become absent-minded, that his gait has become unsteady, and that the family is worried he will fall or burn himself. His daughter says he has "messed up" all his financial records, forgotten to pay his income taxes and bills, and ignored warning notices. Recently widowed, she had been the primary caregiver for her husband, who had a long and painful illness. If Mr. Cohen's daughter contacted you, how would you go about assessing the situation?

What Do We Mean by Assessment?

In the previous chapter we discussed ways of using Schlossberg's (1984) formulations to analyze client situations,

47

especially transitions, and to determine appropriate counseling interventions. This chapter is intended to add to rather than to substitute for that analysis. It focuses on the psychological and emotional assessment of older adults.

Gallagher, Thompson, and Levy (1980) view assessment "as a systematic evaluative process that leads to specific judgments about a given person's (or group of people's) current and potential level of functioning in a variety of settings" (p. 19). They caution that psychological assessment should not be equated with psychometric testing, although standardized tests may be used as part of the process. Although the term *assessment* often conjures up images of formal tests, we will be using the broader definition as we proceed in this chapter. Kane (1985) notes that "the major clinical purpose of assessment is to facilitate decisions about the type and amount of services that should be offered to a particular client."

As you read the descriptions of Mr. Cohen and his daughter, what hypotheses did you formulate? Some of the questions you may have asked yourself include: Who is your client — Mr. Cohen or his daughter? Whichever you decide, can you or someone else help the other? What strengths and personal resources do they bring to the situation? What coping strategies have they developed over the years? What limitations do they have in coping with problems? What is the nature of each of their support systems? Who provides instrumental support? Who provides emotional support?

Considering some of the categories of problems identified in Chapter Two, you might want to think about whether the situation is likely to be temporary or permanent. Would you define it as a normal or abnormal transition, a planned or unplanned situation? Finally, what other information would you need in order to begin to work with each of these people? What assessments do you need to get this information?

Informal assessment is a necessary survival skill learned from the cradle. Snap judgments, prejudices if you will, are needed for navigation of life's course. We ask ourselves questions such as: Am I safe here? Is this person trustworthy? Will we share interests, values, or ideas? Whenever we meet someone new, we form impressions, usually based on scanty data and on comparisons with past experience. In addition, we make judgments about someone's age, gender, social class, level of education, nationality, occupation. We notice these judgments when they turn out to be wrong. The "old man" turns out to be a prematurely gray young man. The "woman" turns out to be a man with long hair. The "nurse" turns out to be the doctor. The "depressed" person turns out to be overmedicated.

Starting with their first meeting, counselors make judgments or tentatively assess many aspects of their clients' personalities, circumstances, and demographics. These initial assessments are made on the basis of appearance and mannerisms as well as on problems or circumstances the clients may describe. Although informal, experience-based assessments may be effective for one's personal life, it is important professionally to make assessment as rational as possible. We suggest here ways to capitalize on one's experience yet avoid misjudgments.

Let us assume that you identify both Mr. Cohen and his daughter as your clients and that you plan on working with them both individually and jointly. What information have your informal assessments given you? For example, if you assume that you are working with a Jewish family with Eastern European roots, you may further assume that there are expectations that daughters should take care of fathers in their old age and that men should be catered to. You may also suspect that, as a former accountant, Mr. Cohen will have done adequate financial planning and may, therefore, be able to afford some paid help. Because the daughter has just seen her husband through a lengthy illness, it seems likely that she may be somewhat familiar with community services. Her reports of constant care of her husband and frustration over repeated calls from her father, however, suggest she may be reluctant to ask for help. You may also assume that other family members may be able to provide financial assistance, take over some chores, or offer emotional support to father or daughter.

All these assumptions must be checked out. A first step is to talk with Mr. Cohen and his daughter separately to get a clear picture of their values and their expectations about intergenerational obligations and sex roles as well as information about family composition and financial resources. In talking with the daughter, it would be important to find out what support she gets from her father, as well as what she provides. It would also be important to try to get some information about her ability and willingness to ask for help, and the priorities she gives to caring for herself. An important step would be to have a thorough medical evaluation of Mr. Cohen. This evaluation should include information about his current status, the prognosis, and suggestions for his care.

Effective counselors are familiar with a variety of assessment techniques. Different situations call for different methods of gathering information. We have just given an example of the simplest and most commonly used technique — interviewing and observing. Observation may take place in a typical counseling interaction or while the client is engaged in other activities at home or elsewhere. It may be informal and general or may employ standardized instruments such as behavioral checklists. Clients may or may not be aware that they are being observed. The ethics of "secret" observation, as when a family member asks the helper for advice, warrant some consideration here. With Mr. Cohen, initial information was provided by his daughter, filtered through her own feelings and fears. A home visit by you would provide additional information as to how Mr. Cohen operates. During that visit you would need to tell him that you are coming with joint concerns — for his safety and for his daughter's increasing fatigue. Because the daughter came to you with expectations of confidentiality, you will have to talk with her and get her permission for you to visit her father and explain the dual concerns. You may also wish to seek outside assistance.

On some occasions a counselor may also want to have a specialist conduct a thorough assessment of a client. An excellent resource, if it is available in your area, is the geriatric assessment unit of a community mental health center. In a personal interview, the head of one such unit explained how they respond to requests for consultation. A first step is to send a clinician to the patient's house to take a social history, get the client's view of the problem, and assess mental status, looking for both judgment and affect. Afterward, the geriatric assessment unit has a psychiatrist do a basic neurological evaluation and look at the patient's physical and medication history.

In a different approach to assessment, counselors may use life-history techniques to look at developmental-task accomplishment or conflict resolution. Life histories may be obtained through autobiographies, through a systematic interview schedule, or through the guided-imagery life-review technique described in Chapter Nine. Sometimes clients bring personal documents such as journals, letters, or artistic endeavors that aid in assessment.

In assessing individuals it is important to look for what they can do as well as what they cannot do. Sundberg (1977) classifies behavior into "excesses, deficits, inappropriateness, and assets" (p. 171). This classification is consistent with the views of M. P. Lawton (cited in Kane, 1985), who talks of assessing competence of functional capabilities. Such an approach, which focuses on the interaction between individuals and the environment in which they function, has much to recommend it.

Many assessment techniques, particularly those based on interviews, can be used by all counselors. Others are appropriately used only by those with special training. These tests include some personality tests, including projective tests, as well as neurological and other medical tests. In such cases, referrals to physicians or psychometricians may be in order. Unless you have special training, we recommend referrals when you see clients who are unable to care for themselves, seem out of touch with reality, or are unable to function. Because a higher percentage of older people than younger people have chronic physical problems and take medications, referral is particularly important when working with this age group.

What Do We Need to Consider in Assessing Older People?

Although the principles mentioned above could apply to people of any age, it is important to consider the differences involved in assessing older people. To begin with, assessment of an older client is more complex than assessment of a younger client because the older client has more life experiences to take into account. In addition, as we mentioned, diagnosis of older people may be complicated by the effect that physiological or medical problems have on cognition, behavior, and affect. Therefore, counselors must, when necessary, consult with physicians and other health care professionals, combining their observations with results of any standardized testing that is done.

Because of the complexity of older people's lives, it is important that assessment be done in many different areas. Kane (1985) identifies several factors to be included in a multidimensional assessment: physical condition, self-care capability, emotional state, cognitive ability, environmental factors, social factors, and preferences. Each is discussed briefly below.

An older adult's *physical condition* and *self-care capability* are keys in determining what that person's life-style can be. Before counselors can help older adults and their families make decisions and set goals, all involved must know the parameters within which they are working. The ability to care for oneself is a reflection of a person's physical and mental capabilities, emotional state, and environmental situation. Counselors can utilize some fairly simple measures to assess a client's ability to perform daily activities. These tests are discussed later in this chapter.

Analysis of a client's ability to perform daily activities may yield information about the kind of help a marginally independent person needs. For example, someone who can answer the telephone but not dial may profit from a daily reassurance call or may even be able to call out if given the kind of telephone with which one can make programmed calls by dialing one digit. Similarly, someone not able to take complete responsibility for medication may be able to function if a caregiver puts a day's supply in vials that are color coded to match similarly coded numbers on a clock, or if a flashing light goes off at the appointed times.

Most counselors are aware that the *emotional state* of clients has a major impact on their ability to function. People with high self-esteem and an extensive support system may need instrumental help and emotional support when problems arise but are in a fairly good position to summon the necessary resources. Depressed clients, however, are less likely than others to learn new behaviors and take control of their lives. This generalization applies equally to a sixty-year-old who needs to make a career change and to a frail older person who must make decisions about what kind of supportive environment she needs. Depressed people may also consciously or unconsciously choose dependence. Counselors can learn a lot about a client's emotional state through interviews. With older people, as with people of any age, appetite loss, fatigue, sleep disturbance, and general apathy suggest depression. Before acting on this tentative diagnosis, however, it is important to check for physical problems, drug reactions or interactions, substance abuse, or inactivity, which may be creating the symptoms. To make this kind of check, the counselor may get permission from clients to talk with their physicians or pharmacists. Or perhaps a case consultation with formal and informal caregivers would be in order. Counselors may also wish to administer one of the instruments for assessing depression that are discussed later in this chapter.

Appraisal of *cognitive ability* is especially important when older people or their family members are concerned about memory or intellectual functioning. A number of mental-status examinations are made up of questions that are simple enough to include in an interview. Some of these questions are designed to see whether a person is aware of time, place, and date, or able to perform simple calculations. Counselors must be selective about the use of such instruments, however, as they can be perceived as demeaning. We know a retired professional who was incensed when a young internist asked him who the president of the United States was and for the address of the office he was in. "I got to this damn office on my own" was his terse reply. The counselor may, rather, find it effective to engage the client in conversation about current events or his or her life, determining orientation by observation.

Assessments of cognitive and emotional functioning must often be compared because brain impairment and depression have many similar symptoms. Many older people complain that they cannot remember things and are unable to concentrate. Not surprisingly, they tend to be highly distressed about these symptoms. The counselor or other person hearing this complaint must decide whether there is any basis to it, and if so whether the problem is medical or emotional. Although consultation with medical people is essential, Gallagher et al. (1980) suggest some guidelines. Complaints about poor memory accompanied by apparent depression and normal performance on objective "memory tests" suggest an emotionally based problem. Poor memory performance accompanied by few complaints about memory and low depression scores suggests that the problem stems from brain impairment. When there are many complaints, depression scores are high, and performance measures are poor, a detailed work-up is called for.

On a different level, some older adults are concerned about intellectual functioning because they want to go back to school, learn how to use a word processor, or make a career change. In such cases the counselor would want to help them find appropriate ways of assessing their capabilities — by taking an aptitude or ability test, taking a continuing education class, attending a one-day seminar on job-seeking skills, or holding an information interview with someone in a field they are considering.

The safety, convenience, manageability, and familiarity of an older person's living quarters can have a major impact on the quality of his or her life. Home visits, in which counselors can see clients operating in their own *environments,* are extremely helpful. Remember Mr. Cohen? A visit to his home would enable the counselor to help both Mr. Cohen and his daughter determine needs and consider alternative community resources. If home visits are not possible, it is important to get information in an interview about the physical aspects of a person's home as well as the client's feelings about the home and the neighborhood. For example, someone who does not drive and wants to be independent may have to be encouraged to think about the availability and safety of public transportation when deciding whether to remain in a neighborhood.

Social factors are defined by Kane (1985) to include activities, relationships, and resources. This is an important area to assess in working with people of any age. Activities include things a person likes to do alone and with other people. Relationships cover interactions with everyone from casual acquaintances to close confidants.

Resources include a client's strengths. Older clients caught up in thinking about their losses may find it difficult — but also worthwhile — to identify these resources. Counselors, particularly those trained in career counseling, can help older people identify their skills, interests, and abilities, and consider how they can transfer them to new situations.

Resources also include the formal and informal support systems of clients (see Chapter Nine). Counselors need to know whom their clients can count on for what kinds of support and also for whom they are a source of support. The support system may include family members, co-workers, or caregivers. Relevant questions here are: What kinds of help is the person getting? from whom? at what cost? To whom is the client providing assistance? What satisfaction is she or he getting from providing this help? It may also be important to consider whether all the help being given or received is necessary and whose needs are being met. Sometimes caregivers, in an effort to be compassionate and a "good" wife, daughter, or significant other, do more for a person than needs to be done, creating a condition of learned helplessness on the part of the receiver. Chapter Nine discusses techniques for assessing the formal and informal support system of a client. It is important to help clients and their family members see themselves as a system, in which a major change for one person affects others. The retirement or illness of one person, for example, can have a significant impact on the lives of other family members.

Kane concludes her analysis of key factors involved in an assessment with a reminder that counselors must always be cognizant of their clients' value systems and life-style *preferences*. Keeping these factors in mind helps counselors to individualize their approach as they consider the theories of adult development and demographic issues discussed in previous chapters.

A Framework for Assessment

To bring the above assessment techniques to life, we will introduce you to four more people, with different backgrounds and different needs, who might seek help from a counselor or other service provider. We assume that each client has had a thorough medical workup and most have no major physical problems or incapacities. As you read each case study, try to plan an assessment approach.

Lillie Phillips is a sixty-five-year-old who lives alone in an apartment in an inner-city neighborhood. She and her husband have been separated for about five years. She has seven children, most of whom live in the metropolitan area. Lillie is legally blind but able to make her way around her house and do the necessary cooking and cleaning for herself. She is active in her church and in the local senior center but must depend on family and friends to drive her back and forth. Her children are worried about her and think she should move in with one of them. Lillie is resistant to this idea and wants to discuss it with you.

Jim Podolski is a fifty-six-year-old semiskilled worker who has been employed by a manufacturing company for the last twenty-nine years. Jim, an active union member, knows that the "thirty-and-out" provision in the collective bargaining contract entitles him to retire with full benefits after thirty years. His wife, who has been a full-time homemaker, has told him that she does not want him under foot all day and that she feels he is too young to quit work. If he retires, he would like to go to a rural area, where he can be a real outdoors person. His wife does not want to leave the grandchildren and her church.

Marian Johnson, a carefully groomed woman in her early fifties, has three adult children, the youngest of whom is about to graduate from college. She and her husband have been putting a little money aside every year so they can take the first extended vacation of their lives after the third child is launched. Three months ago her husband's father died suddenly, and his mother is having a tough time. She refuses to leave her house except to do errands and come to her son and daughter-in-law's home. Because she does not drive, she calls several times a day to ask Marian to pick her up and take her shopping or to the doctor or somewhere else. Marian says she feels guilty and selfish because she resents her mother-in-law's demands and is worried that she and her husband will not be able to take their vacation.

Sylvia Smith is an executive secretary who works in the same building as you do. She meets you on the elevator one day and asks whether she can talk to you for a few minutes. Almost as soon as she comes into your office, she begins to sob and says, "I don't know what to do about my mother. She loses everything, forgets what she's supposed to be doing, says I don't care about her and never have. She called my brother and told him I stole all her jewelry. I go over to her house and clean up her mess three times a week. Each time I come home a nervous wreck. I'm tired all the time."

For each of these cases, what additional information might you need and how would you go about obtaining it? What formal and informal assessment would be appropriate?

Although we have talked about concrete approaches to assessing various aspects of an older person's life, it is also important to have a conceptual framework in which to put assessment information. In some cases Maslow's (1954) hierarchy of needs may be a useful starting place. Figure 2 illustrates how the kinds of problems an older person is experiencing (as revealed by presenting symptoms) may indicate where the person falls on the Maslow hierarchy. This information in turn helps to clarify the client's needs and may suggest appropriate assessment tools and counseling interventions.

Let us consider how this procedure might work with some of our clients. For example, a confused and hallucinatory person like Sylvia Smith's mother is probably operating at the level where she is concerned with safety and security. She may well be suffering from a dementing disease and should be assessed for brain impairment. (Alternatively, she may be suffering from serious drug reactions.) She probably needs a safe environment and may well do better in a setting where she gets regular attention and frequent reminders of where she is than at home alone. Sylvia, however, is experiencing depression, which is a threat to her self-esteem. She needs to increase her control over her own life and to experience success rather than being told that everything she does is wrong. She may not need any formal assessment or she may profit from one of the depression scales discussed later in this chapter.

Figure 2. Maslow's Hierarchy of Needs Applied to the Assessment of Older Adult Clients.

Problems	Symptoms	Level	Needs	Interventions
Social clocks Self-fulfilling prophesies Routinized life	Apathy Rigidity Boredom Ennui	Self-actualization	Self-expression New situations Self-transcendence Stimulation	Creative pursuits Meditation Reflection Fantasy Teaching/learning Relaxation
Social devaluation Lack of role Meaninglessness Little autonomy	Delusions Paranoia Depression Anger Indecisiveness	Self-esteem	Control Success To be needed	Reminiscing Control of money Activate latent interests Allow to help others Identify legacy
Displacement Losses	Depression Hallucinations Alienation Loneliness	Belonging	Territory Friends Family Group affiliation Philosophy Confidante	Significant objects Pets, plants Soap opera families Touch group participation Listening Fictive kin
Sensory losses Limited mobility Translocation	Illusions Hallucinations Confusion Compulsions Obsessions Fear/anxiety	Safety and security	Safe environment Sensory accouterments Mobility	Familiar routines Spaced stimulation Explanations Environmental cues
Homeostatic resilience Poor nutrition Medications Income Subclinical disease Pain	Confusion Depression Fear Anxiety Disorientation	Biologic integrity	Food Shelter Sex Rest Body integrity Comfort	Adequate resources Knowledge of medications Conservation of energy Napping Small, frequent meals Choices of food

Source: Ebersole, P., and Hess, P., 1990. Reproduced by permission from Ebersole, Priscilla, and Hess, Patricia: Toward healthy aging,

Jim Podolski and his wife seem to have concerns about belonging and about self-actualization. Jim is tired of his routine life and wants new stimulation and a chance for a different kind of self-expression. Mrs. Podolski is concerned about losses if they move and afraid she will be lonely. Her major needs seem to be for contact with friends, family, and groups. They need to talk together with a counselor about their mutual and separate interests. A counselor may wish to give them interest tests. A retirement-planning program in which they participated with other couples might be extremely helpful as they could look into information about retirement styles and also have a support group.

Lillie Phillips wants to continue to be independent and to do her volunteer work at the church. Her children's concerns, while understandable, may represent their needs more than hers. Both Mrs. Phillips and her children seem to be dealing with self-esteem issues. In this case, an evaluation of Mrs. Phillips in her home is called for. Perhaps her environment can be made more supportive so that she does not need to move.

In Mr. Cohen's situation, what was perhaps seen as a permanent solution is becoming less functional. The family may need to reassess his capabilities for independent living and consider alternatives as his needs fall at the safety and security level on Maslow's hierarchy. An immediate need exists for assistance with financial matters and perhaps the creation of powers of attorney. While the family's basic needs for safety and legal probity are being met, the emotional problems should also be addressed.

The Maslow hierarchy may also be helpful in analyzing the needs of groups of people. For example, if you are working with a group of retirees who can manage their own lives reasonably well but seem to miss the status they enjoyed at work, they likely have some concerns about self-esteem and the need to matter. Helping them find paid employment or meaningful volunteer work may be a way of rebuilding their self-esteem. Even frail older people whose safety and security needs are met may well be able to operate at higher levels on the Maslow hierarchy. A day-care center we are familiar with attracts many more men than usual, we suspect because it has the men meet around a large wooden table much like the kind found in corporate boardrooms. As they sit at the table they reminisce about their days in the business world.

Although counselors need to be aware of the whole Maslow pyramid, they are most likely to be consulted about problems with belonging and self-esteem. Regardless of where clients fall on the Maslow scale, however, counselors may want to supplement their clinical observations with information from formal assessment instruments, some of which are described below. In many cases, counselors will want to refer their clients to a psychiatrist, a psychometrician, or other specially trained person to administer the instruments.

Assessment Instruments for Use with Older Adults

A general discussion of psychological assessment and the broad array of available instruments is well beyond the scope of this book. Readers interested in that subject may want to look into such standard works as Buros (1989), Sundberg (1977), or Kapes and Mastie (1988) for vocational counseling. Many older people who seek help from a counselor in private practice or in an agency are perfectly capable of responding to standard assessment instruments. However, in using standard tests it is important to remember that many people in this age group are wary of tests. Many have no experience with computer-scored tests, which require people to fill in the spaces between small lines. And, as Myers (1989, p. 31) observes, "Today's older persons were raised in a time when . . . tests were used to assess classroom achievement or work potential. Many view testing as a negative means of evaluation and are uncomfortable in testing situations." Myers also cautions that people who do not understand the value of testing may lack appropriate motivation or may simply give answers they think the examiner would like. "Acquiescent response sets are common when testing older persons, as is easy distractibility and failure to complete sections of the test" (p. 32). Because we know that reaction time slows down in old age, timed tests may pose a particular problem and should be used only if the length of response time is important.

For example, if a person is being considered for a job as an emergency medical-service dispatcher, speed of reaction is an appropriate consideration. In assessing a person's general intelligence, however, speed is largely irrelevant.

In using standardized tests with older adults, consideration should be given to the norm groups used. If older adults were not part of the norm group, questions about the reliability and validity of the results arise and establishment of a separate norm group may be required.

Counselors also should not buy into the myth that intelligence decreases with age. Although it seems fairly clear that the speed of processing information decreases with age, several research studies (Troll, 1982; Stark, 1987) suggest that intellectual reasoning does not and that memory functioning can be improved with appropriate "exercise."

Myers (1989, p. 34) offers a number of suggestions for overcoming some of these limitations. One interesting idea is to involve older adults in selecting instruments that they consider appropriate for themselves. Myers also notes that "ensuring adequate lighting, providing large, readily readable type, and engaging in oral administration may be necessary in some instances."

A number of instruments suitable for use with older adults are briefly described below in three major categories. Much of the information is based on Gallagher et al. (1980) and Myers (1989).

Instruments to Assess Functioning Level. There are two scales for assessing a client's competence to carry out basic tasks. The Index of Independence in Activities of Daily Living (Katz, Ford, Moskowitz, Jackson, & Jaffee, 1963) rates clients as independent or dependent with respect to six basic skills: bathing, dressing, going to the toilet, transferring (getting self in and out of bed and chairs), being continent, and feeding. The Instrumental Activities of Daily Living Scale (Lawton & Brody, 1969) assesses a person's ability to perform somewhat complex activities such as using a telephone, shopping, preparing food, or taking responsibility for medication.

A comprehensive measure of functioning is the Older Americans Research and Service Center Instruments. This 105-question instrument, conducted as an interview with forced-choice responses, measures functional ability in five areas: social resources, economic resources, mental health, physical health, and ability to perform daily activities. It requires trained raters to make evaluations in each of the five areas (Pfeiffer, 1976).

The Multilevel Assessment Instrument is another comprehensive measure. Designed both for research and to determine service needs, it assesses competence in the areas of health, daily activities, cognition, time use, social interaction, and perceptions of the environment (Lawton, Moss, Fulcomer, & Kleban, 1982).

The Wechsler Memory Scale is an easily administered instrument that assesses functioning in seven areas: personal and current information, orientation, mental control, logical memory, memory span, visual reproduction, and associate learning. Two much shorter instruments, the Mental Status Questionnaire and the Short Portable Mental Status Exam, involve ten or fewer questions such as "How old are you now?" and "Who is the president of the United States?" (Gurland, 1980). Cautions about the use of instruments that assess awareness of current events and memory were given earlier in the chapter.

Life-Planning Instruments. Basic interest inventories such as the Strong Interest Inventory, the Career Assessment Inventory, and the Self Directed Search may be useful with people of any age who wish to compare their interests with those of people in the field (Kapes & Mastie, 1988).

The Retirement Maturity Index (Johnson, 1982), a fifty-nine-item instrument, can be administered as a paper-and-pencil test or a structured interview. It assesses readiness for retirement in fourteen areas such as attitudes toward retirement, leisure interests, and perception of health. It is designed to identify people who are at risk of making a poor adjustment to retirement so that appropriate interventions can be made.

Measures of leisure interests, including the Leisure Activities Blank (McKechnie, 1974), the Leisure Well-Being Inventory (McDowell, 1978), the Constructive Leisure Activity Survey (Edwards, 1979), and the Mirenda Leisure Interest Finder (Wilson & Mirenda, 1975), can be helpful in identifying past interests and predicting future ones. They may be particularly useful in retirement-planning programs as well as in helping people who are still actively working become "rounded." This goal fits in with McDaniels's (1982) belief that "career = work plus leisure."

Measures of Life Satisfaction. Measures of subjective happiness or well-being have been used for many years for research as well as for clinical purposes. The Life Satisfaction Index, developed by Neugarten, Havighurst, and Tobin (1961), is an easy-to-administer checklist. The Philadelphia Geriatric Center Morale Scale, developed by Lawton (1975), taps into similar dimensions. A related instrument, which assesses older people's perceptions of the stressfulness of particular life events, is the Geriatric Scale of Recent Life Events, developed by Kiyak, Liang, and Kahana (1976). It can be given as a self-report measure or included in an interview. The Salamon-Conte Life Satisfaction in the Elderly Scale measures eight categories of life satisfaction: pleasure in daily activities, meaningfulness of life, goodness of fit between desired and achieved goals, mood tone, self-concept, perceived health, financial security, and social contact (Salamon & Conte, 1981).

Because depression is a major problem for many older adults, several scales to assess it have been developed. The Zung Self-Rating Depression Scale (Zung, 1965) includes twenty items that yield subscales on well-being, depressed mood, optimism, and somatic symptoms. The Beck Depression Inventory (Beck, Ward, Mendelsohn, Mock, & Erbaugh, 1961) contains twenty-one sets of statements designed to assess a client's mood, pessimism, guilt, irritability, fatigability, and loss of libido. It is read to clients. The Zung and Beck scales are designed for people of all ages. Two others are specifically geared to older adults. The Geriatric Depression Scale consists of thirty items that assess affective, cognitive, and behavioral symptoms of depression. It can be read to a client or given as a paper-and-pencil test (Brink et al., 1982). The Geriatric Hopelessness Scale is a thirty-item, true-false instrument that looks at the extent of negative expectations for oneself and the future (Fry, 1984).

These descriptions suggest instruments that can be used as part of an overall assessment strategy. Interpretations of any of these instruments must be combined with information obtained from interviews and observations of older adults and their families.

To give some idea of how the instruments might be selected, let us return once more to the clients we met previously in the chapter. A counselor might learn more about Lillie Phillips, whose children are worried about her living alone, by administering one of the life-satisfaction scales along with a scale that assessed her functioning level. The life-satisfaction scale might help Lillie clarify her own values and goals, and an assessment of her functioning level might reassure her children or confirm their concerns and the need for her to live in a protected setting. Jim Podolski and his wife might be helped if both were to take an interest inventory and the Retirement Maturity Index. Scores from these scales might be a useful adjunct to the retirement planning they are doing. Marian Johnson's major problem stems from her mother-in-law's depression and dependence on her. Marian might find it helpful if she had an assessment of the amount and type of depression her mother-in-law is experiencing. In the case of Sylvia Smith, her mother needs a medical and psychosocial assessment. We recommend a referral to the geriatric assessment unit of your community mental health center.

Throughout this chapter we have tried to emphasize the need to combine formal and informal assessment. It is also important to remember that assessment needs to be ongoing. With older people changes occur in particular in level of functioning and in psychological well-being. The major purpose of assessment, as discussed here, is to help older people and their families, working with a counselor, to make decisions about the kinds of services needed.

4

Getting Started: Techniques for Working with Older People

The three previous chapters have provided basic information about older people, suggested a conceptual framework for looking at the counseling process, and discussed issues involved in assessing older people's strengths and needs. This chapter looks at practical issues. It raises such questions as how to establish a relationship with a client, make the work site as comfortable as possible for an older person, and arrange contact with the aging network. The focus of this chapter is on individual counseling. Suggestions for group counseling appear in Chapter Nine.

Identifying and Overcoming Barriers

Before we address those questions, we would like you to take a brief fantasy trip with us. After you have read the directions that follow, close your eyes and think about the questions posed: *As you close your eyes, think about a real problem that you have. After pondering the problem for a while, think about what might stop you from discussing it with another person. What kind of messages come to mind? What concerns or fears do you have? Before you read further, make a list of the barriers you identify.* When we have used this activity in training groups, we have heard concerns such as "I should be able to do it myself,"

"They'll think I'm dumb," "They might tell other people," "My problems aren't important enough," "I was always told not to air my dirty linen in public," or "Laugh and the world laughs with you, cry and you cry alone." Such concerns create barriers that may make it difficult for people to seek counseling. The barriers may be particularly strong for older adults, many of whom have the independent spirit and concerns about spending money on themselves that are sometimes labeled "depression mentality."

In a review of the literature, Lasoski and Thelen (1987) identify a number of reasons for older adults' reluctance to use mental health services: "They (a) no longer feel capable or worthy of being helped, (b) wish to avoid the financial consequences and disdain of accepting public aid, (c) perceive available services as inappropriate, or as a threat to their independence, and (d) perceive mental illness differently and as more stigmatizing than younger people" (p. 288).

Let us discuss each of these concerns in turn. Maintaining self-esteem is one of the challenges of aging; it is often difficult because of the variety of losses most older people sustain. In addition, our youth-oriented culture bombards older adults with negative images about aging. These images have often been reinforced even by the helping professionals who ought to be counteracting them. Both helper and client may believe that it's too late to change.

Many of today's older adults take great pride in their self-sufficiency. Having survived the Great Depression is a source of satisfaction that may lead to a sense of superiority over the younger generation with all its entitlement programs. One often hears "I always had food on the table for my family" when talking to older adults about their lives during this period. But this coping strategy, which has served them so well in their lives, may hinder them from getting mental health assistance. Compounding this issue is the often-held belief that even if one can afford such services, it is not an appropriate way to spend money. A ninety-year-old woman whom we know said she had to save as much as she could for her old age!

Independence is of great importance to many older people. As we saw in the poem "My Children Are Coming Today" (Chapter Two), being as independent as possible may be critical to an older person's self-esteem. Asking for help of any kind may be perceived as giving up some of this power. "I can do it myself" is a value much reinforced by American culture. John Wayne is the quintessential American hero. Seeking help may be seen as admitting failure to match this heroic image, although there are gender differences. Men seem more concerned about losing face or losing their sense of their worth than women do. Women have been socialized more to ask for help than have men, although they too often struggle with this issue.

The stigma attached to mental illness by older adults generalizes to all mental health services, including counseling. Ethnic differences also have an impact on how one perceives both counseling assistance and assistance in general. Messages such as "Keep a stiff upper lip," "The Lord gives you only what you can handle," or "We take care of our own" are common in many groups. This stigma may also stem from outdated images of mental health services. Lasoski and Thelen conclude that "a lack of familiarity with psychological concepts and services may be responsible for some of the underutilization of services by the elderly. The elderly may be largely unaware of current trends away from warehousing and toward more active treatment on an outpatient basis. Such unfamiliarity may represent a cohort difference rather than an effect of the aging process and, as such, could be amenable to change" (p. 292). The paucity of longitudinal research leaves this question open.

In addition to the barriers Lasoski and Thelen identify, another obstacle for older adults in their utilization of counseling services may be their perception that helpers are too young to understand. Another barrier alluded to above is a lack of understanding of what help is, how it can be helpful, and who can provide it. "Nothing you say can bring my husband back. What good would it do?" Or "You're not a real doctor, how could you help?" And there are practical considerations too. Lack of mobility or transportation may impede an older adult's search for help. Here again, the high cost or the lack of taxis, unwilling-ness to ask for assistance, or fear of crime may tip the scales against someone's seeking help.

Think back to your own list of barriers. What could an agency or private-practice counselor do to overcome them? How could a helper reach out to you and let you know that help could be useful? In the next section we begin to identify those coun-selor behaviors designed to do just that.

Before we move to such action steps, however, we again invite you to personalize the process by continuing with the fan-tasy introduced above. Once again you may wish to close your eyes after reading the directions and make a list for yourself be-fore you resume reading. *Think of the problem that you identified before. Now mentally sort through all the people you know and select the one person with whom you would be most willing to discuss this problem. What characteristics drew you to this person? Please write your responses down before reading the next paragraph.*

If your answers are like those of many other people, you will have identified someone who is a good listener, is nonjudg-mental, will keep confidences, will take your problem seriously, will challenge you, and has some relevant knowledge or expe-rience. These are all characteristics of a good counselor.

A number of standard counseling texts describe the stages in the development of a helping relationship. For example, Brammer (1988) identifies two broad stages: building relation-ships and facilitating positive action. The flow of this chapter is consistent with his model in that it begins by addressing ways of establishing a relationship. Once a relationship has been estab-lished, counselors may help their older clients move to action as represented by our empowerment model (Chapter One): learn, change, and take control.

Establishing a Relationship

Developing Trust. Before counselors utilize any specific tech-niques in their work with older people, it is crucial that they develop trust. According to Brammer (1988, p. 5), "The degree of trust [clients] feel will determine the extent of their sharing with a helping person." Egan (1986) says that clients make judgments about the trustworthiness of counselors on the basis of their physical appearance, reputation, role, or actual behavior (or combinations of these). Kottler and Brown (1985) identify sixteen steps that are important in the first counseling session; these steps are likely to facilitate the development of trust. They are designed to help the counselor "simultaneously collect needed information and establish a therapeutic relationship that is equitable, productive, and caring" (p. 55). The steps, presented below, are general strategies that are important regardless of the age of the client. As we go through their list, we make some suggestions for adapting the strategies for an older population.

Kottler and Brown suggest that the counselor's *opening remarks* must convey enthusiasm and excitement about the possibility of change. The beginning of the interview may also be a good time to check on the client's physical comfort with a question such as "Is that chair comfortable for you or would you rather have one with a straighter back?" If the counselor senses that the older client is uneasy, it may be helpful to acknowledge this hesitation with a statement such as "Sometimes it's hard to open up to a stranger" or "I'm imagining that you may not fully understand who I am or what we are going to do together."

In working to establish trust with older clients, counselors may need to respond to stated or implied questions such as "How can someone your age really understand?" We find it helpful for counselors dealing with this issue to remind themselves of other demographic lines they have crossed in providing counseling. As one counselor said to a colleague who questioned her ability to work with older people, "No, I've never been sixty-five. I've also never been male, black, or gay, and I have worked successfully with people in all those groups." If counselors hear — or sense — such reticence, they may want to bring the issue up. Sometimes it helps if a counselor says something like "You may be wondering whether I can really understand what you are talking about, since I haven't had the experience of retiring, being widowed, having a child die, having my children leave home, or whatever the situation may be. Although I haven't, there have been lots of times when I felt sad, scared, or angry. If we get to a point where my lack of experience gets in the way, let's talk about it." Such openness on the part of a counselor is likely to help engender trust.

Route and *reason* are closely related steps. It is helpful to discuss why the client is seeking counseling and how you were selected as the counselor. If you sense that the client was pushed or dragged, possibly by an adult child, it is important to both acknowledge the resistance and make a contract with the client — for example, "I sense, Mrs. Miller, that you are here primarily because your children are worried about you and that left to your own devices you may not have come. Since you are here, what can you and I do to make it as productive as possible for you?"

Kottler and Brown think it is important to find out *what the client knows about counseling,* what the client *expects* from it, and how the client *defines* it. In working with older people, it may be particularly important to make sure they do not see counseling as a first step on the way to being institutionalized or as a signal that relatives or other referring parties think they are "crazy."

Assuring clients that what you discuss will be kept *confidential* is crucial to establishing trust. If, however, an older person has been referred to you for assessment and you are committed to providing a report to the referring person, it is necessary to be honest about that commitment.

Kottler and Brown see the initial interview as the place to *search for content* — to identify presenting problems, self-destructive behavior, and unresolved conflicts that may be appropriate topics for the client to work on. Counselors working with older adults may want to be especially attuned to losses, which occur in almost all areas of life. With older people, it is often helpful to begin with concrete, practical issues. "It sounds as if you are really discouraged about the number of turn-downs you've had in searching for a new job, and you are wondering whether you'll ever get a job at your age. You and I can talk about your reactions and perhaps identify some of the problems. Would you like the name of a group that specializes in job development for older workers?" Or "It must be really hard for you to be so dependent on your daughter-in-law to shop for you, bring in your meals, clean your house. You'd like to be more independent. If you think it would be helpful, I can suggest two agencies that will send in home-care workers who can do many of the chores you need done. You might want to interview a couple of people and see which ones you like." Note that the counselor is making suggestions but not taking over, trying from the very first session to give control to the client.

Kottler and Brown suggest finding out about those *people who are most important* to the client, especially those who have an interest in the outcome of counseling. For older adults, the important people are usually family members. Counselors need to provide an opportunity for clients to talk about their feelings about these people. Such feelings are likely to be ambivalent, as older adults may both appreciate the help they get from family and resent their need for such help. "I don't want to be a burden" is a major concern.

As discussed in the previous chapter, assessment of an older person's *functioning* in many areas is crucial. In an opening interview, particularly with an older person who may be wary of tests, formal assessments are not recommended.

Kottler and Brown note the importance of helping the client to identify realistic *goals*, gaining a *commitment* from the client to work on them, and choosing a *way of working* that will be most beneficial. With older people, we suggest these goals be as concrete as possible and be capable of being achieved in short periods of time. If the overall goal is "to have a better relationship with my daughter," subgoals might be to identify the major satisfactions and dissatisfactions in the relationship, to find ways to express appreciation for the satisfactory aspects, and to learn a strategy for addressing one of the dissatisfactions.

In closing, it is important to *summarize* the session, to restate the client's *"homework"* for the next session, and to set the time and place of that session. In working with an older adult, the counselor might want to make sure that the client has available transportation and whatever other support is needed to carry through on the commitments made.

In summarizing the key elements in establishing a relationship, Kottler and Brown (1985, p. 56) talk of "the soft smile, soothing voice, relaxed posture, and interested eyes [that] communicate an authenticity that helps the client to trust, to open up, to feel prized." Such behaviors are important with clients of all ages and may be especially reassuring to older people.

Becoming Aware of Individual Differences. In establishing a relationship with older adults, it is crucial for counselors to assess the personal values of their clients as well as their situations. In the area of preretirement counseling, for example, counselors must explore their clients' values about the meaning of work and of leisure. People's self-esteem depends in part on the extent to which their behavior is consistent with their values. An example occurred during a panel presentation at a preretirement program. Four retired teachers were talking about how they spend their time. One had a new career as a freelance handyperson. One was enjoying the opportunity to make jelly, put up fruits and vegetables, and engage in a variety of arts-and-crafts projects. Two others devoted much time to volunteer efforts, one serving on the boards of several agencies, and the other performing a variety of tasks in a hospital. All four were delighted to have the opportunity to spend their time the way they wanted. A counselor who did not get to know the different goals and values of these individuals would have had difficulty in working with them to identify appropriate retirement activities for each.

Another area in which awareness of individual differences is crucial is that of death. Deeply religious people may wish to talk about their view of an afterlife and a possible reunion with family members who have preceded them in death. Others who want to leave special mementos to family and friends may wish to discuss ways of ensuring the "right" disposition of their prized possessions. Older people who have used a sense of humor as a major coping style may bring this approach into their discussions. One of our mothers, for example, attached humorous labels to some of the things stored in her attic. "At least you'll get a good laugh when you have to sort through all this junk" was her explanation for one label, which read "Selma's old blue formal—what the hell for?" Other older people do not wish to discuss their death in any way. Counselors need to be sensitive to a broad range of styles and remember the injunction "different strokes for different folks."

That injunction fits many different situations. The truism that older people have had a long time to develop their individuality bears repeating. People who survive until old age have had to develop a variety of coping skills that work for them. To be most effective a counselor must help clients remember and tap into these coping mechanisms when they face new challenges.

Adapting Basic Skills and Approaches. Helping people use past coping skills and shape their behavior in ways that are consistent with their values and their life-styles is important in counseling people of all ages. The examples above merely highlight typical arenas in which that task may be carried out with older people. Getting to know clients as individuals involves the basic counseling skills of active listening, effective questioning, and caring confrontation as a prelude to providing assistance with problem solving and goal implementation. Egan's (1986) three-stage model involving problem definition, goal development, and action may be particularly helpful in this regard, although counselors may need to make some adaptations in their usual approach in order to utilize these basic skills with an older clientele.

Dealing with Overdependence. As clients develop trust, they are increasingly likely to discuss their feelings. Because many older adults are not used to doing this, such open expression may represent new behavior and lead to a strong emotional attachment to the counselor. Such attachment, or cathexis, can be extremely valuable up to a point, as emotional attachment increases the probability that the counselor can exert positive influence on the client. A special challenge is to encourage openness without fostering dependence; overdependence on a counselor may make it difficult for older persons to assume the desired control over their own lives.

Establishment and maintenance of control is a basic and lifelong human need. The quest for autonomy is one of the earliest psychosocial tasks identified by Erikson (1950), and concern about autonomy is, according to Butler and Lewis (1983), one of the common themes that emerges in psychotherapy with older adults. Whether or not clients use words like *burden* or *control,* we think it is important for counselors to listen for, and acknowledge, fears of losing control. For many older adults, loss of control may represent a "return to childhood" or "the beginning of the end." Counselors can help clients maintain control by making sure they repeatedly give clients choices about what is discussed in the counseling sessions as well as about behavior changes.

Not only may overdependence on a counselor make it difficult for clients to assume control over their lives, but it may also complicate the termination of counseling. Edinberg (1985) notes that termination may be difficult for both older clients and counselors. "Because the relationship may be one of few if any where there is intimacy and trust, termination can represent another irreplaceable loss for the client" (p. 149). To avoid the devastating effects of yet another loss, counselors may need to prepare clients for the ending of the relationship and also make special efforts to help them find alternative meaningful social contacts. Some strategies for this step are presented in Chapter Nine under the topic of support systems.

Environmental Considerations. In addition to considering adaptations in the way they work with older clients, counselors need to consider environmental adaptations that affect the establishment of a helping relationship. All of us know that the environment in which we work has an impact on our clients as well as on ourselves. For this reason we think carefully about the type of furniture and art we have in our offices and about the atmosphere we create. Counselors who want their offices to be welcoming and responsive to the needs of older people need to consider normal age-related sensory losses as well as the special needs of people with physical limitations.

A sensory-loss simulation is a good way to increase sensitivity to the needs of older clients, and we encourage counselors to do that for themselves. Normal vision loss can be simulated with a plastic bag taped over your eyes or around your glasses. Typical hearing losses can be simulated by placing damp cotton balls in your ears. Reductions in tactile sensitivity can be simulated by wearing latex or surgical gloves or wrapping tape around your finger tips. If you have clients who use canes, crutches, or wheelchairs, you may want to borrow the equipment and use it to tour your office building. Be sure to maintain your simulated old age for a minimum of fifteen minutes. During that time we suggest you go to the bathroom, read bulletin boards or other signs, use vending machines, look at books or pamphlets on literature tables, and use a telephone and telephone book. As you go through your office having "aged," be aware of what you do, think, and feel.

Be aware that this activity may arouse strong feelings. Some people experience fear of becoming blind or infirm. Some become sad thinking of what they fear for themselves or know to be true of family and clients. Others realize how much energy it takes to do normal activities when senses are diminished or deepen their understanding of why some older people withdraw rather than make the constant effort to go out. Do remember, before becoming too discouraged, that in doing this activity you have experienced "instant aging," while in real life people generally experience these losses gradually and usually learn to compensate.

In addition to providing empathy training, this activity is suggested to encourage you to think about what you can do to make your office, materials, and programs appropriate for older people. Such adaptations may be important in helping build a positive relationship. Here are some aspects of the environment you might consider:

Do you have a firm, straight-backed chair for people to sit in? (The soft throw pillows or overstuffed chairs that may appeal to younger people are uncomfortable for people with arthritis and may be almost impossible for them to get in and out of.)

Is your office set up so that clients have their backs to the window to minimize glare?

Does the building use color contrasts to highlight stairs and door openings?

Is the entrance well lighted? Aging eyes take longer to adjust to changes from the brightness of the outside to a dark interior.

Are program materials and signs printed in large type with dark print on light background? Colored flyers may look pretty, but they are difficult for many older people to read.

Is the receptionist's desk in a quiet place? Noise from piped in music or office machinery may make it extremely difficult for older people to hear, particularly as they enter a new place.

Counselors may also help clients make adaptations in their own homes that enable them to function safely and independently. For example, many older adults can profit from having handrails in the bathroom or hallways, a riser on the toilet seat, or an easy-lift chair that facilitates getting up and down. Or they may be able to remain independent if they have hearing-enhanced telephones, beeper systems that call for help in an emergency, or eating utensils with a special grip. Assisting older people and their families in clarifying their needs and identifying sources of help is an example of the action phase of counseling, which we discuss next.

Facilitating Positive Action

Helping Older People Solve Problems. Often when people come to a counselor, they want help in solving particular problems. They may be coping with situations as different as looking for a new job or planning retirement, thinking about how they want to relate to grandchildren or accepting the lack of grandchildren, deciding whether or where to move, considering a return to school, accepting a terminal illness, or deciding whether to get a face lift. Whatever the particular subject may be, the job of counselors is to help clients use all three aspects of the empowerment model—learn, change, take charge.

In encouraging older people to explore their situations, consider alternative courses of action, make and implement decisions, counselors use a variety of techniques. As stated before, basic counseling skills do not need to vary with the age of the client. Although the content may be age linked, the process skills are generally not. People of all ages need to make decisions, and they can profit from learning a systematic approach to decision making, such as this one from Goodman and Hoppin (1990):

1. State the decision you want to make.
2. List your desired outcomes and rank them in the order of their importance.
3. Make a list of possible alternatives (at least three).
4. Gather as much information as you can about each alternative.
5. List advantages and disadvantages for each alternative.
6. Consider which alternative will most likely help you achieve your desired outcomes.
7. Draw conclusions and take action.

Sometimes older adults who are having trouble making a decision attribute their difficulty to age. In fact the reason is likely to be inadequate information, conflicting values, or limited choices (for example, "I don't know whether to stay in my ten-room house or move to a trailer in Florida"; "We don't think Mother can live alone any more, so I guess she'll have to go to a nursing home or move in with us").

When older people have to make decisions that are highly emotional, they may forget their skills as decision makers and be unable to use a guide such as the one above. In such cases counselors may want to help them remember how they made difficult decisions in the past. Some older adults who feel stuck and unable to make a decision can profit from being asked to identify the steps they would go through in making a routine decision. For example, you might ask what the person would do if the vacuum cleaner broke. Many will outline a systematic procedure for deciding whether to have it repaired or to purchase a new one. The goal is to help them identify the decision-making strategies they use and then see whether the same procedure will transfer to the emotional situation.

Working with the Aging Network. In helping clients of any age take action, almost all counselors make referrals. They therefore need to understand the process of identifying and accessing resources for their clients. In helping older clients, counselors must know how to tap into the aging network. The phrase *aging network,* frequently used in gerontology literature, refers to the partnership of public and private organizations at the federal, state, and local levels that are involved in providing services to older people. Although there may not be adequate services to meet the varying needs of all older people, our experience indicates there are many more resources than most older people, their families, or their helpers know about. There is indeed a continuum of care.

Services may be provided for healthy, community-living older people as well as for impaired older people requiring long-term care. Table 1 lists some of the many services provided in different settings to older adults with varying needs. Detailed information can be found by contacting any of the organizations in the Resources listed in this book or by visiting a local Area Agency on Aging.

At the federal level, the Administration on Aging (AoA) is the agency responsible for most programs for older people. AoA was created by the Older Americans Act (1965) and charged with improving the lives of older people, with coordinating agencies responsible for funding, and with planning and monitoring services. In addition to the main AoA headquarters in Washington, there are ten regional offices throughout the country that work with state offices of aging. State units on aging assess needs in their states, set priorities, and develop plans and policy directives. They receive and dispense federal funds and develop statewide programs to complement national efforts.

The over 650 Area Agencies on Aging (AAAs) are the primary implementers of the Older Americans Act at the local

Table 1. A Classification of Services for Older Persons (Focus of Service Delivery).

Degree of Impairment	Community-Based	Home-Based	Congregate Residential and Institutional-Based
Minimal	Adult education Senior centers Voluntary organizations Individual and family information and referral, advice, and counseling	Home repair services Home equity conversion Share-a-Home Transportation Telephone reassurance	Retirement communities Senior housing Congregate residential Housing with meals
Moderate	Multipurpose senior centers Community mental health centers Outpatient health.services Case management systems (social/health maintenance organizations, and so on)	Foster family care Homemaker Meals on Wheels Case management for family caregivers and elderly impaired members	Group homes Sheltered residential facilities Board and care (domiciliary care) facilities Respite care
Severe	Medical day care Psychiatric day care Alzheimer family groups	Home health care Protective services Hospital care at home	Acute hospitals Mental hospitals Intermediate (health related) nursing facilities Skilled nursing facilities Hospice care in a facility

Source: Tobin and Toseland, 1985. Used by permission of Van Nostrand Reinhold.

level. They receive federal money that has been funneled through the state offices and are mandated to monitor and evaluate local policies and programs, and award contracts. As part of their planning process, AAAs hold annual public hearings that address the concerns of older people and service providers in the area. These hearings are a good place for counselors to learn about services and to articulate the needs of clients. AAAs arrange a variety of services such as information and referral, telephone reassurance, and transportation assistance. They award contracts for nutrition programs, in-home care, adult day care, legal aid, counseling, health screening, and other related social services. One of their primary responsibilities is to foster interagency cooperation through meetings and training opportunities for service providers.

In addition to these governmental agencies, many other community organizations and private agencies provide services to older adults and their families. Listings of these services are often found in the yellow pages of the telephone book and are available as well through information and referral services of AAAs and United Community Services. It behooves counselors to check on the reliability of agencies before recommending them to their clients as quality control is excellent in some and absent in others. We strongly encourage counselors to visit senior centers, where community-living older people engage in a variety of educational and social activities, to be aware of nutrition services, medical services, and a variety of housing alternatives, as well as respite services, which may assist caregivers.

Counselors who have basic helping skills and who are knowledgeable about the aging network have the background necessary for working with older adults. It is also important for them to be familiar with the major issues that are likely to be brought up, directly or indirectly, by older adults and their families. Such issues are discussed in Part Two.

PART TWO

Major Issues
Affecting Older Adults

This part approaches counseling needs in a different way than did Part One and looks at major areas that are likely to be the subject of counseling relationships. When counselors meet with older adults and their families, they often talk about self-esteem, work, family relationships, or losses. A chapter is devoted to each of these topics. Within each chapter we provide both general information and specific examples of how the topic might come up in counseling sessions. We also consider what counselors can do to help their clients make decisions in these areas.

Chapter Five underlines the importance of self-esteem to the healthy functioning of people of all ages. It considers threats to the self-esteem of older people, and ways in which counselors can help the elderly develop or restore a healthy view of themselves. It addresses such questions as how retirement, with its consequent role losses, affects self-esteem and what alternative sources of satisfaction can be built into a person's life. As counselors, we want to consider ways in which we can help people accept themselves and gain control over their lives.

Chapter Six discusses planning for work and leisure. It talks of the meaning of work to individuals and poses the challenge of what people can do to remain productive and self-sufficient as long as possible. Helping older workers prepare for and seek new sources of paid and unpaid work can be a satisfying activity for many counselors. It utilizes many skills for promoting personal growth and assisting with career development that counselors typically have and frequently use with youth and young adults.

Chapter Seven examines the many faces of families today and considers various roles older people can play in those families. It also explores the implications of changing family relationships. For example, what is the significance of the fact that many people now have more parents than children?

Chapter Eight looks at loss and grief, which are ever present for most older people as a reality or as a fear. The chapter considers the many kinds of losses older people sustain, from losses of roles and responsibilities to losses of physical stamina. It looks at death as a special kind of loss and discusses ways in which counselors can help people who are grieving over the death of family members and friends or mourning other losses.

5

Developing and Maintaining Self-Esteem

Before people can learn, change, and take charge, they have to believe it is possible. Self-esteem encourages belief in the possibility that one can influence one's world. Growing old confronts many people with the challenge of maintaining self-esteem in the face of loss, change, and subtle or dramatic deterioration of abilities. In this chapter we define self-esteem, discuss the threats to it presented by aging, and then talk about what counselors can do to help older clients maintain, gain, or restore this essential element of mental health.

What Do We Mean by Self-Esteem?

Self-esteem has been defined as the estimate one makes of oneself — one's self-evaluation. Brandon (1969) says, "There is no value-judgment more important to man" (p. 109). McKay and Fanning (1987) state that "self-esteem is essential for psychological survival. . . . Judging and rejecting yourself causes enormous pain. . . . You find yourself avoiding anything that might aggravate the pain of self-rejection in any way. You take fewer social, academic, or career risks. You make it more difficult for yourself to meet people, interview for a job, or push hard for something where you might not succeed. You limit your ability to open yourself with others, express your sexuality, be the center of attention, hear criticism, ask for help, or solve problems" (p. 1).

Clearly, then, motivation depends on self-esteem. Clients often say, "I just can't get motivated." Families exhort counselors to help older people get motivated. Yet one can never really motivate others, just help them find the conditions and internal belief system to develop their own motivation.

Self-esteem includes two essential components—self-concept and self-worth. Self-concept is the cognitive element of the self—the thoughts and ideas about "who I am." It is developed throughout our lifetimes as we interpret and internalize all the messages we receive from others, particularly our parents, close relatives, early teachers, and others whom we encounter when we are children. Self-concept is not immutable, but it is resistant to change. New messages are often distorted to agree with an already established framework. In a delightful short book called *How to Be Your Own Best Friend,* Newman and Berkowitz (1971) discuss this issue. "You can't do anything if you believe you can't. . . . If people want to see themselves as unable to do something, they manage to forget the times they actually have done it. . . . It gives us a sense of security to keep on in the same old self-defeating ways. . . . We know what to expect" (pp. 39, 46).

Rosenberg (1979) describes four ways that people develop their self-concept: "(1) Reflected appraisals. People come to view themselves as they are viewed by others. (2) Social comparisons. People judge themselves by comparing themselves to others. (3) Self attribution. People observe their own behavior and draw conclusions about themselves. (4) Psychological centrality. People value particular qualities of themselves." For social comparisons, adults use the groups found at work. But when older adults leave the formal work setting, new social-comparison groups become a part of their lives. These new groups can be a positive or a negative influence on self-concept. An important role for counselors, therefore, is to help their clients find groups in which they can succeed.

In addition, much research has focused on the necessity of continuity of self-concept for maintaining mental health (for example, Cohler, 1982). Clark and Anderson (1967), however, found that older adulthood created conditions requiring flexibility to maintain self-concept. Kaufman (1986) investigated this paradox and found that "though sociocultural demands for change are inevitable in late life and do present dilemmas of being and action, people, in describing the meaning of their lives, are able to create continuity of self" (p. 6).

Self-worth, the second component of self-esteem, has been defined as the emotional element of the self—the feelings and values that we attach to our self-concept. Self-worth often relates to how we compare ourselves with an ideal: "Am I good enough?"

Erikson's (1950) conflict orientation, described in Chapter Two, is generally accepted as a meaningful way to look at development. Positive self-esteem is linked to successful achievement of generativity in midlife and integrity in old age. Societal forces often mitigate against generativity. People may be forced to retire; they may be told they are too old for certain activities; they may be told, "Don't interfere!"; they may be relegated to an onlooker role. Those who successfully avoid stagnation tend to have positive self-esteem. They believe that they have something to contribute to society and therefore make an effort to do so. Similarly, those who find roles and arenas in which to be generative receive messages that they are valuable and needed, which in turn help foster positive self-esteem. Thus we find not a vicious but a beneficial cycle.

Brine (1979) defines Erikson's integrity as "the ability to accept one's life and to face death without undue fear, to integrate present circumstances with past history and feel reasonably content with the outcome" (p. 70). If one generally feels that one's life has been good, one is likely to experience integrity. The life-review procedure discussed in Chapter Nine can be extremely helpful in this assessment process.

Although older adults face many assaults to their self-esteem, moving through old age does not usually bring about drastic changes in self-concept and self-worth (Brine, 1979). Life satisfaction, a closely related concept, is also somewhat resistant to change, even in the face of serious losses, reductions in income, or other stress. One hypothesis is that because "dissatisfaction represents a discrepancy between real and aspired conditions of life, it can be reduced either by bolstering achievements or lowering aspirations. . . . Older adults are apparently masters of the art of lowering their aspirations to meet realities" (George, 1986, p. 7). On a positive note, however, George concludes that "the data suggest that euphoria is the prerogative of youth whereas contentment is the reward of old age." Going back to Erikson's concept of integrity, we might also hypothesize that those who look back over their lives as a whole indicate high satisfaction even if their present circumstances are not what they would wish.

Threats to Self-Esteem

As alluded to above, growing old in the United States, as in many parts of the world, opens one to a number of threats to one's self-esteem. Several of these threats are discussed briefly below; we then counter with how counselors can help individuals improve or protect their self-esteem.

Many of the threats to self-esteem experienced by older adults were discussed in Chapter Two; others will be elucidated in Chapter Eight. We discuss here exactly how these experiences threaten self-esteem. In a society that places as high a value on youth as does ours, aging presents a continuous chain of assaults on narcissism. The advertisements in magazines begin by warning the over twenty-five(!)-year-old that she needs to take care of her aging skin. By old age, when cosmetics and even face lifts no longer conceal reality, adults must face the fact that they no longer look young. A handsome eighty-year-old man whom we know saw himself on television. He was devastated, saying, "I look so old!" Somehow he had avoided that confrontation with his mirror—perhaps seeing there only his remembered self—but could not avoid recognizing changes on the television screen. Television perhaps heightened this discrepancy, as he and we are used to seeing young faces there. For him, the assault on narcissism was sudden; for most people it is gradual. In all cases, however, self-esteem that is tied to appearance—smooth skin, shining hair, athletic build—is threatened by the aging process.

Losses are also assaults on one's self-esteem, particularly losses of one's abilities, roles, or autonomy. Sometimes the losses are seemingly trivial — for example, loss of the ability to do fine embroidery or to beat the "flatbellies" at tennis — but to people who have valued that ability the loss may create a hole in their sense of self-worth as big as that created by losing the ability to have sex whenever they want or to drive whenever and wherever they want.

Another assault on an older adult's self-esteem is led by the media, often supported by older adults themselves. The equations of young and attractive (good) and of old and ugly (bad) were not created in a vacuum. Complicity exists each time we are flattered or say "thank you" when told we look young, think young, act young. Why is "old at heart" not an exciting compliment? Ageism and its corollary, group self-hatred, must be confronted if self-esteem is to be maintained in old age.

What Can Counselors Do?

According to Maloney (1985), healthy self-esteem has four parts: self-acceptance, a sense of having clear values and goals, a sense of control over one's life, and a feeling of being special or unique. Each implies specific interventions by counselors. As we look at each of these areas, let us remember that in promoting all of them counselors must use their basic helping skills of listening, acknowledging feelings — anger, sadness, joy, fear — and encouraging exploration by asking open-ended questions.

Encouraging Self-Acceptance. Self-acceptance is perhaps the most commonly recognized aspect of self-esteem and the one with which counselors are most familiar. Gaining self-acceptance involves taking a good look at ourselves, the parts we like and the parts we do not like, and coming to terms with what we see. It does not imply complacency. Acceptance does not mean abandoning the desire to learn, change, and take charge. Rather it is a necessary precursor to change, a base from which to move. In addition, self-acceptance usually increases acceptance of

others. When we can acknowledge that we have flaws and are
still, in the parlance of transactional analysis, OK (Berne, 1964),
we can allow others to have flaws and also be OK.

Most people have areas of their lives in which their self-
acceptance is strong and areas in which it is weak or less strong.
A particular challenge comes when a strong area is lost or its
importance is diminished. "I know I'm a good cook, but what
good is that since my husband died? There is no one to cook
for anymore. I don't do anything else well; I always was terri-
ble at making new friends."

Counselors can help people who are having trouble with
self-acceptance identify areas where they do accept themselves,
both their strengths and their weaknesses. If people recognize
that they have come to accept themselves as poor dancers, they
may be able to forgive themselves for having dropped out of
school. They are reminded that they have the ability to accept
themselves and come to realize that this ability can be applied
to other areas of their lives.

A useful tool for promoting such acceptance, particularly
in group counseling, is the Johari Window (Luft, 1963), a pic-
torial representation of the relationship of one person to other
people (Figure 3). The upper left quadrant contains information (thoughts and feelings) each of us has about ourself that
we are often willing to share with others. People may talk freely
about certain aspects of their jobs, families, food preferences,
and so forth. The lower left quadrant contains information each
of us has about ourself that we do not usually share with other
people ("I worry a lot about becoming a burden"; "I think I could
do a better job than my boss"). The upper right quadrant contains information other people have about a person of which
that person is unaware ("You really seem to be friendly"; "The

Figure 3. Johari Window.

	Known to self	Not known to self
Known to others	Free	Risk
Not known to others	Private	Unknown

Source: Adapted from Luft, 1963.

frown on your face makes me think you are angry"). The lower right quadrant contains information, often unconscious, that is known to no one and may be brought into awareness only after fairly deep therapy. As a result of individual or group counseling, the size of the boxes may change. Typically the first box increases in size. As people become open with each other, they are willing to provide more information from the private area and absorb more feedback from the risk area. In the process of learning how other people see them, individuals may become increasingly accepting of themselves, particularly in group situations where positive and realistic feedback is encouraged.

Counselors can encourage self-acceptance in other ways. For example, they can encourage clients to make a list of their strengths as they see them or as they imagine someone who likes them might see them. When people are too hard on themselves to be able to construct such a list, counselors can start by asking them to list their best friend's strengths. People tend to list attributes they have or wish to have. Alternatively, counselors may ask clients how their best friends would describe them. (Or the process of self-acceptance may begin with the confrontational question "Why does such a nice person [your friend] put up with you if you are so worthless?"

Think back to Mrs. Jones, whom we discussed in Chapters One and Two. Her old self-concept — a woman who works hard and has many people needing her — is no longer applicable. She is now facing the challenge of developing a new self-concept that fits her limited capabilities and roles. The counselor's task in this process is to help her develop a positive self-concept that is focused on what she can do rather than on what she could do.

Self-acceptance is aided by outside acceptance. An accepting counselor can go a long way toward helping clients see themselves as worthwhile. In addition to demonstrating acceptance with words and facial expressions, counselors may want to touch their older clients. Tobin and Gustafson (1987) suggest that touching may be appropriate and useful with older people who may "feel untouchable and unlovable because of bodily deterioration that makes them feel unattractive" (p. 116). They believe that elderly clients experience touching as caring, a form of symbolic healing. As mentioned elsewhere, touching may also be a way of alleviating some of the "skin hunger" experienced by the lonely elderly.

Group counseling may be particularly effective in fostering self-acceptance. As discussed in Chapter Nine, a major value of group counseling is that clients may discover not only how much they have in common with other people but also what they can contribute. Both discoveries are likely to increase self-acceptance. Clients may need help in finding groups or individuals who appreciate them and see them as competent. They may also need a great deal of assistance, encouragement, and prodding to leave groups where they are not accepted.

According to Atchley (1988), many older people enjoy a high degree of self-acceptance and fulfillment because they have broken the ties that bound them to roles and their culture. "They reach utter faith and trust in themselves. They learn that by understanding and accepting themselves, they no longer need to fear themselves and they no longer need to rely on the various identities society provides. These people answer the question, 'Who am I?' with the reply, 'I am.'" For those older adults "who are still searching, we must nurture and support purposeful introspection aimed at self-acceptance, development of identity with enduring qualities such as gentleness and kindness, . . . and awareness of one's completeness and at oneness with the universe" (p. 12).

For many people, self-talk is another powerful technique in the search for self-acceptance. People can learn to replace negative messages — "I just don't belong here"; "I'm never any good at cards" — with positive messages — "If I talk to two new people today, I'll feel more at ease"; "I am good at learning handicrafts."

Assessing Values and Goals. Having values of our own is one of the things that makes us distinct, uniquely ourselves. Wearing someone else's values is like wearing someone else's shoes; we can do it for a while, but we will begin to feel phony, uncomfortable with ourselves, and ultimately less worthwhile as a result. Think of a time when you have gone along with the crowd against your beliefs and how you felt afterward. In addition to wearing someone else's values, many older adults continue to wear values that do not quite fit anymore for fear of being valueless or because they have not taken the time or energy to reexamine their beliefs. Or they may be acting in ways that violate their values because they think they should. For example, an older adult who values service to others has stopped helping a neighbor because his children tell him that he is just being taken advantage of. Whenever he sees the neighbor, he feels ashamed and less worthwhile. Another older person who places a high value on independence is allowing her daughter to do her grocery shopping because she does not want to hurt her feelings. Meanwhile she is feeling increasingly less in control of her own life. All these actions take their toll on self-esteem. Counselors can help people assess their values and make choices about their behaviors in relation to those values.

Having goals is another foundation stone in the building of self-esteem. The old saying "If you don't know where you are going, how are you going to know when you get there?" acknowledges the importance of goals. To feel good about ourselves, we must know where we are going and have a plan to get there. Often people whose self-esteem is low set goals that are either much too high or much too low. Either way, they lose. If a goal is too high, they cannot reach it; they say to themselves, "See, I knew you couldn't do it," and their self-esteem drops again. If the goal is too low, they say to themselves "Anyone could have done that," and they deny themselves pride in achievement. Older adults often resist setting goals. They may say, "What's the point? I don't have much longer to live." However, when told, "It will take me two years to do that. I'd be eighty-five before I could complete it," counselors can reply, "In two years you'll be eighty-five anyway, why not have that under your belt by then?" The same argument stops people in middle age from beginning new things. How silly that seems to an older adult who now thinks of forty as young!

Maintaining a Sense of Control. Having control over one's existence, or, in the words of our empowerment model, taking charge, is a critical element in establishing and maintaining Erikson's integrity; the loss of control often engenders its opposite, despair. Indeed, one of Erikson's earliest conflicts is autonomy versus shame and doubt. From childhood, therefore, our struggle to maintain control over our own lives is paramount. Older adults may be increasingly challenged in this area. Physical and intellectual deterioration, major or minor, may induce others to take over, whether or not it is really necessary. Institutionalization — for example, entering a nursing home — may lead to even greater reductions in control.

Community services and environmental manipulations may help older adults remain independent longer. As discussed in Chapter Four, home-delivered meals or telephone reassurance may allow someone to stay at home rather than move to supervised care. Building an entrance ramp or replacing the bathroom scatter rug with carpeting may make living at home safe.

Counselors can help clients assess areas of their lives they can control and help them come to grips with areas of their lives they can no longer control. In assessing areas of control, it often helps to look at what is still manageable rather than what is not. As counselors we can help people change such thoughts as "I can't go to church when I want because I am dependent on my neighbor for rides" to "I can choose how to pay my neighbor back for the kindness — I can pay him, cook him a good dinner, or make wooden toys for his grandchildren." Counselors also need to provide opportunities for clients to solve their own problems, thus enhancing control. As discussed in Chapter Four, a systematic problem-solving technique may be taught as an adjunct to this process. Counselors can also act as advocate for their adult clients in these areas with adult children or other caregivers. Often having choices helps older persons both feel and be in charge of their lives. For example, a frail elderly person may still wish to choose between the red shirt and blue shirt; a recent widow may wish to spend time alone even if her children think she is moping too long.

Promoting a Feeling of Being Special. Finally, each of us needs to feel that we are special, and counselors can help in the discovery and appreciation of this uniqueness. Many of us felt special in childhood. Being the best at jumping rope in the second grade may no longer seem important, but the feeling of being special stays with us. Counselors can ask clients to remember what made them feel special in the past and to try to reconnect with those feelings. They may also suggest that clients notice what kinds of help they are asked to give by family or friends. Those are probably areas in which they are particularly good.

However, many older adults never did feel special. Here, new activities or skills may be mastered that add to their sense of competence or specialness. Imagine the pride that can result from being the oldest graduate of Central High School or from being the person who takes up community theater in retirement.

Other Techniques. Counselors may use a variety of other techniques to help older clients boost their self-esteem. Behavioral techniques and cognitive restructuring have been found to be useful in this regard. Sometimes it helps to have clients think about what they would say to a friend who had a similar problem. Counselors may also assign homework to their clients, asking them to make lists of strengths, learn new skills, or talk to themselves positively. Consider the following dialogue from an individual counseling session:

Counselor: Mr. O'Hara, you have been talking about all the things you can no longer do. I'd like you to spend some time this next week thinking about what you can do.

Mr. O'Hara: I try to think about that, but I can't. There really just isn't anything any more.

Counselor: Why don't you try keeping a pad and pencil near where you sit and carry one in your pocket. Here are two small pads you can use. Every time you do something new or find you can still do something you used to, write it down. You may also wish to jot down positive things others say about you, even if you don't believe them. Bring these with you next you come.

This excerpt from a group session illustrates the technique of cognitive restructuring:

Counselor: Miss Kelly, I wonder why everyone in this group greets you so warmly each week when you are so worthless.

Miss Kelly: Well, I didn't exactly say I was worthless. But I really don't have much to offer anyone. I can't bake for them anymore or even babysit my grandnieces and grandnephews. I used to help out at the church bake sales and knit for the craft fair. I can't do any of that now.

Counselor: Maybe it would be useful for you to ask some of the people in this group what they look forward to when they imagine seeing you again. Are you willing to do that?

Miss Kelly: Sure, but they'll just say nice things.

Counselor: Are you saying they'll lie to you?

Miss Kelly: I guess maybe I was. I'll try to listen and believe.

Counselor: Group, why don't each of you tell Miss Kelly something about her that you think about when you imagine seeing her here again, something that makes you greet her with the warmth I see.

Group members: You listen to me and always seem to accept me. . . . You have a warm smile for me each time I see you. . . . You have good ideas about how to talk to my daughter about her daughter. . . . You tell me when I am cutting people off and not hearing them. My daughter says I do that less since I've been coming to the group. . . . You're so loving. I just feel good about me when I'm with you.

Counselor: Miss Kelly, what did all that say to you?

Miss Kelly: I guess I have to rethink what it means to be helpful to someone. Maybe it's not only what I do for them but who I am and what I do with them.

Similar techniques can be used both to confront negative self-talk and enhance positive belief systems.

Another useful approach is that of reframing. Perhaps an anecdote can best describe how this technique can be useful. After having her hair cut, one of the authors went to the salon desk to pay her bill. The amount was considerably more than she was used to paying. When queried, the receptionist looked at her and said, "Well, you got your hair frosted didn't you?" She had not previously thought of her graying hair as a free frosting! This new frame around the picture changes our perception of the picture.

On a more serious note, a widow we know once discussed her full and satisfying life after her husband's death. "I loved him very much," she said, "but I find I really enjoy the freedom to make my own decisions and do what I like, not what he liked." Although the famous man who describes his first major failure as critical to his success has become a cultural cliché, his ability to reframe that failure was probably the critical factor. The Chinese pictograph for crisis, "threatening opportunity," again illustrates this idea. Counselors' jobs are to help clients find the new frame that will maintain or enhance their self-esteem.

Support systems are another necessary component of self-esteem. Older adults' support systems are often disrupted by death, distance, or shrinking of activities and relationships (Schmidt, 1980). As one older adult put it, "As my relatives age, we maintain our relationship, but they cease to be a support system for me." Counselors need to help clients assess their current support systems, perhaps complete a mourning process for what was, and plan ways to develop new supports. Some specific techniques are presented in Chapter Nine. It is also important to encourage people to think about their ability to give as well as to receive support. Being helpful to others makes people of all ages feel needed and good about themselves.

An additional, and difficult, aspect of helping clients enhance their support systems is that of assessing not only the nourishing aspects but also the draining ones. If the water is running out of the pool faster than it is running in, the pool will soon become empty. People need to look at the drainers in their lives, decide whether and how much contact is necessary, and take steps to reduce the draining flow. If the drainer is someone for whom the older adult is a caregiver, additional

assistance may be appropriate. Caregivers may need to learn
the skill of asking for specific help: Instead of, "You don't help
me enough," try "Will you take Father to the doctor at 2:00 on
Tuesday?"

All these techniques require that the counselor be ready
not only to explore feelings but also to help clients plan a specific course of action. Helping older adults maintain or improve
their self-esteem is valuable in and of itself. It also assists them
in family and work relationships and in coping with losses, as
we will see in the next three chapters.

6

Planning for
Work and Leisure

Throughout this book we have talked about individual differences and variability among older people. In no area of life is this variability greater than with respect to careers. (We define the term *career* as McDaniels [1982, p. 3] does, to include both work and leisure.) We begin this chapter by considering a subject counselors can help older adults explore, the psychological meaning of work and retirement. Then we move to a broader framework and examine the societal context in which older people work, considering such factors as the effects of demographic change on workforce needs. We also enumerate some of the career choices that are open to older adults and, finally, discuss ways in which counselors can help older adults with career and retirement planning.

Psychological Meaning of Work and Retirement

Work has widely different meanings to, and places in the lives of, older people. We now have the paradox of people retiring earlier than ever before at the same time as legislation is being passed to end mandatory retirement.

Work has been defined as "an activity that produces something of value for other people" (O'Toole et al., 1973, p. 3) and has always been seen as central to existence. During the Protestant Reformation, work was considered service to God. Freud saw work as part of the central trinity of work, love, and play. O'Toole et al. (1973) summarize: "It is clear from recent research that work plays a crucial and perhaps unparalleled psychological role in the formation of self-esteem, identity, and a sense of order. . . . The opposite of work is not leisure or free time; it is being victimized by some kind of disorder. . . . Besides lending vitality to existence, work helps establish the regularity of life, its basic rhythms and cyclical patterns of day, week, month, and year. [Consequently,] . . . the retired suffer a crucial loss of identity" (pp. 4–8).

Many people, however, look forward to and enjoy retirement. Perhaps the apparent paradox is the result of how retirement is defined as well as of how each individual feels about work. People retire in many different ways. Some collect their last paycheck, say good-bye to their co-workers, and never again seek paid employment. For others, retirement means leaving a job they have held for a long time, receiving benefits, and doing something else, often for pay, usually with a lesser commitment of time. People in this group naturally do not have to deal with the loss of identity, at least not to the same extent as do those who cease all "productive" activity.

Soumerai and Avorn (1983) measured the effects of paid part-time employment on the perceived health status, morale, and activity level of aged retirees. In comparing program participants with randomly assigned controls, they found highly significant differences in perceived health and happiness. Older adults wish to work for some of the same reasons younger adults do, and the primary reason is financial, especially as inflation has diminished the spending power of retirement income. Other reasons are the increased length of life after age sixty-five, improved health after age sixty-five, and the relatively young ages at which more and more workers retire. The National Alliance of Business (1985) found that "more than two-thirds of older persons would prefer at least part-time employment to full retirement after age 65."

Troll (1975) uses Erikson's stages as redefined by Gruen (1964) to discuss how successful and unsuccessful resolutions of the conflict between industry and inferiority are enacted in adulthood. The unsuccessful resolver of this stage "is passive; leaves things undone; feels inadequate about ability to do things or produce work" (pp. 6–7). The successful resolver "likes to make things and carry them to completion; strives for skill mastery; has pride in production" (pp. 6–7). What happens then to older adults who are not working in the traditional sense of paid employment? How do they maintain "pride in production" and "skill mastery?" To what extent can leisure pursuits meet these needs?

Myers (undated) says that "the loss of employment at retirement can be equally as devastating to the older individual as job loss at *any* time in life" (p. 13). Schlossberg's transition theory, however, postulates that such on-time and voluntary transitions are not so traumatic. No one, however, disputes that retirement is a major transition. For many people, the retirement transition is a positive experience, providing relief from unpleasant work or an opportunity to pursue meaningful interests. For others, even for those who voluntarily chose retirement, the sudden availability of large amounts of time can be a shock (McDaniels, 1982). Atchley (1988) sees retirement as a do-it-yourself stage of life. He states that "many people satisfy their thirst for fulfillment with social roles or activities. . . . But genuine fulfillment runs far deeper. . . . If the individual has no experience with living life from the vantage point of this more basic self, then the prospect may be a fearful one — fear of the unknown" (p. 12).

Because a major factor in retirement adjustment seems to be a positive attitude, retirement planning is useful. Counselors assisting clients with this planning can offer more than the traditional "money, health, and housing" programs that may be conducted by employers. The counseling perspective of looking at life-style, relationships, and internal needs and values can lead to a positive adjustment. In many ways, leisure planning is a form of career planning, with which counselors are already familiar.

In demographic terms, positive adjustments correlate with being male, having adequate income, working in a semiskilled job, having good health, and higher education. Negative adjustments correlate with being female, having a mid- or upper-level position, and having a high work commitment. Women's poorer adjustment is usually based on lower income. They generally earn lower wages while working, have fewer years in the work force, and are less likely to be covered by a pension plan (Myers, 1989, p. 98). The pay gap for women in the work force widens with age. In 1988 women in general earned 68 percent of men's wages, but women over forty-five earned 61 percent and women over sixty-five earned 57 percent. In addition, only 20 percent of women received pensions, compared with 43 percent of men, and only 2 percent of widows received their husbands' pensions (Nussbaum, 1988). Homemakers are another group to consider when looking at the retirement of women. How do you retire from a job that you must continue to do? Often the issue faced by these women is how to manage their husbands' retirements. "I married you for better or worse but not for lunch" has become a humorous summary of this problem.

"Retirement has been found to be a less disruptive and less stressful experience for members of disadvantaged minority groups. This is so because the occupational roles they have to relinquish tend to be less intrinsically meaningful by virtue of the fact that greater proportions of minority elderly work at menial jobs. However, after the initial shock of retirement, the more advantaged White retirees are better able to adapt to life without work because of their greater educational and financial resources" (Markides and Mindel, 1987, p. 201). Blacks are more often forced out of the labor force than whites. Their precarious economic situation, however, "often makes it necessary for them to continue working into advanced ages despite declining health. Many of these people never had the kinds of jobs that entitle them to benefits in old age" (p. 185), "Retirement for Mexican Americans—particularly lower class males—is not a specific event, but rather a gradual withdrawal from the labor force characterized by intermittent periods of unemployment" (p. 189). Both Native American and Asian retirees face a time of cultural change. These groups' traditional respect for the elderly is gradually changing as they become more similar to white Americans. The financial and emotional support for these elderly, formerly provided by their extended families, must now come from other sources.

Older People at Work

We have seen that older individuals, for a variety of reasons, often remain in the work force or wish to continue working at least on a part-time basis. In this section, we look at ways in which society aids and hinders older individuals in their attempts to find and keep jobs.

Exactly who is included in the category of older workers? Are older workers those over forty? over forty-five? over fifty? over sixty-two? over sixty-five? Each of these, and several other ages, has been used as a criterion. The federal government prohibits discrimination against older workers after the age of forty. AARP has publications relating to workers over forty, forty-five, and fifty. At the upper limit, sixty-two is currently the age for early retirement with Social Security, and sixty-five is the age for retirement with full benefits. Beginning in 2000, however, this age will gradually increase until, in 2027, it will be sixty-seven. Many organizations — universities, for example — consider seventy an official retirement age. Others — for example, the armed services, police and fire departments, and school systems — provide for retirement after twenty to thirty years, which often means that retirees are in their forties or fifties. Several unions, notably the United Auto Workers, have negotiated a "thirty and out" policy, allowing workers to retire while still middle-aged.

The average age of retirement has decreased about as sharply as the increase in the proportion of elderly people in the population as a whole. In 1955, 40 percent of men over sixty-five were still in the labor force; in 1985, fewer than 16 percent were. In 1955, 83 percent of men between sixty and sixty-four were in the labor force; in 1985, only 56 percent were. Women's participation has similarly declined — from 11 percent of those over sixty-five in 1955 to 7 percent in 1985. For women aged sixty to sixty-four, participation has remained about the same, after rising slightly between 1955 and 1965. Retirement takes place even earlier among employees of large companies with private pension plans. In 1986, 84 percent of retirements in these companies occurred before the age of sixty-five, up from 62 percent of such retirements in 1972 (Crystal, 1988).

Why are people leaving work early when, as we discussed above, work provides so many satisfactions? The foremost reason is that improved Social Security and increases in both private pension plans and homeownership make it financially possible for people to retire early. There have been financial incentives for early retirement, bonuses for older, higher-paid workers to leave to make room for younger, lower-paid workers. Additionally, the bias of many employers against older workers and the stress of many low-satisfaction jobs work together to decrease retirement age. Furthermore, leisure opportunities beckon to many. As a society, we now need to decide whether early retirement is good or bad.

Although unemployment in at least some areas of the country is still high, growing evidence indicates that we will need more workers in the future than are available in the pipeline. Fewer young people are entering the work force; the seemingly inexhaustible supply of women to fill the gap no longer exists. Therefore we will need older workers. We will need their "maturity, commitment, stability, and well honed skills" (Stepp, 1988). In addition, we will need workers to stay longer in the work force to continue to contribute to their own pension plans rather than drawing from them. Today we have 3.3 workers per pension/Social Security recipient. In 2000 it will be 2.9 to 1; in 2050 it will be 1.9 to 1 (Stepp, 1988). At Ford in 1988 there were 1.6 active workers to each retiree or surviving spouse (Savoy, 1988). At Chrysler the ratio was 1.3:1 (St. John, 1988). Clearly, younger workers are going to rebel at reducing their own standard of living further to support a growing retired population, particularly when they see that group as healthy and capable of working.

When we look at early retirement from the perspective of the individual, we find that many workers who have retired, even those who freely chose that state, feel that they did so prematurely. "They complain that without work and the associations they had at work, they lack a daily focus and sense of purpose, feel isolated, and consider that they lack worth in the eyes of their families and others" (Kieffer, 1986). Many of these workers, added to those who find they cannot sustain a reasonable standard of living on their pensions, wish to return to some form of work. An increasing number of individuals and organizations are exploring creative options to meet this need. Part-time work, flexible-time work, part-year work, internal consulting, all are ways of satisfying business's need for experienced workers and older workers' need for and expectation of leisure.

However, when we throw into this broth of societal and individual needs for older people to work the still pervasive stereotype of older workers as "over the hill," we have the makings of a poisonous concoction. What exactly are the myths or stereotypes that employers have about older workers? Eleven were identified and debunked in *Older Workers: Myths and Reality* (U.S. Department of Health and Human Services, 1984); five of these are: Older workers are less productive than the average worker; older workers do not get on well with others; older people are unwilling to learn new jobs and are inflexible about the hours they will work; the costs of employee benefits outweigh any possible gain from hiring older workers; and older workers are prone to frequent absences because of age-related infirmities and above-average rates of sickness. Each of these reasons can be shown to be faulty or easily countered.

To examine these stereotypes in a systematic way, AARP commissioned a study from the firm of Yankelovich, Skelly, and White, Inc. The report of this study, *Workers over 50: Old Myths, New Realities* (1985), discusses in great detail the opinions of human-resource decision makers about older workers, defined in this case as workers over fifty. They summarize, "In general, older workers are perceived very positively by gatekeepers. They are particularly valued for their experience, knowledge, and work habits and attitudes. The salary and health insurance costs of older workers in most companies are not seen as being higher than those of younger workers. There are some negative perceptions of older workers, centering around questions about their flexibility, adaptability to technology and aggressive spirit—all imperatives of the current focus on competitiveness in American business. There are few if any signs of overt or systematic discrimination against older workers, and gatekeepers do not believe that new Federal legislation is necessary to protect the rights of older employees" (p. 5).

To be fair, however, we need to point out that the stated beliefs of the gatekeepers may be in contrast to the actual practices of their companies. Or, in situations where the chief executive officer is unprejudiced, as found in the Yankelovich study (Yankelovich, Skelly, and White, Inc., 1985) other hirers may still be misinformed. The AARP received 26,000 unfair treatment complaints in 1987 (Gamses, 1988), and 70 percent of surveyed adults believe that "most employers discriminate against older people and make it hard for them to do a good job" (Harris & Assoc., 1981). A fifty-six-year-old man who lost his job and was denied another because of his age has founded an organization, Justice for Age Discrimination, to assist professionals with similar complaints.

There are significant differences in the ways large and small companies view different aspects of older-worker costs and benefits. Yankelovich, Skelly, and White, Inc. (1985) attributes these differences to the differing needs of large and small companies. For example, a small company may be more worried about attendance because the absence of one person has a big impact; a large company may be more concerned about health care costs because large companies generally have more comprehensive policies.

In discussing some of these myths directly, Pifer (1986) states, "In regard to intellectual functioning, a series of studies supported by the Institute on Aging in Washington shows actual *improvement* with aging under certain conditions, namely, if the work situation is challenging, if people continue to use their skills, and if the social environment provides incentives and opportunities for learning" (p. 9). Pifer (1986, pp. 9–10) continues his demythologizing by analyzing the costs of older workers.

Another misconception on the part of many employers is that it is not cost effective to retrain older workers, since the expense of their compensation, as a result of seniority, is greater than that of young workers. This, of course, is true only if one overlooks the value of experience and if one disregards the costs of benefits provided to retirees, especially health care costs. The point here is that, as long as employees remain on the job, they continue to earn their benefits and play a part through their productivity in helping meet the overall burden of the retired. Once they, too, retire, however, they simply become part of that burden. Finally, to the degree that a company pays federal taxes, it has a strong interest in seeing that as many older persons as possible stay in the workforce, thereby restraining the growth of federal spending on the elderly.

Further evidence for older workers' abilities was found by Kovar and LaCroix (1987). Of those adults aged fifty-five to seventy-four who were surveyed, 73 percent of those still working and 58 percent overall had no difficulties with ten work-related activities (such as walking a quarter of a mile, lifting twenty-five pounds, and standing on one's feet for two hours). Furthermore, 60 percent of retirees who had retired for other than health reasons were also able to perform all ten tasks. In other words, not only intellectual but physical tasks are usually within the reach of older workers.

Stepp (1988) concludes, "Research has shown no relationship between age and productivity except in cases of unusual physical or sensory demands. But 1) people need continuous retraining, 2) there is a need to redesign jobs ergonomically [designing equipment and work settings to better fit the human body], 3) people need an opportunity to scale down, e.g., shared jobs or part time work, and 4) pension portability is a necessity."

In response to these issues, AARP developed two booklets: *How to Recruit Older Workers* (1988a) and *How to Train Older Workers* (1988b). The recruitment booklet "describes various groups of older workers and what motivates them. It suggests ways to analyze and modify jobs, benefits, and work environments to make them more attractive to older workers. It outlines strategies for reaching older persons and recruiting them" (p. iii). The training booklet addresses such issues as motivating older workers, helping them gain self-confidence as learners, and designing special audio and visual aids to compensate for possible hearing and sight loss.

In summary, we are in a time of flux for older workers. The trend toward earlier and earlier retirement seems to be slowing down or reversing. More older people wish to work, for personal as well as economic reasons. Society may need older workers as fewer young people enter the work force and fewer people are available to support a growing pool of retirees. But older workers may need or want accommodations of schedule or work requirements so that they may combine work and leisure. These accommodations will require adjustment on the part of traditional employers. How these sometimes conflicting needs will be met is yet to be seen, but a number of model programs, described briefly below, address these issues.

What Career Choices Do Individuals Have?

The range of options for older people in the area of work is expanding rapidly. In past years the choice was between working full time or not working at all. Today's older adults may work full-time or retire full-time. Or they may work part-time or for part of the year. Many of these people may call themselves retired, but in reality they have a restructured work life. A man who sold insurance now harvests Christmas trees in late fall and helps build motels in Florida in the winter. Some "retired" persons may move to a less demanding role in their present career. We know of an attorney who moved "down" from partnership in his firm to salaried and therefore less demanding status. For some retirees with appropriate skills, consulting part-time during retirement is a viable alternative. For many, however, "consulting" is a euphemism, protecting the retiree from responding to the question "What do you do?" with the answer

"Nothing." Other retirees begin a business or expand on one in which they have been moonlighting. A retired shop teacher works as a handyperson; a retired nurse helps mothers of newborns during those first few difficult weeks; a retired auto worker manages a trailer park in the Sunbelt.

Other retired persons may volunteer in roles related to their previous work or in totally unrelated areas. A former letter carrier now volunteers as a peer counselor in senior centers. A former auto worker reads for the blind. A former counselor builds homes for Habitat, and her husband, a former engineer, keeps the records on his computer. A retired school counselor volunteers as a counselor in a small school near his rural retirement home.

All these alternatives provide a middle road for the retiree who is not financially or emotionally ready for complete separation from the world of work. Whether the trend toward early retirement continues or whether it reverses itself, we expect these kinds of alternatives to continue to grow. Some companies even provide for phased retirement. A Varian Associates program involves a reduced workweek ranging from twenty to thirty-two hours for employees who wish to retire within two years (AARP, 1986a). Bird (1988), writing in *Modern Maturity,* summarizes: "Part-time work is as varied as the people who perform it; but for more than 3 million people over 55, it offers the best of two worlds: the satisfaction of work and the time for whatever else they want to do with their lives" (p. 43).

For those individuals seeking new full-time work after retirement, the still-persistent myths about older workers may create barriers. The U.S. Department of Labor (1980) puts out a pamphlet entitled *Memo to Mature Jobseekers.* In it they state, "The basic techniques of an effective job search are the same for workers of all ages. . . . The difference is mainly in what a particular worker has to offer an employer. . . . As a mature jobseeker, you have assets that are of value to an employer. You have proven job skills and practical experience, plus a record of reliable service to offer." The search may nonetheless be a frustrating one. In this arena, as in the others we have been discussing, counselors may be of assistance.

How Can Counselors Help?

It has been widely recognized that counseling is a critical component of an effective approach to an aging work force. The American Society for Personnel Administration (1988) and Commerce Clearing House conducted a survey of effective management practices for an aging work force. They conclude that "more than 75 percent [of surveyed companies] said career counseling, training and development for older workers was needed, but less than 30 percent of those same companies had such programs in place" (p. 3). The report focuses on the necessity to retain older workers in a work force in which younger workers are entering in smaller numbers and older workers are rapidly retiring.

Synchronous with this trend is the growing program area of job development for older workers. Combining training and advocacy, these programs report high rates of placement or other kinds of participant satisfaction. Texas alone has eight separate older-worker demonstration projects funded through the Job Training Partnership Act (1982). These programs include teaching job-search skills, on-the-job subsidized training in the private sector, placement, and counseling. In targeting job-search programs to the needs of older adults, it is often useful to include practice in answering or anticipating employers' concerns about older workers. An assertiveness-training approach has been found to be effective; through it job seekers learn to avoid either a defensive (aggressive) or full-disclosure (passive) approach. The assertive response acknowledges the employer's need for an active contributing employee and the possibility that the employer believes that age is a relevant factor in that regard. The job seeker then presents his or her credentials and capabilities in a way that overcomes the objections (Goodman, Hoppin, & Kent, 1984). The Los Angeles-based Council on Careers for Older Americans has published a job-search manual specifically targeted to older adults (Merrill, 1988).

Operation ABLE (Ability Based on Long Experience) is a nationally recognized model for older-worker programs. Its missions are "to strengthen existing non-profit older worker employment agencies and develop new services in areas without them, to serve as an advocate for older workers and promote public awareness of their value in the work place, and to develop new strategies for job development through employer conferences, pre-retirement planning, etc." (quoted in Rugg, 1987). There are over ten Operation ABLE projects throughout the country providing these training, placement, and advocacy functions.

Another national program is the Senior Community Service Project, "designed to demonstrate the feasibility of employing older persons, who are able and willing to work, as paraprofessionals in the fields of education, health and social welfare" (National Council on Aging, undated, n.p.). Some of the jobs they have developed include homemaker assistants for the elderly, paralegal aides, bilingual teacher aides, mental health aides, and home-repair aides.

Many private companies have created special employment programs for older adults. McDonald's is probably best known in this category as their television advertisements promote the idea of employing older workers. Many other large and small businesses have discovered the advantages of hiring older adults: their availability during hours when traditional minimum-wage workers, students, are not available; their willingness to work for low wages, even with good experience; their maturity and good attendance; and their gratitude, sometimes, for a job.

In addition to helping older workers find jobs, counselors can also assist with retirement planning. Atchley (1980) details six phases of retirement. They are summarized below with suggestions for appropriate counselor interventions at each stage.

The *preretirement* period includes a remote phase, in which retirement is seen by the individual as a vaguely positive thing that will happen some day, and a near phase, in which individuals orient themselves toward a specific retirement date. In the remote phase, those workers who do plan ahead usually think about their financial future and sometimes consider issues such as health insurance or housing. Counselors can be helpful to workers at this stage by encouraging them to think about lifestyle decisions, to develop avocational interests, to make connections in the community that do not depend on children or work, and to discuss retirement plans with their spouses.

In the near phase, people begin to gear themselves for separation from their jobs and the social situations associated with their jobs. They may develop a "short-timer's attitude." They also develop detailed fantasies of what they think their retirement will be like. If these are realistic pictures of the future, they serve as a dry run that may smooth the transition into retirement. If they are unrealistic, they may thwart a smooth transition. In this phase the counselor interventions mentioned above become critical. People need to move from thinking about developing other interests and connections to acting on such plans. Counselors may need to assist clients with the concrete actions required as well as occasionally to provide a tender loving kick in the pants. In situations where married people have different views of retirement, counselors may need to do short-term marital counseling.

The retirement is often followed by a *honeymoon,* a euphoric period in which the person who is positively oriented to retirement is busy doing all the things he or she never had time for before. However, sooner or later, the hectic phase of the honeymoon ends, and the retirement routine begins. If the individual is able to settle into a routine that provides a satisfying life, then that routine will likely stabilize. This phase of retirement rarely involves counseling.

For some people, a *disenchantment* period begins after the honeymoon is over. The more unrealistic the retirement fantasy, the more likely that a period of emptiness and even of depression will follow. Individuals may be overwhelmed by the evidence that they must start over to restructure life in retirement and give up the dreams with which retirement was begun. Counselors may help people in this phase mourn for the loss of their dream as well as to approach again the planning of their retirement transition. Schlossberg's (1984) transition analysis may be helpful to both the counselor and the client as they jointly assess the situation, the individual involved, and the support system available. Clients may be encouraged here to remember how they coped with past transitions and to plan similar coping strategies for this one.

During the *reorientation* phase, disenchanted people take stock and begin to pull themselves together. They are able to use their experiences as retirees to develop a realistic view of alternatives available to them. Reorientation also involves exploring new areas of involvement. Groups in the community can be helpful to these individuals if they are willing to explore such options. For the most part people seek help from family and close friends. Counselors can help people develop a set of realistic choices that can establish structure and routine. Fortunately, most counselors know how to assist clients with goal setting and decision making.

For the most part, life in the *stability* stage is predictable and satisfying. Many people pass directly from the honeymoon stage into this one. At this point, people have mastered the retirement role and are no longer in a state of uncertainty. They know what is expected of them, and they know their capabilities, limitations, and resources. They are, for the most part, self-sufficient. Counselors' roles during this stage include helping people with the continual reassessment necessary to keep life satisfying, helping to develop new activities as others become less satisfying or less possible, and helping people plan ahead for the termination phase.

The *termination* phase occurs if people reach a point where the retirement role is no longer relevant to their lives. They may return to work or may become ill or disabled. When returning to work terminates retirement, the counselor may need to assist with job finding, as discussed above, and may also wish to help clients plan for their next retirement transition. When an individual is no longer capable of engaging in major activities such as housework and self-care, the retirement role, which depends on independence and physical well-being, is replaced by the sick and disabled role. Counselors here can help their clients make the decisions necessary to arrange for their own care and to maintain maximum control over their lives.

Let us look again at Jim Podolski and his wife, the clients we first met in Chapter Three. It is clear that in the preretirement phase Jim's fantasies are positive but without much thought. It is also clear that he and his wife are not approaching this transition as a joint event and that her feelings are quite different from his. If Jim has come to see you, the counselor, what should you do? Obviously your first step is to encourage Jim and his wife to express their feelings fully, including their fears and their hopes regarding Jim's new status. This step could lead to negotiation between them about their new roles. If it does not, you should probably encourage this type of interaction.

Next, you will probably wish to give Jim information about alternatives for his retirement. These will range from the "rocking chair" to new full-time work. You might want to help him consider meaningful volunteer work as one of his options. Many communities have volunteer referral offices, usually run through United Community Services. Or he could contact the AARP Volunteer Talent Bank, "a computerized volunteer-to-position referral project designed to provide AARP members, and others who are age fifty or older, with appropriate volunteer opportunities (AARP, 1987a). You might also wish to help Jim with his decision making, perhaps using a model like that in Chapter Four.

Throughout this process, we must remember that our goal is to empower Jim. He needs to learn about the options available to him as well as to learn more about himself, his values, his interests. He needs to change his behavior by taking charge of his own retirement. It appears that up to now he has been a somewhat passive participant, assuming all would work out. He must indeed learn, change, and take charge.

7

Relationships
with Family Members

To quote Howard (1978), "The trouble we take to arrange ourselves in some semblance of families is one of the most imperishable habits of the human race" (p. 15). Throughout our lives, our family situation strongly affects our sense of ourselves and our well-being, as well as our living arrangements.

The relationships between older people and their families, including adult children who are caregivers, is one of the areas of gerontology where cooperation and exchange of ideas between practitioners and researchers is most important — and most difficult. Family relationships can be the proverbial elephant, as perceptions are affected strongly by the vantage point from which the relationship is viewed — which group is studied, who the client is, or which generation the researcher or counselor identifies with.

In this chapter, we first discuss the importance of families to older people, then look at families as systems and examine some of the family relationships that are most important for older people. The last section outlines the role of counselors in dealing with older people and their families.

Importance of Families to Older People

During the course of their lives most people play many different roles — child, spouse, parent, employee, co-worker,

supervisor, union member or leader, professional association
member, community leader, neighbor, friend and so on. As
these roles change, people experience the joys and pains of transitions. After retirement, and with advancing age, people may
voluntarily or involuntarily give up many of these roles. Although older people often disengage from roles outside their
families, they rarely disengage from involvements inside their
families. Indeed they may put increasing amounts of energy into
this area of life. The stories are legion of men who happily make
formula, read and reread favorite books, and generally spend
time with grandchildren or great-grandchildren in a way they
never did with their own children. People who have made the
transition to retirement may find that the luxury of having time
to spend with their families can be a major source of satisfaction.
That same time can be a burden or a source of sadness for those
older people who do not have family members nearby, do not
have positive relationships with family, or have not developed
a quasi-family network of friends.

Many older people evaluate their own lives, to a considerable extent, on the basis of the perceived success of their progeny.
Success can be measured by occupational attainments ("My son,
the doctor"; "He wanted to be a tool and die maker just like
his dad"; "She was the first black teacher in the district"); family behavior ("He's a wonderful father"; "She's the most patient
mother"; "He picked a wife just like his mother"); or attentive-
ness to parents ("He calls me every week"; "She stops in every
day"). As we have mentioned, in delineating the developmental tasks of adulthood, Erikson (1950) talks of generativity versus
stagnation as the task of midlife and integrity versus despair
as the task of old age. To the extent that older people evaluate
themselves by how well their children have done, these two tasks
blend. Indeed a major source of satisfaction for many older people is the belief that they were good parents.

People often think about their lives as a series of key family events. Hagestad (1986) states, "We place ourselves on the
axis of chronological time by orienting ourselves to key transitions: when we graduate, marry, have children. In such tem-
poral construction and reconstruction, family members play key
parts: 'It was the year Pete started school, so it must have

been . . . ' In the work of creating an autobiography, we need the help of family consociates. Some of them know our pasts better than we do . . . [as] we constitute integral parts of their life stories" (p. 691).

Perhaps the major reason for studying older people in the context of their families is because that is where they live most of their lives. As average life expectancy increases, siblings may share eight decades of life, and most parents and children will have about half a century of overlapping lives (Hagestad, 1987). This lengthy period presents a tremendous opportunity for sharing the large and small triumphs of life. It can also lead to serious conflicts, as people in middle generations are torn between their own needs for self-fulfillment and the needs of family members of earlier and later generations. As Troll (1987) puts it, "In the midst of our efforts to be independent and perhaps even greater efforts to realize our potential, we can find ourselves overwhelmed by guilt that we are neglecting our family, even though we may be doing more for them than either we or our family can take." A major myth in our country is that older people are neglected by their families. Brody (1985) calls this myth "the hydra headed monster" because it will not go away despite evidence to the contrary. Study after study has shown that older people are in frequent contact with their adult children. In the balance of this chapter we investigate the nature of that contact.

What Do Families Look Like?

Although it may be a cliché to say that families are changing, counselors must understand this basic fact if they are to be helpful to older people and their families. Hagestad (1986) identifies three major demographic trends that have affected family relationships: increased life expectancy (the majority of the population now survives into old age, and about three-fourths of all deaths occur among those over the age of sixty-five); decrease in family size (currently mothers bear an average of 1.8 children as compared with 3.9 at the beginning of this century); and the increased gap between male and female mortality rates, which has led to a seven-year difference in life expectancy. *demographics*

Increased life expectancy means that an increasing number of adults will have responsibilities for parent care. It is becoming, to use Brody's (1985) phrase, "a normative family stress." On a positive note, increased longevity means parents and children have many years together when the child is chronologically an adult and may well be a parent. In Hagestad's (1986) view, parents and children experience increased rapport and empathy once the children become parents themselves. Because of the smaller number of children in the average family, relationships tend to be intense.

Multigenerational families are becoming common. The term *sandwich generation* refers to the generation in the middle. In contemporary society it is likely to be a club sandwich, as about half of all people over sixty-five are great-grandparents. Such families have three sets of parent/child connections, two sets of grandparent/grandchild ties, and two generations who are both parents and children. For the first time in history the average married couple has more parents than children.

Multigenerational families lead to considerable role ambiguity. One of the questions posed by Hagestad (1986) is, Who has the right to be old? Old age is often considered to have certain perks such as deferential treatment from young family members. The sixty-five-year-old woman who has been looking forward to such treatment may experience disappointment or anger when she finds the deference flows instead to her eighty-five-year-old mother or mother-in-law. Other questions that may get sticky include: Who gets to — or gets not to — host the holiday meals? Who is the guest of honor on Mother's Day? Which special birthdays do you celebrate? Is an eightieth birthday less significant when the octogenarian has a living parent?

Four out of five older people in this country have living children. And 94 percent of those who have children have grandchildren. Most of these older people have frequent contact with their children. Shanas (1980) conducted a national study that indicated that three-fourths of older people with children had seen one of their children during the week before their interview. In addition to seeing children and grandchildren frequently, most older people who have families help and are helped by family members. Seventy percent of older people report that they provide help to children and grandchildren, and an equal percentage reports receiving help (Shanas, 1980).

Such statistics do not hold for all ethnic groups. Because many Chinese and Filipino men came to this country and either left wives at home or never married, there are large numbers of childless older men among these groups who have special needs and problems. Indeed Markides and Mindel (1987) note that in 1970 there were 132 Chinese men over sixty-five for every 100 Chinese women as compared with 71 males for 100 females among elderly whites. The Chinese men may or may not be part of extended kin networks that can provide informal support and serve as a link with formal support networks, an important function of family members. In the absence of family members, counselors may need to be active in reaching out to single or widowed people and referring them to appropriate resources.

Many older people who have no children are helped by other relatives or may become part of "pseudofamilies" or families of choice, which provide them with emotional and instrumental support. Such groups may get together on holidays and other occasions or may share living space. In the movie *Wrinkled Radical,* Maggie Kuhn, founder of the Gray Panthers, and her housemates talk of the values of intergenerational shared housing. In an article about the childless elderly, Johnson and Catalano (1981) note that caring for a frail relative who is not one's parent may produce special strains. Distant relatives who assume caregiving functions may serve more as intermediaries between the older person and the formal support system than as direct caregivers. When nieces and nephews provide care, they typically do so out of loyalty to their deceased parents rather than to their aunts and uncles.

In some cities social agencies have arranged communal housing for single older people who are not able to function on their own but do not need institutionalization. In Southfield, Michigan, for example, the Jewish Family Service (JFS) rents a number of apartments in a high-rise, barrier-free apartment building. JFS furnishes the common living areas and residents furnish their own bedrooms. This set-up provides a somewhat protected environment, yet permits assimilation amidst a normal population. Program managers screen applicants in order to locate people who have the capacity to share with others but also have the need to be taken care of because of their frail physical condition. Staff also make considerable efforts to involve family members, sometimes asking them to assist with outings as well as attend social events. "One of the goals of our program is to help the family to ease some of the tension and to be able to spend these few remaining years in bringing to resolution some of the past problems" (Daitch & Lerner, 1984).

Foster care for the elderly is another alternative to both traditional family life and institutionalization. However, it is not without problems. Kosberg (1985) points out that neither foster homes nor foster-care providers are licensed and that older persons in such homes are subject to abuse. He also raises serious questions as to whether foster homes are more like families or more like small businesses.

Troll, Miller, and Atchley (1979, p. 5) state that "families today can include same-sexed and opposite-sexed cohabiting partners, children of previous marriages (or of more informal pairings), as well as more 'legitimate' great grandparents, great nephews and cousins." Counselors may be helpful to older people in helping them sort out their feelings about the many nontraditional relationships they see.

Major Family Relationships

Because of the complex network of relationships in which most older people are involved, they, and the counselors who help them, need to think carefully about the meaning of their various roles. Some of these roles and relationships are discussed below.

Husbands and Wives. Although 95 percent of all Americans are married at some time in their lives, there is a gradual reduction with increasing age, particularly for women, in the percentages of people who are married. In 1987, 77 percent of older men and 41 percent of older women were married (American

Association of Retired Persons & Administration on Aging, 1987). As counselors or family members we clearly are concerned not just with the statistics but with the nature of marital relationships. As longevity increases and family size decreases, many couples have a much longer period of being alone together again after the children leave. Troll and others (1979) cite contradictory reports on this period of life, with some writers seeing it as a time for a second honeymoon and others as a time when divorce rates rise. Both may be true; older marriages may be characterized by extreme diversity. Those in older marriages have, after all, had longer to develop their similarities and their differences!

A variety of factors affect the marital satisfaction of older husbands and wives. Partly it depends on their expectations. Troll et al. (1979) suggest that spouses who perceive few options are likely to view their marriages as satisfactory in order to reduce cognitive dissonance. They also cite research that indicates changes in marital satisfaction over the life course. A number of studies show a reduction during childbearing and child-rearing years. There is also evidence (Gilford, 1986) of an upswing in satisfaction among older couples. Gilford summarizes strengths and strains in marriages in later life. On the positive side, she notes that married persons appear to be happier, healthier, and longer-lived than widowed or divorced people of the same age. Marriage can be a buffer against the stresses of retirement, reduced income, and declining physical capacity. In Atchley's (1985) view marriage can meet the needs of older people for intimacy, interdependence, and a sense of belonging. Gilford (1986, p. 19) cautions, however, that "although some couples may have built reserves of intimacy and belongingness on which to draw," other couples may experience conflicts and see their partners as burdensome. A more recent study by Lee and Shehan (1989) found no indication of a beneficial impact of retirement on the marital satisfaction of husbands or wives. The clearest finding was that the marital satisfaction of employed wives whose husbands had retired was lower than that of any other group in the study. The authors suggest that the dissatisfaction of these wives may be related to feelings about the unequal division of labor in the house.

The retirement of either or both marriage partners presents new challenges and opportunities for many couples. A host of new decisions may have to be made such as: Who decides how money is spent? Who decides how often visits to children and grandchildren are made? Who baby sits, and who makes the offer? Many people resent having their services volunteered by their spouse. Counseling may help older couples talk through some of their differences and renegotiate their relationship. This is another arena in which our framework for helping may be useful. Both partners may learn about their situations and about negotiating techniques in order to change some behaviors and take charge of getting the marriage relaunched in this new life stage.

Parents and Children. Relationships with their children are extremely important to most older people. As Troll (1987) phrases it, "Parents and children are not easily divorced." They usually share similar values, even though they may express these values in different ways. Relationships with children are particularly important for women, partly because women are less likely to grow old with a spouse than are men. Older women tend also to be the kinkeepers in American families. They typically arrange family get-togethers and spread family news, letting family members know who needs help or merits congratulations. At this stage of life, as in their younger years, women seem to perform these "executive" functions regardless of whether they are working.

Additional evidence points to the different family roles played by women and men. Because older women are the kinkeepers and daughters the primary caregivers when parents need help, the mother/daughter relationship is a crucial one. This conclusion fits Kastenbaum and Aisenberg's (1972) observation that while dying men mourn the loss of their bodies and their selves, dying women grieve that they are abandoning their spouse and children.

Just as it is important to consider strengths and strains in relations between spouses, it is crucial to look at the benefits and the problems of relationships between parents and their adult children. Although counselors' offices may be full of people experiencing difficulties in relationships with family members, most studies report good feelings between different generations within a family. Hagestad (1984) believes that many families make special efforts to preserve these good feelings, partly by avoiding controversial topics, creating what she calls a demilitarized zone.

Long-term illnesses and the inability of people to care for themselves obviously present major problems for families. The stresses experienced by caregivers are subjects in the popular press as well as in publications on gerontology. AARP (1987b) has developed a checklist of concerns of caregivers. They range in seriousness from "My relative really needs to get out and do something" to "My relative has a terminal illness and wants to return home instead of dying in the hospital." Next to each statement is a brief description of services that might be relevant to that need, readings that may be helpful to caregivers, and resources that might be tapped. A special section of the checklist is devoted to feelings of the caregivers, including being overwhelmed, resenting other family members, and being concerned about the impact of caregiving on work, personal life, and health.

Corporations are beginning to be concerned about the responsibilities of their employees for aging parents as well as for children. A study at the Travelers Corporation in Hartford found that 8 percent of employees over thirty spent thirty-five or more hours a week caring for elderly relatives and 20 percent spent ten or more hours (reported in *Parent Care,* 1988). Such pressures on employees can lead to absenteeism, low productivity, and resignations. Therefore, some businesses are experimenting with ways to provide assistance including holding lunch-hour seminars where people exchange information and share feelings, paying for respite care, allowing flexible schedules for caregivers, creating adult day-care centers, and granting sabbaticals with job guarantees to help employees through difficult times. Such programs underline the fact that families are systems and that problems with one member may have a significant impact on others.

Grandparents and Grandchildren. For most people, becoming a grandparent is an exciting and heartwarming experience, a reminder of the continuity of the generations. The general expectation in this country is that people become grandparents at a time when they have been freed from the commitments of their own child-rearing years, have attained a certain level of economic security, and are still healthy and vigorous. When those conditions hold, it is indeed fortunate for members of all generations involved.

When one is handed the grandparent role off time (and clearly individuals do not have control over when they become grandparents), it may have different consequences. Hagestad and Burton (1986) report a study of black women who became grandmothers on time and off time. Not surprisingly the on-time grandmothers were much more positive about the role. Early grandmothers expressed discomfort, saying that grand-motherhood interfered with parenting, work, education, friend-ships, and romantic involvements. Some early grandmothers actively rejected the role, which had implications for other generations in the family. Hagestad and Burton (1986) note the absence of research on late grandparenthood, but they raise questions about whether delay of childbearing creates tensions between parents and adult offspring and how it affects the resolutions of life tasks for both generations. Such tensions may take the form of nagging by the older generation or careful avoidance of the topic.

However, although they may have trouble with their children's values, many grandparents are extremely flexible and accepting of the values of grandchildren. We overheard one delightful conversation in which a woman in her mid-eighties was talking to her thirty-five-year-old granddaughter about her plans for a family. When the younger woman indicated she was not in a hurry, the older woman, whose own children were born over a twenty-five-year span, said, "Well, having a baby really is a good way to get through menopause."

It is somewhat of a paradox that as more and more people become grandparents, the role becomes less and less clear. Today's grandparents range in age from thirty to over one hundred, their grandchildren from newborns to retirees. The image of the gray-haired, matronly looking woman in a house-dress who dispenses cookies and kisses with infinite patience is not an accurate representation of many of today's grandmothers. Although today's grandmothers may be gainfully employed, physically active, and socially involved women, old stereotypes still prevail. The disparity between the stereotype and the reality brings delight to some families and poses difficulties for others. Many grandparents experience considerable conflict between their desire to be independent and live their own lives, and their desire to be responsive to their children's needs for help with the grandchildren. When communication is not open, grandparents may feel ignored or imposed on; parents may feel burdened, cheated of the help they need, or confused because their parents are not elated at the prospect of being regular babysitters.

Although such problems clearly exist, most grandparents feel close to and visit frequently with grandchildren, at least those in their geographical area. In discussing the frequency of visits, Cherlin and Furstenberg (1986, p. 27) state that "this strong sense of obligation to keep in touch usually is overlaid with love, concern, and assistance; but even when the sense of obligation is unsupported by these props, it is often still honored." In the absence of family crisis, most grandparents seem to see their role as being emotionally close to the grandchildren but not interfering with the way their children raise their children, although some evidence indicates that black grandparents, particularly grandmothers, play a more parentlike role in relation to their grandchildren than do white grandparents.

In times of family crisis, grandparents often step in to provide assistance to parents and grandchildren. If the crisis is a divorce, grandparents on the custodial side, typically the parents of the children's mother, are most likely to be involved in providing financial as well as emotional support, housing or regular child care. Providing such support may bring these grandparents into close contact with their grandchildren.

Grandparents on the noncustodial side, typically the father's parents, may have a difficult time maintaining close relations with their grandchildren. The magazine *50 Plus* (Lindeman, 1987) ran a poignant article entitled "Nana, I can't visit you," which dealt with the plight of "abandoned" grandparents and of grandchildren cut off from one set of grandparents. In recognition of this problem, a number of self-help groups now provide information about legal options and suggestions for improving relationships. Grandparent-rights provisions are also sometimes written into divorce agreements. Because concerns about such issues are often brought up in counseling sessions, counselors need information on lawyers skilled in this area and on groups that can be supportive. (See Resources.)

Brothers and Sisters. For most older adults, the people with whom they have the longest shared relationship and history are their brothers and sisters. Sibling relationships can be an ongoing source of support or a continuous arena for hostilities and rivalry. They may be particularly important to never-married older people. Studies of sibling relationships in old age (Gold, 1988) indicate that most brothers and sisters grow closer as they grow older. One reason is that siblings who communicate through a parent, usually a mother, can no longer stay in touch this way when the parent dies. Old age may also be seen as a time to put aside childhood rivalries. Typically it is also a time when the demands of career and family are reduced.

Talking with brothers and sisters about early shared experiences can be an important part of a life review (discussed further in Chapter Nine). Siblings who shared those experiences are in a unique position to help each other remember parents and make sense out of recollections of growing up. Maybe old age is finally the time to laugh, rather than cry, about feelings that "Mother always loved you more," particularly if both siblings had the same feeling.

Widowed persons may look to siblings for emotional closeness after the death of their spouses, and old women are more likely to have a living sibling than a spouse. Some older siblings choose to live together. Sisters are more likely to do this than brothers or siblings of opposite sex, perhaps because there are more unattached sisters and perhaps because women are more willing to acknowledge their dependency needs. However, despite the increased closeness that comes with old age, most older people look to their children, rather than to siblings, when they need help with problems of daily living. It will be interesting to see whether this pattern still holds when the baby boomers, who have more sisters and brothers than children, become old.

Old age may also be an important time to resolve hostilities, whether they stem from childhood rivalries, jealousy over differing life-styles, dislike of each other's spouses, resentment about inequalities of efforts devoted to parent care, or inheritance disputes. As people age and become conscious of their own mortality, they may want to reconcile. Just as many married people think you should not go to bed mad, some older people think you should not die mad. This need to deal with unfinished business is one of the areas in which counselors may be helpful. Often clients need to talk through their hostilities so they can understand them and let go of built-up resentments.

Gay and Lesbian Relationships. Research on older gays and lesbians is limited and recent, partly because most homosexuals who are now old discovered their sexual orientation at a time when homosexuals tended to be closeted. The degree of social integration or isolation experienced by homosexual older people depends on a number of factors, among them acceptance or nonacceptance by family members of the homosexual's life-style. Lipman (1986) cites several studies that show that both older gay men and older lesbians have more friends than do heterosexuals of similar age. Strong friendships may supplant or supplement traditional kinship support. In any event, such friendships provide important social integration into the community.

Support groups are important to homosexuals, just as they are to heterosexuals. The extent to which such supports are available is related, in part, to geographical location. In urban centers, where the gay-rights movement has had more impact and where there are simply more people than in rural areas, older homosexuals are likely to form networks and engage in collective action. The larger pool available in urban areas is important, as elderly gays and lesbians tend to associate mainly with other gays and lesbians (Lipman, 1986).

Another factor that may affect the life-style and counseling needs of an older gay person is the presence or absence of a partner. For older homosexuals, as for heterosexuals, the presence of a committed partner is a source of satisfaction and a buffer against stress. When the relationship is longstanding, a reservoir of experience and cooperation can be drawn on. Problems may arise when one member of a gay or lesbian couple is hospitalized or institutionalized because the partner may not be perceived as "family" by the bureaucracy or the family of origin. In these cases both the ill older person and the partner may be denied opportunities to support each other, to enjoy continued intimacy, and, in cases of terminal illness, to say good-bye. Gay and lesbian couples, like any nonmarried partners, may also have difficulty with respect to wills or giving each other durable power of attorney. In some areas the situation is beginning to change. In 1989 New York City passed an ordinance that allowed the surviving nonmarried partner to remain in a rent-controlled apartment after the death of the tenant with the lease. It is helpful for counselors working in this area to keep abreast of such developments and to be advocates for legislation that will favorably affect their clients.

The Role of Counselors

What Do Counselors Need to Know? The complexity of relationships between older people and their families and the importance of such relationships to all parties make this an important arena for adult counselors. Fortunately, most counselors are trained to help people improve communication and to understand and accept complex and conflicting feelings. In working with families of later life, the client may be the older person, an adult child or other member of the family, or the family as a whole. Often counselors are sought as consultants, helping adult children make appropriate decisions and deal with their feelings about an aging parent.

Working with older families — or members of those families — requires some specific knowledge to supplement basic counseling skills. Counselors must understand the complexity of family systems and realize that in treating one member of a family they have an impact on, and may disrupt, the whole system.

Interventions are still appropriate, but they must be done thought-fully and with a realization of possible consequences.

Counselors also need to be keenly aware of their own values about "taking care of one's own," responsibility to older people, and the need to take care of oneself. Although knowing your own values is important in all counseling situations, it may be essential in this complicated area. Without such clarity, counselors can easily see other people's situations through the filter of their own perspective on families and may unwittingly impose their own values. Because of differences in personality, family history, or ethnic background, their clients may operate with different values.

On a concrete level, counselors must also be knowledgeable about the aging network, community resources, and the referral process. Families of older people who are experiencing difficulty may think they have no choices other than a hospital or nursing home if they are unable, or reluctant, to care for their relative at home. In most communities, particularly those in urban areas, there is a continuum of care available for the short and long term for persons at home or in institutions. Counselors must know about such formal community supports as well as be able to encourage clients to use them. A comprehensive picture of services is found in Huttman (1985). On a local level, Area Agencies on Aging are a good contact point.

Counselors also need to be aware of elder abuse as an increasing problem. Students of family violence have termed the sixties the decade of child abuse, the seventies the decade of spouse abuse, and the eighties the decade of elder abuse. It is not clear whether there is an increase in the incidence of such abuse or just in the awareness of it. The major cause of elder abuse seems to be family stress, but there is a high correlation between child abuse and elder abuse. Not surprisingly, battered children often grow up to be abusive. Hayhow (1983) reports that victims of elder abuse are usually from the most dependent part of the population, typically over age eighty with multiple problems, including incontinence. Substance abuse is involved in 40 to 50 percent of the cases. Service providers need to be attuned to the possibility of abuse because it is seldom reported by the abused older person, probably because of dependence on the family and fear of reprisals. One indication of the extent of the problem is that there is now a special publication, the *Journal of Elder Abuse and Neglect,* published by Haworth Press in New York.

How Do Counselors Work on Family Issues? In addressing family concerns, counselors may work with individuals, groups of nonrelated persons, or families. Adult children are more likely to come for individual sessions — often starting with a request for a consultation — than are aging parents. Requests can be for information about community resources, nursing homes, or symptoms of Alzheimer's disease. In the process of seeking such information, clients may reveal a need to talk about their own feelings and concerns.

For example, in Chapter Three, we met Sylvia Smith, who was terribly upset over both her mother's highly impaired functioning and the fact that she accused Sylvia of stealing from her. An interview with Sylvia might go like this:

Counselor: It sounds like your mother is no longer the same person she used to be.

Sylvia: She sure isn't! She used to be such a sunny, fun person to be around. All my friends used to enjoy visiting her. Now I almost dread going into her house.

Counselor: That must be agonizing for you. Tell me what it's like when you do go there.

Sylvia: The place is always a mess with dirty dishes and half-eaten food all over the place. Clothes are usually strewn all over the house. If I can be honest, I sometimes hope she's asleep so I can just clean the place up and not have to talk to her because if she is awake, she screams at me for not coming over. She never remembers that I was there two days ago. The worst is when she says she's been searching her house for her jewelry or some money she had put away, says it's not there and I must have taken it.

Counselor: No wonder you dread the visits. You must feel like you are doing as much as you can and get nothing but grief and accusations in return.

Sylvia: That's about it. I'm exhausted from working full-time and taking care of her house as well as mine. I'm at my wit's end and don't know what to do.

Counselor: I can see why. Tell me what you have done so far to find out just what is going on.

Sylvia: Not much. She has all but refused to go to the doctor.

Counselor: I think as a first step we should get an assessment of her level of functioning. Ms. Robinson is the head of the geriatric assessment unit of the community mental health center. They work with people like your mother all the time. If you would like I'll call and alert her to expect a call from you. While you'll want to find out what is going on, it sounds from your description like your mother is suffering from dementia. If that's true, she really can't control her erratic behavior. I know that doesn't make it any easier for you.

Sylvia: Actually, it does help a little to have someplace to contact.

Counselor: It sounds like you have been dealing with this problem pretty much by yourself. Do you have any other family members whom you could involve?

Note that in this interview the counselor attempted to assure Sylvia that her feelings were understandable. The counselor also referred her to a resource for help and offered to pave the way but still indicated it was Sylvia's choice. As the interview continues, Sylvia and the counselor may explore her reluctance to ask the rest of the family for help. It may be appropriate to help Sylvia become assertive with her family or to arrange for a session with the whole family after the report is in from the geriatric assessment unit.

Adult children who seek help are often experiencing role overload. Although all of us like to matter to other people, adult children who find themselves in the middle of the club sandwich described above may matter to too many people. Marian

Johnson, another of the clients we met in Chapter Three, is a
good example. Caught between the needs of an aging mother-
in-law, her young adult children, her husband, and her own
desire for self-fulfillment, she is in a crisis. Her counselor can
help her see that she is not selfish to resent these demands or
uncaring because she does not want to have her mother-in-law
live with her. Often people in Mrs. Johnson's situation have
made promises to a parent such as "I'll never put you in a nursing home." Or, even without such promises, they may think,
"My grandmother lived with us for years; how can I not take
my mother or mother-in-law in?"

In working with adult children, a primary job is to help
them realize that they can both love their parents and resent
their demands. Caring for frail older people can exact a terri-
ble toll, physically and emotionally. Brody (1985, p. 22) states
that although taking care of a disabled parent may lead to declines in physical health and financial hardship, "study after study
has identified the most pervasive and more severe consequences
as being in the realm of emotional strains. . . . Depression, anxiety, helplessness, sleeplessness, lowered morale, and emotional
exhaustion are related to restrictions on time and freedom, isolation, conflict from the competing demands of various responsibilities, difficulties in setting priorities, and interference with
life-style and social and recreational activities."

Sometimes adult children have trouble understanding how
they can be so accepting of the dependence of young children
and so distraught over the dependence of aging parents. Counselors can help them understand some of the actual differences
between these two experiences and some of the differences in
the internal meaning of these events. For one thing, children
can be expected to outgrow their dependence, while frail or impaired older people probably will not. It is also hard for many
of us to accept the fact that our parents or older relatives are
no longer able to take care of us. Although we can never be
a parent to our parents, we may become their caretakers, and
it is hard.

In addition to helping adult children express and accept
their complex feelings, counselors can help assess the extent of

the problem and make appropriate referrals to various agencies. Adult day-care centers, respite-care organizations, Meals on Wheels programs, visiting-nurse or other services may provide sufficient support to enable older people to stay in their own homes. Such supportive services can also help improve the quality of time adult children spend with dependent relatives. If adult children spend all their available time on chores, they may not have opportunities to provide the love and emotional support that is harder to hire. Male caregivers, in particular, often concentrate on instrumental assistance (fixing the roof, dealing with insurance and banking needs, or even doing the shopping). (A project at Bryn Mawr College developed a guidebook for involving men in caregiver support groups [Jacobs, 1989].)

Although counselors are more likely to be approached by adult children than by aging relatives, older people can clearly benefit from the help of counselors. Some older people are resentful of what they consider lack of attention from family members; others are concerned about becoming a burden on their families. Supportive counseling may help older people who are concerned about intruding on their children's lives see that they still belong and matter, and have a role to play. Older adults who feel neglected by their families may be helped to understand their children's needs for some degree of privacy and may also be encouraged to develop new interests or rekindle old ones. Both groups can benefit from training in communication skills so they express thoughts and feelings directly. Often such training is most effective when done in groups, as we see in the next section.

Group and Family Counseling. In addition to working with individual family members, counselors can offer group experiences that improve communication within families. Wheeler (1980) makes a case for assertiveness training as a way to prevent depression as well as improve communication. In Wheeler's view, when older people are taught to counter slights and put-downs, they are not likely to internalize the criticisms and allow them to affect self-esteem negatively. Burnside's (1984) book contains a great deal of information about group work with both community-living and institutionalized older people. Although the book is not focused on family, relationships with family are discussed in many of the chapters.

Sometimes the intervention of choice may be family counseling, in which a counselor works with several or all members of a family. Gwyther (1986) urges that an adequate assessment is a necessary first step in family therapy and that the assessment should begin by answering the questions, Who is complaining about what? Why now? What does the family hope to accomplish with the visit? Gwyther also suggests that work with older families may well begin with an attempt to see that family members gain a common understanding of the condition and prognosis of the identified patient. This technique is helpful with families who may be resistant to the idea of therapy but willing to come for interpretive information.

Florsheim and Herr (1990) and Genevay (1990) provide models of problem-focused approaches to family counseling. Consistent with our concerns about nomenclature, Florsheim and Herr suggest that family members may be more willing to attend "family meetings" than "therapy sessions." Genevay's approach, which she labels "A Summit Conference Model of Brief Therapy," may involve friends, neighbors, and caretakers as well as family. She states that the most common topics are the current situation, including decisions that must be made; unfinished business and past losses; family rules; family communication styles; division of labor; and exploration of communication skills.

In working with families, counselors must be able to help members communicate honestly. In family counseling, unclear communication patterns can come to light. For example, family members may see that they have been tiptoeing around each other, with one generation afraid to ask for help for fear of intruding and the other generation feeling slighted because they are not being asked. Or the counselor may need to help a family confront a member who is making unfair demands, resisting a needed nursing-home placement, or refusing to follow a medically prescribed regimen.

An issue that frequently arises in couple or family counseling is that of the balance between work and family commitments. In most families the work/family connection is a dynamic issue that has to be renegotiated at various stages of the life cycle. Adult counselors often see a problem that we have labeled the "out-of-sync career-commitment curve." This problem emerges as gender differences and sex-role expectations interact with career stages throughout the life cycle. In many two-career families, changing career commitments can be graphically depicted as one "hump" for men and two for women. We have characterized this as the dromedary-versus-camel phenomenon (Goodman & Waters, 1985).

For the family in which both the man and woman start off, typically in their twenties, with a strong investment in their careers, the career-commitment curves may begin the same. During the childbearing and child-rearing years, many women, including those who are working, become less career-committed as they face conflicting demands on their time and emotions. When the children get older or leave home, many women feel an increased career commitment and a desire to find new challenges. As career counselors know, this spurt of enthusiasm on the part of a woman often coincides with a reduced career commitment by the husband. Thus men in their forties and fifties may make the same complaint, "All she thinks about is her job," as their wives had made about them ten or twenty years earlier. Families who weather this storm may then have to renegotiate the work/family balance if one wishes to retire and the other does not or if parent care becomes an issue.

Whatever the situation, whether working with individuals, couples, groups of unrelated people, or families, counselors must be keenly aware of the values and dynamics of each family. As indicated throughout this chapter, families come in many shapes and sizes, and members of families have different relationships with each other. Sometimes these relationships are the primary source of satisfaction for family members; other times they are the primary source of pain. Helping older adults examine and rethink these relationships is an important arena in which counselors can help families to learn about themselves, change maladaptive behaviors, and take charge of their lives.

8

Adjusting to
Loss and Grief

As indicated in previous chapters, loss and the fear of loss become increasingly salient for many older people, even though losses are not a new phenomenon in old age. We suffer losses throughout our lives, and we grieve over those losses throughout our lives. We may grieve over any perceived loss, not just the loss of a loved one. We may grieve over the loss of a job or a piece of jewelry, the loss of a softball game, the failure to get a promotion, or a forced move to a new community. We may also experience grief during happy times when they involve a loss. For example, graduation from school typically represents the achievement of a goal but also involves the loss of a familiar routine, place, friends, and clearly defined norms, as well as loss of the goal itself. For older adults a move to a condominium may represent both the fulfillment of a dream and the loss of lifelong friends and services in the old neighborhood.

This chapter is divided into three major sections. The first, which deals with losses in old age, distinguishes between normal or common age-related losses and abnormal or less common losses. It also discusses the interplay of losses and fears. The second section focuses on death as a special kind of loss. The third section is practitioner-oriented; it addresses the question of what counselors can do to help older adults cope with losses and death.

Losses in Old Age

Although we experience losses at all ages, loss in old age may differ in significant ways from earlier loss. First, older people must adjust to losses in many different areas of their lives. Some older people are confronted with the loss of a job, and all the associations that go with that job, at about the same time that they experience health problems, move from the family home, and have some of their age mates die.

Second, losses seem to be cumulative over the life span. When older people suffer losses they tend to relive previous losses. Although people of all ages may relive other losses, younger people typically have fewer losses to relive. To understand this situation on a personal level, picture yourself at the last funeral you attended. Chances are, particularly if you attend many funerals in the same religious institution or funeral parlor, that while you were involved in one funeral service, you recalled others you had attended in the same place and relived some of that previous grief.

Understanding the cumulative nature of grief is important for older people. Sometimes what appears to be a relatively minor loss (for example the loss of an object or the death of a casual acquaintance) may trigger intense grief reactions. Older people may question their sanity after such an overreaction. In these cases, the latest loss may be the proverbial straw, and people need help in understanding what has happened. Another effect of cumulative grief is that losses in old age may trigger grief that was never expressed over previous losses. Frequently we encounter older people, particularly women, who lost a spouse or a child many years before and had to keep on going. The submerged or unresolved grief may then pour out at a later time when they do not feel forced to, or are unable to, keep on going.

Third, older people may find it more difficult to replace losses than do younger people. Although there are clearly exceptions, it is easier for most twenty-five-year-olds who are laid off to find another job than it is for most fifty-five- or sixty-five-year-olds. Similarly, it is usually easier for a thirty-year-old divorcee or widow to remarry than it is for a sixty-five-year-old in the same situation. Moreover, older people often have a diminished support system because they play fewer roles in the community than do younger people. In the sections that follow we amplify each of these themes, considering how they apply to normal and abnormal losses.

Normal Age-Related Losses. As discussed in Chapter Six, work is a central part of the lives of most men and many women. Most of these working adults retire and therefore lose their job or work role. For some people retirement is an overwhelmingly positive experience. For others, the series of losses it triggers is devastating. (For the vast majority, the reaction is somewhere in between.) What are some of the losses that accompany this change? In addition to diminished self-esteem and identity, which we discussed previously, the loss of work may mean losing contact with colleagues, lunch out, a drink after work, social events tied to work; it may mean losing a certain structure to the day, a reason to set the alarm clock, a timetable for the year; one may lose physical or intellectual challenges, praise or recognition, and the necessity of keeping one's mind and body going at full strength. The loss of status that comes with working is often the hardest to bear. Some people grieve for the end of their job as they do for many of the other losses described in this section. It is important for them to know that this reaction is appropriate and normal. Even those who are pleased to be retired must handle many of these losses.

For women whose job has been full-time homemaking, their husband's retirement may mean an increase in responsibility and an accompanying change in life-style. Some women see their husbands' retirement as an invasion of their privacy and their "turf." For many women, the pleasure of increased time with their spouse outweighs the problems. That fact, however, does not eliminate the need for couples to think about problems and to negotiate new ways of being together. As mentioned in previous chapters, counseling and retirement-planning programs can be extremely helpful in this area.

Most older adults also experience sensory losses, such as reduction in the adaptability of the muscles of the eye, which makes it difficult to go from light to dark. Other sensory losses may include a reduction in acuity of taste, smell, and touch, as well as a reduction in hearing for higher tones or other hearing and sight problems. Although these changes occur gradually, the awareness that they have taken place may be sudden. "Mom, you're putting an awful lot of salt on your food!" or "Dad, didn't you hear the phone ring?" may catapult the older adult into unhappy knowledge. As with other losses, an older person needs both to grieve for the loss and to plan for whatever compensations the loss necessitates. The loss of appetite, for example, may require a person to eat on a schedule rather than as hunger dictates. With mild losses, compensation may be as simple as getting glasses, a hearing aid, or a telephone with volume control; greater losses may necessitate medical attention or extensive planning. All such changes are likely to engender strong feelings that can be explored productively in counseling. Physical losses create the need for older adults to learn about the nature of the problem and make appropriate behavioral changes in order to regain control of their lives.

The loss of perceived physical attractiveness, of stamina, and even of height can be damaging to the self-esteem of an older adult. Particularly if one has determined one's worth largely on one's looks, athletic prowess, or sex appeal, such physical losses can be difficult to bear. The increased popularity of cosmetic surgery and of face, eye, and tummy tucks attests to the power of this loss. When "You look so young!" is no longer perceived as a compliment, older adults will not have to mourn this loss. In the meantime . . .

Despite the old joke about life beginning when the children leave home and the dog dies, the death of an animal can be a traumatic event for an older adult, particularly someone who lives alone and who counted on the pet for companionship. The person may be reluctant to replace the pet: "I'm too old to take care of it." "I don't want to care that much again." Whether or not the dilemma is resolved by the acquisition of a new pet, the emotional aspects of the loss remain the same. The counselor must remain sensitive to the power of the loss; clients may be saying or thinking, "It's only an animal," and wonder at the strength of their reaction.

The loss of the ability to drive or, as has been mentioned previously, to drive at night is a serious loss for many older persons. Driving is associated with adulthood in our society. Teenagers come of age with their first license. To lose that ability and that privilege may feel like a demotion to childhood. It also seriously restricts people's ability to choose their activities, schedules, and friends. This serious loss of independence must be mourned and not belittled. As Miller said in *Death of a Salesman* (1949), "Attention must be paid!"

Finally, the loss of mobility that often follows physical deterioration is a serious loss for many older people. When getting to the kitchen or bathroom takes a great amount of energy, going out and involving oneself in social activities may become too difficult to contemplate. Thus the loss of mobility, like the loss of the ability to drive, can result in diminished relationships with others and therefore increased isolation.

Less Common Losses. Although some loss of visual or auditory acuity is to be expected in old age, extreme loss is not. Becoming totally blind or deaf is an enormous loss for anyone. For an older adult it may be catastrophic. When other resources are already reduced, when other losses have taken their toll, these handicaps may lead to complete withdrawal or severe depression or both. It is important for the medical profession to be on the alert in these cases and to refer the older person for counseling assistance. Fear of becoming blind or deaf may become a self-fulfilling prophecy. Some people with impaired hearing are reluctant to seek medical assistance because they do not want to use a hearing aid. In such cases the condition may worsen seriously. Similarly, those who avoid glaucoma checks or cataract surgery may lose their sight unnecessarily.

Indeed, the fear of losses is in itself an important characteristic of loss in old age. As old friends die, older people may be reluctant to invest too heavily in other people, for fear of being hurt and left once again. Although we may not agree with Franklin Roosevelt that the only thing we have to fear is fear itself, fear adds to actual losses. For example, although being confined to a wheelchair means a loss of mobility, the attendant fear of being further incapacitated and the concern about having to ask for help may add greatly to an older person's sense of loss. Fears of falling, of becoming ill, of being a victim of crime, of being a burden on family members cause some people to act as if the feared event had already happened. Here again we often have a self-fulfilling prophecy. Fears of becoming an unwanted hanger-on in the work group or community organization may indirectly cause a person to adopt unfriendly or belligerent attitudes. Fear of contracting AIDS or hepatitis through blood transfusions may deter some older people from agreeing to needed operations.

Other less common physical losses are the amputation of toes, feet, or other body parts, a frequent consequence of diabetes. In addition to the pure physical pain or disability, the emotional loss is great. Friends and relatives' well-meant comments about how lucky one is to be alive may make it hard for older persons to express their anger, fear, or panic. Counselors need to be alert to this squelching of emotion and provide opportunities for clients to discuss their feelings as well as plan appropriate actions.

When there is a divorce in a family, the potential losses are numerous. When older men or women themselves get divorced, they may lose touch with a set of in-laws who have been lifetime relations. Nieces, nephews, brothers-in-law, and sisters-in-law with whom they may have spent every holiday or every Sunday may suddenly or gradually disappear from their lives. As with any divorce, friends often stick with one member of the couple or the other. When one has had one's friends for fifty years or more, this loss can be devastating.

Similarly, if one's child gets divorced, relations with the spouse usually cease. Initial anger at the child's spouse may drive an older person to cut off relations, a move the person may later regret. When the divorced child is a son, and his ex-wife, as is usually the case, gets custody of the children, contact with grandchildren may be lost or reserved for an annual visit or other rare occasion. Even though grandparent-rights organizations are springing up nationwide, this problem remains a serious one.

Death: A Special Kind of Loss

Although death is one of many losses we experience, it is clearly different from others because of its finality. In earlier times, death was a natural part of everyday life. People of all ages were cared for and died at home. Today, most people die in hospitals or other institutions, and their actual death is witnessed by few. Hence death is difficult for some people to understand or discuss.

Kalish (1985) introduces his book on death with a parable entitled "The Horse on the Dining-Room Table." A group of people at a dinner party enter the dining room and discover a horse sitting on the table. All are obviously discomfited by the presence of the unexpected horse but decline to mention it for fear of making other people, particularly the host and hostess, uncomfortable. As a result of the conscious effort to avoid discussing the obvious, the guests enjoy neither the food nor each other's company. Kalish then recommends an alternative course of action. "If you speak about the horse, then you will find that others can also speak about the horse—most others, at least, if you are gentle and kind as you speak. The horse will remain on the dining-room table, but you will not be so distraught. You cannot make magic to have the horse disappear, but you can speak of the horse and thereby render it less powerful" (p. 4). We encourage you to think through your reactions to this parable before continuing to read this chapter.

Within the last twenty to thirty years death has indeed been moving off the list of taboo subjects. A number of factors have contributed to what has been called the death-awareness movement. Among these factors are the cultural emphasis on openness and interpersonal communication and the rapid advances in medical technology, which can increase both the length of life and the length of the dying process.

Definitions of Terms. Despite the fact that it is increasingly acceptable to talk about death, many Americans still use euphemisms such as "passed away," "lost," "gone to his maker," or "gone to her just reward." In this chapter we use Kalish's (1985) definitions. He distinguishes death, which is a transition, from being dead, which is a state, and dying, which is the process. He also defines grief as the feelings of sorrow, anger, guilt, and confusion that often follow a significant loss; bereavement as a state involving loss; and mourning as the overt expression of grief and bereavement.

One of the questions often debated is when dying begins. Although the easy answer may be "at birth," this answer is neither meaningful to most individuals nor helpful to counselors. Kalish (1985, p. 26) notes that "subjectively . . . my dying begins when I learn that I have a condition that will eventually cause my death." Similarly for friends and relatives "my dying begins when you learn that I have this condition." (The definitions do not imply that individuals cannot influence their own health or diseases or that they cannot recover from serious diseases. A number of writers such as Siegel [1986] and Pearsall [1987] talk of the vital importance to one's health of a positive attitude and of the strong connections between mind and body.) Two major issues that arise are the right of individuals and their families to know of an impending death and the desirability of letting them know. Conspiracies of silence between family members and physicians are becoming less common than they once were. When patients are aware of their prognosis, they are able to discuss with family members and health care professionals their feelings and preferences about the type and extent of treatment.

Different Views of Death. In training students and service providers we often ask them to draw a picture of how they see death. We are always struck by the variety of pictures and the vastly different views of death they represent. We believe that it is important for counselors to be aware of their own conceptions of death and what they believe to be "appropriate" ways to grieve so they are not likely to impose their own values on other people.

The variety in conceptions of death stems from many different factors, including religious beliefs and ethnic-group membership. Differences between the sexes and among age groups also surface. Religious beliefs, particularly views as to whether there is an afterlife, can have a significant effect on how people view their own dying as well as that of others. Research on the effect of religiosity on death anxiety is not totally clear. Most such research (Kalish, 1985) suggests that having religious beliefs diminishes the fear of death. However, members of groups that believe strongly in punishment may be fearful. Other studies (for example, Aday, 1984–1985) indicate that death anxiety is lower among both people who adhere closely to traditional religious beliefs and those who reject such beliefs, and is higher among people who are undecided.

Religious and ethnic differences are often reflected in traditions surrounding funerals. Some Catholic wakes are festive occasions, while others are somber, depending on local norms. Among Protestant groups, the stiff-upper-lip tradition prevails in some churches, while loud weeping is not only condoned but expected in others. Traditional Jewish customs include the practice of sitting shivah for one week, during which immediate family stay home and are visited and brought food by friends and other family members. During that period, mirrors in the house of mourning may be covered, and pillows may be removed from couches. With respect to clothing, Koreans wear white for mourning; traditional Greek widows dress in black for the remainder of their lives; some African tribes don brightly colored garb; while other groups think that brightly colored clothing is inappropriate. The Navajo view death as a sacred journey to the spirit world (White, 1986). Funeral customs designed to ensure the safety of this journey prescribe specific behaviors for mourners for several days after a death. Different religious and ethnic groups also respond differently to a suicide. Some clergy address the fact directly during the funeral oration; others talk around the fact.

Sex differences are also important. Atchley (1980) reports that men tend to see death as an antagonist, while women tend to see it as merciful. As mentioned in Chapter Seven, women are more likely than men to worry about the people they leave behind. Women are also much more likely to be widowed than are men, and perhaps in recognition of this fact many women "rehearse" for widowhood. Because there are over five times as many widows as widowers among people over sixty-five (AARP & Administration on Aging, 1988), older women have little opportunity for remarriage. The large number of widows, however, increases the likelihood that widows who wish to find a support group can do so. Widows and widowers who have been involved in gender-stereotyped marriages may experience different kinds of problems. Women may be at a loss about financial matters or household repairs, men about domestic duties and arranging for social activities.

Death has somewhat different meanings to people of different ages. People who have lived a long time have undoubtedly experienced the deaths of many friends and family members. Also, Atchley (1985) reports that the elderly see themselves as having little time left, living on borrowed time. Some looked on those extra years as a bonus. Other older people, particularly the old-old, may welcome rather than dread death. They may be more concerned about how they will die (in pain, alone, confused) than about their nonbeing. Many older people plan for their deaths. They speak openly of their wills and funeral arrangements. Atchley (1985) states that 40 percent of the aged have purchased cemetery plots, and preplanned funerals are becoming common for those with moderate and extensive incomes. The young, however, often feel cheated when they learn of impending death. Concern about their dependents may be all-consuming. They typically yearn to remain active, complete goals, and find a miracle cure.

For many reasons, the death of an older person is typically seen as less tragic than that of a younger person. However, Gadow's (1987, p. 16) provocative article notes that "the consequences of accepting a natural connection between death and aging are troubling." In her view health professionals are obligated to provide treatment measures that are in keeping with the individual patient's view of death, regardless of age. Most of us have an expectation of death order—that is, we expect older people to die before younger people. When young people die, those around them often are devastated. They speak of how unfair the situation is for one in the prime of life.

What Can Counselors Do?

The wide variety in views of death among individuals and different groups poses a challenge for counselors. In this section we focus on the implications of the information about death and losses presented in the previous sections and suggest how counselors can be helpful to dying and grieving people. Perhaps the most important recommendation we can make is that counselors use their basic skills. Although the subject of loss is a heavy one and the feelings associated with death and grief can be extremely painful, the process skills involved in counseling dying and grieving people are the same as those used in helping people experiencing other problems. Listening is crucial and may sometimes be all that is necessary. People who have lost a loved one often need to tell their story over and over again and may seek a counselor because they worry about being a burden or a bore to their families and friends.

Often counselors need to articulate concerns to which clients are alluding. For example, if a bereaved client says, "I don't think I can stand this. I don't do anything but cry all day. My life has no purpose," a counselor might want to respond with "Sometimes you wish you had died too." Such an intervention might make it possible for the client to discuss her desire to be dead or her thoughts of suicide. Clients may dance around many highly charged words such as "death," "suicide," "cancer," and "AIDS." Sometimes such clients are acting somewhat superstitiously, half believing that if they use the words, the fear will become a reality. In such cases, if the counselor uses the words, the clients may feel free to use them. To return to the parable of the horse on the dining-room table, use of such words may render the horse less powerful.

Dying and grieving people often need reassurance that their feelings and behavior are normal. Both counselors and clients need to realize, for example, that grief is a necessary reaction to loss, not a sign of mental illness. Fostering such awareness is one way in which counselors can help to return some degree of control to people who likely feel powerless and out of control.

Working with People Who Are Dying. In working with dying people and their caregivers, it is important to think about the needs of the dying person. The American Health Care Association (undated) has published a pamphlet, *Here's Help! Death and Dying,* which identifies four categories of needs: physical, social, emotional, and religious or spiritual. Physically, the dying, like the rest of us, need food, water, shelter, and comfort. Caregivers are advised to be alert for signs of discomfort in patients, as they may not express themselves openly. Social needs may be especially important as dying is a lonely experience and many patients fear abandonment. Counselors can encourage family and friends not to stay away from someone who is dying, even though they may be at a loss for words or fear they will "catch" the disease. Social contact is particularly important to emphasize for people who have AIDS. Despite the medical knowledge that AIDS is contracted only through an exchange of body fluids, many people are reluctant to be in a room with an AIDS patient, let alone touch that person. Such reticence on the part of family and friends can deprive a dying person of much-needed physical contact. In most cases, open communication between patients and their loved ones helps to meet these social needs. Emotional needs can be extremely complex. Counselors can help dying people get their affairs in order, express appreciation and regrets, and say their last good-byes. A counselor's role may be to assure the dying person or the family or both that such statements are helpful and appropriate, not morbid. Religious needs are quite personal and varied. As indicated in the previous section, individual beliefs and preferences for rituals vary tremendously. A counselor can help by listening to the dying person and the family and helping them make plans consistent with their views.

Kübler-Ross's landmark book (1969), *On Death and Dying,* has had a considerable impact on both lay people and professionals by encouraging discussion of what was once a taboo subject. Prior to writing this book, Kübler-Ross conducted a series of interviews with cancer patients who were terminally ill. Many expressed a fear of going home, as well as concerns about the amount of pain they would experience, what would happen in an emergency, and whether they would become a burden on their families. She found that many patients expressed a need to talk about themselves and their illnesses. From the information gained from 200 interviews, Kübler-Ross devised a theory of developmental stages in the dying process. Those stages are outlined here along with suggestions for helpers interacting with people at various stages. Several of the suggestions come from Henderson's (1978) personal account of his experience as a professional counselor with a terminal disease.

The first stage is *denial and isolation*. Denial is viewed as a healthy way to deal initially with the shocking news that one has a terminal illness. This temporary response is usually followed by loneliness and a sense of isolation. Henderson suggests that helpers need to be patient and wait for the denial to pass.

Anger is the second stage. Typically, patients project their anger in many directions, including sometimes toward God. Caregivers who are dealing with their own anticipatory grief may find it particularly difficult to handle the anger. Counselors can be helpful by encouraging family members and other helpers to stay involved with the angry patient and to try not to take the anger personally.

The third stage is *bargaining;* the patient attempts to postpone the inevitable and be rewarded for good behavior. These bargains are usually attempted with God and may be kept secret from all except religious personnel. Often the bargains are on the order of "If you just let me live until my daughter's wedding (the birth of my grandchild, my husband's retirement party), I won't complain." Or people may promise to give their bodies to science in exchange for medical treatment that will extend their lives. Such proposed bargains are a clue to counselors to encourage patients to talk about how much they would like to be around for the birth, wedding, or other event. Perhaps they can also encourage the dying persons to write down their thoughts so they can be represented at the special event.

Depression marks the fourth stage as full realization of the losses being experienced or contemplated comes. Henderson urges helpers to stay with dying people and to care for them while allowing them to struggle with their deep feelings. Counselors may work more with other caretakers than with the dying person at this and other stages of the process. Many caretakers experience feelings of helplessness at not being able to do anything for the dying person, and these feelings may be heightened when the patient is severely depressed.

Last, *acceptance* will come if the patient has had enough time and adequate help in the struggle through the other stages. Henderson (1978, p. 9) says that for him "acceptance is not having all your questions answered, . . . is a sense of peace . . . not to be confused with resignation. Acceptance of death is based on feelings I can neither prove nor express in any meaningful way. . . . Generally, the way you accept death is closely related to the way you accept life. . . . If you have reached acceptance, you are never again afraid to die." A major role for counselors at this stage can be to help dying people with any unfinished business they may have — expressing appreciations, regrets, or apologies to family members; planning their funerals; or giving away their possessions. We saw a wonderful example of this recently when a friend, a retired English teacher with terminal cancer, found "homes" for all her favorite books.

Kübler-Ross's stage theory can help us assess the thinking and feeling of dying people and therefore provide a guide to how to respond to them. It can also lock people in. People do not always pass through these stages in an orderly fashion, and both patients and family members may therefore feel they have failed if they do not proceed according to this or some other set of stages. These stages may also be irrelevant to very old people who believe it is time, or even past time, for them to die. Another concern about stage theories is that they may cause people to assume that they do not have to take any action, that the stages will just occur in the prescribed order. Perhaps the major message is that all helpers need to take their cues from the patient and not be like one enthusiastic young nurse who sat down on the bed of a cancer patient and said, "I've just finished a course in death and dying and anytime you want to talk about your death I'll be glad to." In addition to being startled and offended, the patient, who was expecting to recover, then spent a lot of time wondering what the nurse knew that she did not.

Working with the Bereaved. In addition to being involved with older people who are dying, counselors are often called on to

extend help to people who are grieving. Worden (1982) outlines four major tasks that need to be accomplished in order to
move beyond grief. First, the grieving person must come to accept the reality of the death. Denying the loss may lead to
prolonged or unhealthy grief. (Jones [1986] suggests that a counselor can help the person accept the reality of the loss by asking
the person to say that the deceased person is dead [insisting on
the use of the deceased's name].) Worden's second task is for
the grieving survivor to accept the fact that grief is painful and
must be dealt with. Reliance on tranquilizers or avoidance of
feelings related to the loss only prolongs the process. Third, the
grieving person must adjust to an environment that no longer
includes the person who died. The person may have to take on
new tasks (for example, handling finances or housekeeping
chores) or otherwise function on his or her own. Fourth, the
grieving person must eventually begin to invest energy in other
relationships and to understand that having other relationships
is not a betrayal of the deceased.

   Two small books that focus on stages of grief are recommended for grieving people as well as for counselors. Westberg's
Good Grief (1976) posits a ten-stage model that can help grieving people understand the wide range of feelings they are likely
to experience. It also emphasizes that grieving takes enormous
amounts of time and energy and assures people that although
they will never be their old selves again, they will be able to
live, laugh, and love again. *Living with an Empty Chair* (Temes,
1984) offers a simple three-stage model of the grief process that
is particularly useful because it includes suggestions for helpers
(see Table 2). Temes's model underlines a point made above,
that helpers need to be responsive to the changing needs of a
grieving person. For example, in the early stages of grief, mourners may need assistance with basic chores. When grieving people have let in the fact of the death, they may want someone
to listen to all the details of the death itself and to talk at length
about the deceased. When they are beginning to reorganize their
lives, grieving people can use assistance in reaching out to other
people and groups.

   Grief is expressed in many ways—physically (sleep disturbances, appetite changes, symptoms of illness), emotionally

Table 2. Stages of Grief.

Stages of Grief	Duration	Characteristics	Needs	Developmental Task	Helper Functions
Stage One: Numbness	Several weeks or months	Mechanical functioning Insulation	Emotional distance	To protect self from feeling impact of loss	Assist with chores
Stage Two: Disorganization	Many months	Painful feelings: loneliness depression weeping Sleep and appetite difficulties Sorrow for self Hallucinations	Intimacy Ventilation of feelings	Acknowledge impact of loss	Permit expression of *all* feelings Listen to talk about life together and details of death
Stage Three: Reorganization	Several weeks or months	Occasional peacefulness Less intensity of feelings	Encouragement to reenter life's mainstream	Complete emotional relationship with deceased	Expand social network

Source: Temes, 1984. Reprinted by permission of Irvington Publishers, Inc.

(sadness, fear, guilt, confusion, despair, anger at being abandoned), and behaviorally (detachment, forgetfulness, prolonged
crying or sobbing). We concentrate on the emotional reactions
here. Heikkenen (1981) asserts that fear is at the heart of the
grief process, that the pain of grieving may be so intense people fear they will not survive. As counselors we must be able
to help people understand and express their feelings, especially
feelings of such depth as fear of survival.

People who are grieving also often feel out of control, and
that feeling contributes to their fear. Sometimes people are afraid
that if they allow themselves to cry, they will not be able to stop.
We often hear people talk about "breaking down" when they
mean crying. It is important to indicate that crying is a normal
expression of grief and not a breakdown. The different expectations we have as to how men and women express grief can
create special problems for men. Jones (1986) has observed that
in funeral homes when women start to cry, they are often held
by friends and family, while men may be taken out of the room
until they "get control of themselves." In neither case, however,
are people encouraged to continue their crying.

As helpers we can talk about the normality and healing
qualities of tears, but we must respect people's differences. Some
people are exceedingly uncomfortable crying in front of others.
In working with such people, helpers may need to suggest ways
in which people can cry on their own terms and in their preferred
location. Although it may be difficult to cry "by appointment,"
there are methods of triggering tears such as looking through
old photograph albums or listening to sad music.

Grieving people also sometimes feel guilty. In cases of
prolonged illness, survivors may experience relief that their own
burdens of caregiving are over, and then guilt over their relief.
Family members who have experienced anticipatory grief may
feel guilty that the death itself provokes little additional sadness.
Assurance of the appropriateness of such feelings is important.
Counselors may also need to help people feel all right and not
selfish about such concerns as: "Now that my husband is dead,
will we have enough money for Christmas presents?" Or "Will
I be able to take the trip we'd planned?"

Counselors can also help people distinguish between regret and guilt. Regret is a statement of fact and feeling, while guilt is usually an inappropriate way of punishing oneself. In this regard, grief counselors hear many "if onlys" — "If only I had told him I loved him," "If only I had made one more trip home," "If only we hadn't had that silly argument." Sometimes it is helpful to encourage people to write out a ledger sheet, balancing each regret with something they did that pleased the person who died.

Many grieving people need to talk about the deceased and repeatedly describe the details of the death. Although this process can be highly therapeutic, it is important that they not deify the dead person. Such deification creates a paragon that no survivor can possibly live up to and may add to the survivor's guilt. Survivors may worry about why they were allowed to live when such a superior person died.

Counselors also need to be aware that survivors often blame themselves for the death; they need assurance that the death is not their fault. Children, in particular, may worry that a parent or grandparent died because they made too much noise when the person was sick or because once when they were very angry they thought or said, "I hate you, and I wish you were dead."

In encouraging people to acknowledge all these emotions, counselors often find that humor can be helpful. Laughing about funny things that happened with the deceased person or recalling absurd situations can help avoid deification. A minister we know who often calls on families shortly after a death has occurred told us that shared laughter frequently opens the doors to shared tears. The combination can be most healing.

Although grieving is always painful, some circumstances increase the pain. One such circumstance is the death of a spouse. When a spouse dies, the survivor loses more than a mate. Survivors lose part of their own identity as half of a couple, as a member of an intact family, as the partner of someone with a significant role. They also lose their dream of a shared future. Shuchter (1986) describes many aspects of the grief experienced when a spouse dies and suggests a variety of interventions, including family therapy and widow or widower support groups, which can supplement traditional psychotherapy.

Other circumstances can also make grieving especially difficult. In cases of accidents where no body is available, it may be hard for survivors to accept the reality of the death. When the survivor has ambivalent or negative feelings about the deceased (for example, in the case of a troubled marriage), the grief process may be complicated by excessive guilt. When a family member commits suicide, survivors may feel punished. They may have extra burdens to bear, particularly if they blame themselves for not spotting the signals. Social and religious beliefs that restrict outward expressions of grief and demand control may also prolong the grief process. In addition, counselors may need to work with unrecognized mourners — that is, people who were close to the person who died but are not now or were never recognized as family. Ex-spouses or extended family members separated by a divorce or family feud are clear examples. Unacknowledged close friends or lovers, of the same or opposite sex, may feel particularly sad and isolated when they are not welcome to participate in funeral or memorial services.

Helping People Cope with Nondeath Losses. At the beginning of this chapter we mentioned that people grieve over all kinds of losses, not just death. Consequently they may also need help in coping with those losses. From the counselor's point of view, the process of assisting people grieving over losses of any kind is essentially the same.

One of the biggest losses people can experience is loss of a job. People in this situation may lose their sense of identity as productive people or as members of a team, along with some of their self-esteem. To help such people, counselors need to be aware of stages of grief over job loss. The emotional reactions have been described by Goodman and Hoppin (1990) as a six-stage process, outlined below. Although people do not move through these stages as neatly as described, the stages do provide a useful scheme for counseling.

Some people at first feel *relief* that the job, which they may have anticipated losing, is over. Many others experience *numbness*. They do not believe they have really lost their jobs. They hope for recall even when that is unlikely. They do not act because they do not really accept their loss. The counselor's role here is gently to remind people of the truth of their loss and to be patient while they take the time they need to absorb it.

In the next stage, *emotional release,* people feel angry, sad, frustrated, jealous of others who are still working. Holding in feelings may lead to physical symptoms. Counselors must help people to release their feelings and to begin to make plans.

People may feel *depressed* and be in *physical distress.* They may doubt their abilities, feel hopeless and helpless. They may show physical signs of stress like sleeplessness, loss of appetite, or back and stomach problems. The counselor here needs to be alert for serious depression, referring if necessary. It is helpful to encourage people to develop and to begin to carry out action plans.

People in the stage of *panic and guilt* may have trouble thinking and be unable to plan effectively. They may feel responsible for the layoff even though they had no control over it. They may keep thinking "if only" and try to do everything at once and nothing effectively. Counselors need to help them set goals and priorities, and make step-by-step plans.

Anger and hostility may be an important part of the recovery process. Anger can be positive but may be directed at those around the person. Clients may need help in learning to use these strong feelings productively to provide the energy to make plans to move on to the next stage.

People can then begin to *plan for a new life* without the old job. They can take constructive action toward finding work or other new activities. They may let go of strong anger and false hopes and feel somewhat in control of their lives again. At this point, counselors may need to provide instrumental support, information, and encouragement. When clients seem reasonably in control of their lives, it is time for counselors to wish their clients well and encourage them to be independent.

Chapter One referred to by-the-way counseling as an important technique in working with older adults—listening for the unstated question or the somewhat veiled request for help. This kind of sensitivity on the part of counselors may be especially important in helping older adults discuss their concerns about sensory losses, sexual problems, or other physical losses. Counselors need to hear these concerns, reassure people that their worries are understandable and normal, and then help them find ways to prevent, minimize, or get help with the problem. For example, with sexual problems, counselors may need to hear about the fears (of reduced desire, inability to achieve erection or to lubricate), the concerns about loss of a sexual partner, or the guilt about attraction to another person. Once the feelings have been legitimized and discussed, counselors can provide information. This help can range from making referrals to sensitive health care personnel to reminding clients of the availability of such products as vaginal jelly.

Developing Programs and Utilizing Community Resources. The previous discussion focused on what counselors can do in direct interaction with grieving people. Additionally, counselors can tap into their educational and presentation skills and develop programs that help older people cope with losses. For example, counselors can develop special programs on job-seeking skills for older workers who have lost or think they may lose a job. Counselors can help start and serve as advisors to self-help groups for persons experiencing a variety of losses (stroke victims, caregivers of Alzheimer's patients, widows and widowers, persons with AIDS).

Because their lives are rich in experience, older adults themselves may be ideal candidates to help their peers acknowledge and deal with the pain of loss and grief. Blue Cross and Blue Shield of Michigan offer an innovative program entitled Healing and Growing Through Grief in senior centers in metropolitan Detroit. The program utilizes a film on loss and grief as a springboard for encouraging interaction in small groups facilitated by trained, older-adult peer counselors.

Counselors need to be familiar with grief-counseling and bereavement-support services in their communities. Many family service agencies, churches, and community groups offer assistance to and social outlets for the bereaved. A number of funeral homes now offer grief-counseling services. In describing her work as a grief counselor, Jamerino (1987) notes that her initial contact with families occurs while funeral arrangements are being made. At that time her role is primarily supportive. Three weeks after the funeral, she contacts surviving spouses and invites them to attend an initial meeting of a widow support group. This group meets for six weeks in a structured program designed to build coping and adapting skills. At the conclusion of this program, participants are invited to join Widows Together, a social organization that meets on a monthly basis.

Counselors should also be aware of hospices as a resource for dying people and their families. Started in Great Britain, the hospice movement has spread quickly. In the United States the first hospice was established in New Haven, Connecticut, in 1974. Currently there are well over a thousand hospices throughout the country, and hospice care can, under some conditions, be covered by Medicare.

Hospices are designed for people for whom getting well is no longer an option. Thus the hospice philosophy emphasizes comfort and quality of life (Mor, 1987). A hospice brochure (Hospice of Southern Michigan, undated) explains that "the main purpose of hospice care is to provide a life-affirming climate in which the dying person can maintain control over his life, prepare for death in his own way, and live his life in comfort and with a sense of personal worth. Care is also extended to the family through the provision of emotional support, encouragement of their participation in patient care, and support during the bereavement period." Although the hospice philosophy is compatible with the needs of many older adults, it is not always possible for them to use hospice services, usually because older people often suffer from multiple chronic conditions that lengthen the period during which they are dying and hospice policies usually stipulate that patients must have fewer than six months to live.

In sum, in order to be effective with older adults who are experiencing or anticipating losses, counselors need not only an understanding of the grief process but also the ability to use this knowledge with their individual- and group-counseling skills, program-development skills, and contacts with the aging network.

PART THREE

Action Strategies for Counselors

Each of the chapters in Part Two ends with suggestions about ways in which counselors can listen for particular issues or respond when clients bring them up. In Part Three we take a different approach, focusing on techniques gerontological counselors need as part of their repertoire. Effective counselors work on several different levels. At the first and most obvious level they interact directly with clients, helping them to understand their situations, to accept and articulate their feelings, and to take action on their own behalf. Second, counselors work at the organizational level, seeing to it that their employers have policies, programs, and practices that are maximally responsive to the needs of older people. Typically, they assess client needs and then develop or advocate programs that will meet those needs. Third, counselors function at the societal level; they are aware of the context in which their clients live and do what they can to make that environment supportive. At this level, counselors are acting as advocates or change agents. The chapters in Part Three suggest activities at each of the three levels and specifically describe certain procedures with which readers should become familiar. It is the "ditch digging" part of the book in that it describes the hands-on work counselors should do in order to become most helpful to older adults.

Chapter Nine begins with a section on group counseling. It includes a discussion of the values and limitations of group work for older people along with suggestions for adapting usual group-counseling techniques to an older clientele. Activities that we have found helpful at various stages of a group's development are included. These range from get-acquainted activities useful in the beginning stages through imaging activities for the middle stages to closing activities for the termination stage. A particularly valuable technique for use with older adults is the life review. We emphasize the importance of the life review and suggest how to encourage people, individually or in groups, to engage in this process. We also present strategies for analyzing the support systems of older people because support can be particularly important, and often threatened, in old age.

Chapter Ten is designed to help counselors broaden their traditional roles to include educational and administrative functions. In many agencies, counselors can have a positive impact on the lives of older people by designing comprehensive programs for them or by designing, marketing, and presenting workshops. The program-development section of the chapter discusses the importance of building evaluation into the process. The workshop section presents factors to consider in making educational experiences appropriate for older people. Sample workshops in several different areas, including personal development, education, and work, are described, with a special section devoted to self-help groups. Finally, we talk about using older people themselves as part of the service-delivery system. We list advantages and limitations of peer counseling, and discuss ways in which professional counselors can work effectively with peer counselors.

Chapter Eleven discusses the role of counselors as change agents. It presents methods counselors can use to intervene for older adults with private and public organizations, as well as ways in which counselors can empower older adults to act on their own behalf. It suggests how counselors can help older adults make their way through bureaucracies and considers a number of ethical issues. It also looks at the role of organizations of older persons and of professional associations in advancing the interests of older adults. It challenges counselors to become passionate in their devotion to political action as part of their commitment to empowering older people.

9

Employing
Special Techniques

In previous chapters of this book, we have referred to the value of group counseling and other specialized techniques for working with older people. In this chapter, we focus on those topics, turning first to a discussion of both the advantages and disadvantages of group work. In addition to considering ways of adapting familiar group-counseling skills, counselors need to know how to use some techniques that are of particular value with older clients. The life review is included here because of its special salience to older people and its relation to the achievement of integrity in the Eriksonian (1950) sense. The other specialized technique to be discussed is an analysis of support systems. Although support systems are important to people of all ages, they are crucial for many older people and may be in jeopardy because of the variety of changes and losses sustained by the elderly. Both the life review and the analysis of support systems can be done individually or in groups.

Considerations in Setting Up and Conducting Groups

Brown (1988) classifies group-work modalities on a continuum ranging from the educationally oriented discussion group with "normal" clients to the medically oriented therapy group with psychotic clients. In between these extremes are guidance groups, human-potential groups, counseling groups, and groups for neurotic clients. Corey and Corey (1987) identify six types of groups: therapy groups, counseling groups, personal-growth groups, t-groups or laboratory-training groups, structured groups, and self-help groups. It is important for gerontological counselors, as it is for all counselors, to be clear about the purposes and structure of any group they form.

Brown (1988) suggests several steps in starting a group. The first two are developing a proposal, which forces one to think through goals and objectives, and formulating and following a selection process. He recommends having a private meeting with each potential member to screen out inappropriate members and to "plant positive expectations and goals." Counselors need to ask themselves whether an individual will benefit from the group and whether that person will detract from the growth of others.

The next step is to determine the composition and scheduling of the group. Consideration needs to be given to five issues. The first is heterogeneity versus homogeneity. Homogeneous groups are useful if the focus is on a special need. Heterogeneous groups are a good microcosm of society, which might be helpful, for example, if learning interpersonal skills is a goal. The second issue is group size. Brown suggests eight to ten members as optimal. Given the sensory limitations of some older people and the difficulty many older adults have in sitting for long periods, we recommend a group of six to eight, with an even smaller number if the members are seriously impaired. The third issue is voluntary versus involuntary membership. If membership is involuntary, screening and orientation become particularly important. Brown suggests using structured activities, especially at the beginning, to reduce the anxiety of reluctant members. The fourth issue is whether the group should be open or closed. Brown strongly urges counselors to have closed groups. However, in working with older adults this arrangement is often impractical. In structured group programs at senior centers, we have occasionally had new members at the last session! Certainly developing trust becomes critical in situations like these. Brown's last issue for counselors to consider is that of the duration and frequency of their groups. In working with older adults we have found one to two hours to be the maximum duration for physical comfort. Frequency may be determined by how often members have transportation to the site of the group meetings.

Special accommodations should be made for older people. Those who are frail may need short groups. In addition, counselors can be more flexible and allow behaviors they would not permit in groups of younger people. Older people who fall asleep may not be "resistant" but very tired or over-medicated. Rather than confronting seemingly inappropriate behavior the counselor may want to help the client identify the cause of the problem.

Discussing the participation of older adults in groups, George and Dustin (1988) suggest that "older adults are more likely than individuals in other age groups to be struggling with some particular themes: loneliness; social isolation; feelings of loss (either of individuals or of physical capabilities); poverty; feelings of rejection; dependency; feelings of uselessness, hopelessness, and despair; fears of death and dying; depression; and regrets over past events" (p. 142). They also assert that older adults have a high incidence of alcohol and other drug abuse, and high levels of suicide.

Let us look back at some of the older people we described in Chapter Three and consider whether group work would be an appropriate intervention strategy for each of them. Samuel Cohen is clearly too disoriented for a counseling group, although he might benefit from a structured reality-orientation group. His daughter, however, might be helped by a discussion or counseling group, where she could both express her feelings and gain information about practical support services. Lillie Phillips might benefit from an assertiveness-training group to help her talk to her children in an appropriate but firm manner. Jim Podolski might profit from a retirement-planning group or a couples' counseling program to help him and his wife deal with their differences about postretirement life-style. His wife might also benefit from group counseling to help her work through her feelings about this new conflict and perhaps learn some communication skills to negotiate her disagreements with Jim.

Marian Johnson might benefit from a caregivers' support group, as might her husband. Her mother-in-law might also benefit from a group-counseling program. She clearly seems to be struggling with some of the themes listed by George and Dustin (1988). And, finally, Sylvia Smith is clearly in need of information about the probable dementia of her mother. A group with a topic such as "You and Your Aging Parent" might well be an appropriate forum in which she could gather this information and also begin to deal with her feelings. The support offered by a group might be helpful to her as she sorts out what she can and cannot do for her mother. Because Sylvia is feeling so fragile — her instant tears are our clue — she would probably benefit from some individual counseling before the group begins. Individual counseling would enable her to feel together enough to be a full participant in the group.

Major Benefits. Our experience and that of other writers such as Burnside (1984), Capuzzi, Gross, and Friel (1990), and Sargent (1980) indicate that group counseling can be valuable in working with older people. Some of the benefits are summarized here; we use Yalom's (1970) classic work as a point of departure.

At almost any age people can benefit from *discovering commonalities,* from realizing that they are not alone. Such a realization, sometimes referred to as a sense of universality, typically comes when people in a group learn that many others have shared similar experiences and feelings. This awareness, or "outsight," can bring significant relief to people who thought they were the only ones to harbor particular feelings. The increasing awareness of others and their feelings is an important addition to the "insight" that is usually focused on in individual counseling.

An anecdote may illustrate how discovering commonalities works. In one group a man reported his discomfort during dinner at his daughter's home the previous day. "I don't understand," he said, "why I always feel so much better when she comes to my house than when I go to hers." Two other group members reported similar strong preferences for being in the host, rather than guest, position. After considerable discussion, they realized they were worrying about whether they would get to the point where they were unable to serve as hosts and would

become dependent on their children. The discussion proved helpful at both a content and process level. It was reassuring to group
members to realize that their fears of becoming a burden were
widely shared. Moreover, the process of discussing their common fears drew the group together.

Groups can be *an antidote for loneliness*. Loneliness is a common problem among older people, who often have lost significant
roles and close friends. Counseling groups provide not only a
setting in which people can get together but also a structure that
fosters intimacy. Groups can get people in the habit of talking
to each other. They can also help combat loneliness in the short
term by providing a time for people to be with others. In the
long term, as discussed next, they can teach the skills to combat loneliness without the prop of the group.

Groups can be *a laboratory for teaching intra- and interpersonal
skills*. People of any age are often drawn to counseling because
they need help with interpersonal relationships. Older people
who have experienced transitions and role losses may find it particularly difficult to reach out and form new relationships or to
replenish a diminished support system.

As a forum for teaching social skills, group counseling
has several advantages over individual counseling. In groups,
members relate to each other as peers as well as to the counselor as an authority figure. Although the counselor can and
should model effective communication, members need a safe
laboratory in which to practice communicating with each other.
This rehearsal is often an important part of the learn and change
aspects of our empowerment model. In groups people can focus
on the process of communication, on how people communicate,
not just on what they say. These process skills are transferable;
older people who learn how to communicate effectively may be
able to use that skill in other situations.

A major value of groups for people of all ages is that members typically share resources; they give both emotional support and suggestions to each other. Such support may take the
form of assurance of the normality of feelings or affirmation of
the ability to handle problems. At a concrete level, group members may exchange such information as which drugstore gives

the best discounts for seniors or which clerk at the Social Security office is most helpful. Older people who see themselves and their fellow group members as helpful gain two benefits. First, defining oneself as helpful often leads to an increase in self-esteem. Second, members who perceive their peers as worthwhile companions may lessen their own ageism or group self-hatred. When older people are eager to attend groups with their age mates, they are less likely to say, "I'm not one of them."

Groups also provide an *opportunity for catharsis*. Many older people have a lot to be angry, sad, and frightened about. Despite the reality of their situations, including the likelihood of many losses, some older people are reluctant to express such feelings for fear of being seen as crotchety old men or women. In groups, people can share their complaints and fears in a safe and supportive atmosphere.

However, the mere telling of one's story may not in itself be helpful. Once the client has had adequate time to ventilate, the counselor then has the often difficult job of redirecting the client from expression of feelings to *development of a plan of action*. Counselors who are overly concerned about respecting their elders may find such confrontation difficult. In one program, we used a picture of an apple with several bites removed as a metaphor for developing a plan. The idea came from a peer counselor and former teacher who told the group how she had helped a grandchild who was immobilized by a homework assignment. After the child declared herself unable to even start the paper, her grandmother handed her an apple with the instruction to eat the whole thing at once. When the child said she could not, the grandmother asked how she would eat it. "One bite at a time" was the answer, and the point was made. In using the apple metaphor, we asked participants to label the various bites as step 1, 2, 3, and so on.

Groups can be *a source of inspiration*. Yalom (1970) talks of the instillation of hope as one of the primary curative factors in group therapy. When people of any age talk with people who have coped with problems similar to theirs, they often find encouragement. Providing inspiration is part of the rationale for many self-help and peer-support groups. Widow support groups or

groups for people who share an illness or have a common problem, such as caregiving, are clear examples. In groups of older
people, members can be encouraged and inspired by seeing
others cope with problems they fear. For example, people who
fear losing their sight are often amazed at the coping abilities
of blind group members.

Cautions. Although group work can be extremely valuable, it
is clearly not appropriate for all people. In discussing the disadvantages of group counseling in general, Gazda (1971) notes
that the same factors that make group counseling potent may
also add risk. "The presence of several counselees in a group
decreases the counselor's control and thus subjects the counselees
to greater risks of the group's ostracism, pressure, rivalry, breaking of confidence and the like" (p. 47). For older people, the
issue of confidentiality may be a special concern, particularly
when the group meetings take place in a residential facility or
senior center where members tend to know each other. People
who wish to discuss delicate issues may do better with individual
counseling.

Burnside (1984) suggests several other categories of people who may be inappropriate for group counseling, including
those who are disturbed and prone to wandering, incontinent,
manic-depressive, psychotic, deaf, or hypochondriacal, as well
as those recommended solely by the staff. In our view, however,
many of these people can be included in groups if proper adaptations are made. For example, incontinent people may simply
be encouraged to wear extra protection; deaf people who know
sign language may be included if a signer is present or if much
of the communication is written.

Brown (1988) believes that the following types of people
are not appropriate for groups: paranoid, obsessively self-cen-
tered, out of touch, suicidal, highly hostile, aggressive, psychotic,
and those in crisis. (Others feel that these people can be served
in sophisticated therapy groups but not in counseling groups.)

We believe that groups also are not the treatment of choice
for people who are so preoccupied with their own problems that
they are unable to listen or respond to others. People who are

extremely narcissistic also may be unable to relate to the problems of others. People who are sufficiently disoriented that they cannot understand the idea of taking turns or are otherwise unable to follow the thread of a conversation may be detrimental to group functioning.

Experience with community-living older people suggests that most for whom groups are inappropriate know that about themselves. Counselors may do well to hold an orientation session before beginning a group to provide a sample of the way the group will work. Both counselors and potential group members then have an opportunity to make an informed decision as to the appropriateness of the group experience. As suggested above, an individual session with a client can also be a valuable screening device.

What Do Counselors Do? Doing group counseling with older people does not require counselors to start all over any more than individual counseling does. Here again the challenge is to think of ways of adapting familiar techniques to meet the needs of an older population. A few examples follow of activities appropriate at various stages of group development. Stimulus activities may be particularly useful in working with a group of people who are relatively unaccustomed to self-exploration and to discussing feelings. As mentioned throughout this book, many, but clearly not all, older people have such an orientation.

As an introductory activity or icebreaker, the values-clarification strategy Forced Choice (Simon, Howe, and Kirschenbaum, 1972) is excellent in many different group settings. Group members are asked to decide which of two alternatives they are more like and to indicate their choice by moving to a designated side of the room. Group members are then asked to talk with another person about the reasons for the choice. By paraphrasing a few responses from each "side," the group counselor models reflective listening and helps the group get off to a lively start. The activity can be adapted to the needs of different groups by changing the choices. For example, retirement-planning groups might use choices such as "Are you more of a spender or a saver?" "Are you more like a condominium or a cabin in the woods?" If group members are not mobile, they can be asked to designate their choices by a show of hands or in some other way.

In the early stages of a group, counselors should reward interactions and expressions that contribute to the growth and development of individuals and the group and ignore those that do not. It is best to avoid confronting inappropriate behavior if possible for two reasons. One, simple ignoring often is enough to extinguish the behavior. Two, not only might the offending member withdraw from the group if confronted too early but other members of the group may feel the chill and reduce their contributions. This withdrawal may result particularly with older adults who are often not too knowledgeable about counseling and therefore not sure of appropriate group norms.

In the initial stages of a group it is also helpful to discuss expected behavior or even to develop a group contract jointly. This contract can include such items as confidentiality and honesty.

We have found it helpful at this stage to teach the skill of personalization through an activity called I-You. Each participant is asked to take a general statement such as "People are always uneasy with new people" and change it to "I'm always uneasy with new people." The person is then asked to take a statement about another person such as "Sue always has such good ideas" and change it to "Sue, I always find your ideas helpful." In processing this activity, we ask people to notice differences in voice tone and facial expression when they make the personal and general statements and to analyze the differences in their feelings as the senders and receivers of both kinds of messages. This activity reminds people to personalize their statements as the group continues. We cannot stress too much the importance of this personalization, as it contributes strongly to the empowerment we work toward.

In the action stage of a group, worksheets that encourage people to think about their interests, skills, and accomplishments as an aid in planning are appropriate for all ages. In working with older people such worksheets need to be printed in large type. An activity we have found useful is to have participants list "fifteen things you really like to do." Adapted from Simon et al.'s (1972) Twenty Things, this activity invites participants to code their fifteen things in areas such as preference for doing the activity alone or with others, cost of the activity, and date of the last time they engaged in this activity. The codes help participants to consider how these things fit or might fit in with their current life-styles. Often people leave this session with new or renewed leisure plans.

Another useful activity for the action stages of a group—one that encourages self-exploration and self-disclosure—is a fantasy in which participants are asked to imagine themselves as a tree. After instructing members to get comfortable and close their eyes, the group counselor suggests, "Imagine yourself as a tree," then slowly asks questions such as: "What kind of a tree are you?" "Where are you growing?" "What time of year is it?" "What do your roots look like?" "What is around you?" "What do you hear?" "Is there anything in your branches?" "Can you smell anything?" In processing the fantasy, group counselors ask such questions as: "How is the tree like you?" "What do you like about your tree?" "What would you like to change?" As can be expected, the fantasy is often a description of how individuals are experiencing their lives. Some group members understand this concept easily; others need help in making the connections; and some never see how their fantasy is like themselves.

The termination stage of any counseling group calls for an acknowledgment of feelings, an assessment of progress made, and an opportunity to discuss next steps. In ending groups for older people, counselors need to help members develop replacements for the group so that the group's end does not represent an additional loss. The Strength Acknowledgment exercise developed by McHolland (1972), in which people identify strengths they see in themselves and other group members, is a particularly good one. A major adaptation needed with older adults may be to help them overcome the "don't brag" message with which many of today's older people were socialized. If group members are unable to read and write in the major language of the group, the leader may need to serve as secretary to help people record their own strengths and those of their fellow members. A written record of this type can serve as a symbol and reminder of the good feelings engendered by the group. It is one way of having the group carry on after its official ending. For older-adult groups meeting at a senior center or other place where they congregate regularly, it is important for people to be clear that the group as it has been has ended. The members may continue to talk to each other and have a different level of communication; they may continue for a while to meet as a group, but it will not be the same.

In addition to having a repertoire of activities appropriate at various stages of development, group counselors working with older adults need to be aware of general principles of group management. Harvill, West, Jacobs, and Masson (1985) suggest four basic group-management skills: drawing out, shutting up, focusing, and changing the focus. Drawing out may be particularly challenging with older adults because, as mentioned before, many older adults are unused to expressing personal feelings and concerns. Efforts on the part of the leader to reflect actively what people say in the group, emphasizing feelings that are expressed or implied, can be especially valuable in this respect. Equally important are interventions that identify links between members. The lack of group savvy on the part of many older adults also makes it possible for one or two members to dominate a group and speak for the others. Firm but tactful methods for "shutting up" or reining in the dominating members are crucial. The leader may get less assistance from older group members in this endeavor than would be likely in groups of younger people because of the widespread acceptance of such messages as: "If you can't say anything nice, don't say anything." Nevertheless, group members will clearly be watching to see how the group leader manages monopolizers and may learn from the leader's modeling how to deal with similar situations outside the group. Group leaders also need to be active in focusing the group or changing the focus if the group seems to be wandering or to be nonproductive.

Self-Help Groups. The above discussion has focused on groups led by a professional counselor. An additional role for counselors may be that of advisor or technical assistant to self-help groups. We have seen a tremendous growth in the number of self-help groups, which typically form around a common problem. Napier and Gershenfeld (1985) categorize self-help groups as crisis, permanent, or addiction-oriented. Crisis groups provide emotional support for individuals trying to cope with a major change in their lives. Included here are groups for widows, the unemployed, or accident victims. Permanent self-help groups focus on long-term problems that may interfere with normal existence. Groups for patients — or family members of patients — with a particular illness fall into this category. Addiction-oriented groups help members learn new behaviors and gain control over such self-defeating habits as gambling and substance abuse.

Although membership in self-help groups is usually not restricted to a specific age group, widows' groups, in particular, often have large numbers of older women. Silverman, Mackenzie, Pettipas, and Wilson (1974) describe the procedures used for beginning, conducting, and evaluating widows' groups. Throughout this scholarly work, as well as Caine's (1974) popular work, an understanding of the special assistance widows can offer each other emerges. The authors suggest that the depth of pain and agony and the fears of many newly widowed people that they must be going crazy can be best understood by people who have shared that particular experience. Whether this belief is true or not, many widowed people are drawn to the credibility of a peer.

Similar factors seem to operate in other self-help groups where members have a bond because of their common problem and can share reactions, cry, and sometimes laugh together over similar experiences, and exchange tips on coping with particular situations. A good example is the support groups that have been formed in many communities by the Alzheimer's Association for family members of Alzheimer's patients. These groups provide assistance in coping with the practical matters of daily living, distribute useful information such as a family guide entitled *The 36-Hour Day* (Mace & Rabins, 1981), and sometimes offer respite care as they build a support network.

Conducting a Life Review

Although people of all ages talk about and periodically take stock of their lives, this activity has special meaning in old age. Butler and Lewis (1977) postulate the universal occurrence of an inner review of one's life that accounts for the increased reminiscing done by older people. In the process, people examine their lives through existential questions such as: "Who am I?" "Who have I been?" "How did I live my life?" It is as if life were a balance sheet and they are asking the question "All things considered, how did I do?" When the answer to this question is positive, people often experience a sense of serenity and a general acceptance of themselves. However, if the balance sheet comes out negatively, people may become discouraged and depressed. Thus the life review relates to Erikson's choice between integrity and despair. Integrity, in his scheme, conveys an acceptance of one's life as having been meaningful. Clearly counselors want to find ways to help their clients achieve such acceptance. When a retired English teacher, responding to this impetus, wrote her memoirs, her recognition of the process was reflected in the title, *Inscape, a Search for Meaning* (Young, 1983).

Interestingly, attitudes toward reminiscing may be a function of who is doing it. Famous people are revered for writing their memoirs, while ordinary people may be criticized for "living in the past" or "telling war stories." Happily, the increased interest in oral history provides a favorable atmosphere for life reviews. This atmosphere can facilitate intervention by counselors or family members when they hear a story being told repeatedly. Such repetition can be a valuable clue, indicating that the person needs to explore the significance of the story and its meaning at the present time.

According to Butler (1975), the realization of approaching death triggers a life review. Therefore, it is more common among older people, but also happens to younger people who anticipate dying. In Butler's words, the process is "characterized by the progressive return to consciousness of past experiences, in particular the resurgence of unresolved conflicts which can now be surveyed and reintegrated. The old are not only taking stock of themselves as they review their lives, they are trying to think and feel through what they will do with the time that is left and with whatever emotional and material legacies they have to give to others" (1975, p. 412).

A first step in facilitating a life review is often to listen for clues that someone is beginning the process and then to capitalize on the opportunity. Counselors can assist life reviewers to resolve conflicts they have identified or to complete unfinished business. Sometimes they help clients contact relatives to express appreciation, to apologize for past transgressions, or to reconcile. Sometimes counselors encourage clients to make wills or to talk with family and friends as to who wants which special possession. Life reviews can also help people recall old interests and abilities that can be rekindled.

In guiding a life review, counselors can help clients gain a sense of pride from looking at the people they have influenced, the events they have survived, and the crises they have weathered. In the process, older people may begin to acknowledge and accept previously unrecognized strengths. Sometimes this realization helps people move in the direction of self-sufficiency and androgyny. Older men report increased acceptance and enjoyment of their emotional and tender feelings, and women begin to appreciate their organizational abilities. Stated differently, men may become more affective and women more effective. These are positive moves for anyone and can be especially important for people who may have to live alone and can no longer depend on a partner. Another valuable outcome of a life review can be increased family closeness. Sometimes people who have lived together for many years tell previously secret or suppressed thoughts. Such communication can lead to increased intimacy.

Although life reviews typically lead to positive outcomes, they can be extremely painful for people who view themselves as failures or who have done serious harm to other people. Life reviews may also be difficult for those whose self-esteem has been closely tied to a vigorous body or physical appearance or who have spent more time planning for the future than living in the present.

Although the life-review process is usually a pleasurable and therapeutic process, most people encounter some memories that trigger feelings of guilt, anger, despair, regret, or sadness. Edinberg (1985) points out that a mental health practitioner working with a life reviewer has choices as to whether to comfort the person, encourage further expression of feelings, or move the client away from the subject. The strategy chosen obviously depends on the counselor's view of client needs at the time (p. 163).

Life reviews can be conducted individually, in a family setting, or in a counseling group. The process can be aided by stimuli of various kinds. Edinberg (1985, p. 164) lists a number of such triggers, with examples of how each can be used.

1. Music—using records or a sing-a-long.
2. Scents—bringing in spices, flowers, perfumes. For many people, the olfactory sense is the quickest route to memories.
3. Imaging—group members can be asked to recall particular events such as holidays, parties, historic occasions, or times when they felt especially happy or scared.
4. Memorabilia—members can be asked to bring to the group old photographs, school yearbooks, newspapers, greeting cards, election buttons, old household appliances, or favorite knick-knacks.

Ambitious life-review activities may involve clients in an active way. Strimling (1986) says that "doing talking"—including oral history, autobiography, theater, dance, and poetry—is becoming an important part of gerontological practice. He cites a number of oral-history projects taking place in New York City including those run by Columbia University, the American Jewish Committee, the Chinatown Oral History Project, and the Centro de Estudios Puertorriquenos of Hunter College. All of these programs focus on gathering history and using it in art, theater, or literature. The Life Stories project that Strimling directs at Hunter College is designed to help older adults in their quest for continuity, which Strimling views as the central task of old age.

An unusually complex life-review project involving researching, writing, and presenting a play is reported by Perlstein (1984). Her poignant description of *Three Generations,* an original play performed by fourteen older women, illustrates the value of theater as a form of life review. The group met weekly for three years to share stories, develop dance and theater skills, put together and rehearse plays. In Perlstein's view, the project not only validated the lives of the older people involved but entertained and educated community residents. Although long-term projects such as this play are exciting to know about, they are beyond the scope of most counseling groups. We describe below two relatively simple life-review activities that counselors can use with short-term groups or in individual counseling.

The *learning-from-your-past* approach to a life review is most appropriate for community-living older people who may wish to develop new interests or activities. It can be useful in career-development programs, including pre- or postretirement planning. The counselor distributes a worksheet that says: "Throughout your life you have engaged in many activities. Some you have really liked and some you have disliked. Reviewing these past activities can help you identify those elements that you might want to include in your future plans. In completing this worksheet, consider aspects of both those previous activities that afforded you personal satisfaction and those that you might want to avoid" (Stone & Penman, 1988).

As the example in Table 3 shows, this worksheet asks counselees to fill in information about activities from previous stages of their lives and encourages them to think about how past activities have helped them develop skills and express values. After about ten minutes the group reconvenes to discuss what they have learned. Particularly if group members have been trained to listen actively to each other, the sharing of recollections can be both affirming and suggestive of new possibilities. We have seen people who recalled their pleasure and success in school activities decide to take up new learning, those who remembered their pride in making furniture decide to embark

Table 3. Sample Life-Review Worksheet.

Past Activities (educational, vocational, leisure)	What You Liked	What You Disliked	Skills That You Developed, Values They Represent
Babysitting	Earning my own money	Cranky kids	Patience, independence
Basketball	Winning, competition	Losing, fights	Quick decision making, "practice makes perfect"

on a new handicraft project, and those who had been in singing or drama groups in high school look for community musical groups with which to affiliate. People also often recognize a continuity in their life's activities that they find affirming.

Although this worksheet is much simpler than a work autobiography, it can lead to some of the same outcomes. Crystal and Bolles (1974, p. 2) state that "self-esteem and good feelings about oneself come from remembering past achievements and strengths. You begin to see that you have a veritable army of talents and skills at your command." When people recall past accomplishments, they can begin to identify transferable skills that they can use in a new paid or unpaid endeavor.

A *guided life review* encourages clients to do a brief life review and then to discuss their recollections. When done in a group, the discussion usually promotes feelings of closeness among the members. To begin the activity, the counselor gives an explanation such as the following: "You will have an opportunity to think back through your lives about the people and experiences that have been most significant to you. When you have finished, you will have a few minutes to jot down some of your memories so that you can share them with the group. Get comfortable in your chair, put your belongings on the floor, close your eyes if that is comfortable for you, and take a few deep breaths." When members seem to be comfortable, the leader begins the journey back with such words as "Picture yourself as a child. Where are you? Is anyone with you? What sights and smells are you aware of? What are you thinking about? How are you feeling?"

As with any guided imagery, the leader needs to go slowly, pausing and allowing people time to think. After an appropriate interval the leader continues with a request to members to picture themselves as young adults and asks the same or similar questions. The leader continues encouraging members to see themselves at various stages of their lives and at the present. When this last image has been completed, the leader asks group members to open their eyes and reminds them where they are.

Although engaging in this kind of reminiscence is often intrinsically pleasurable for people, the major value comes from discussing the recollections with others. All group members should get a chance to tell their stories. During the discussion the leader and other group members can help people identify themes that run through various stages of their lives as well as personal strengths and coping techniques they have developed and can continue to draw on. The continuity in people's lives was dramatically illustrated in one group in which a woman who always "tracked" the statements of other members, reminding them of how what they said one day fit in with what they had said previously, described her role from childhood on as that of family historian.

In many groups we have seen this personal sharing activity foster intimacy. It often leads to comments such as "I have known Sally for several years here at the senior center and learned more about her today than I have ever known." This is an argument for using activities like this as part of a group counseling program, although it can clearly be done with an individual as well.

Analysis of Support Systems

When counselors help clients review their lives and heighten awareness of all the changes they have weathered, both clients and counselors learn valuable information about past and present support systems. What do we mean by the term *support system?* Caplan (1974) defines it as the "health-promoting forces at the person-to-person and social levels which enable people to master the challenges and strains in their lives" (p. vii). He identifies three vital components of a support system: "The significant others help the individual mobilize his psychological resources and master his emotional burdens; they share his tasks; and they provide him with extra supplies of money, materials, tools, skills, and cognitive guidance to improve his handling of his situation" (pp. 5–6).

In less academic terms, a support system consists of people who are in your corner or who are there for you when help is needed. A careful examination of the support system of an older adult may be especially important as that system is likely to have been disrupted by death, distance, or shrinking of activities and relationships (Schmidt, 1980).

Pearson (1980) defines a personal support system as that "network of people whose presence . . . provides support, confirmation, encouragement and assistance. . . . The common element . . . is that our relationship to [these people] . . . contributes to our *positive feelings about our life situation and ourselves*. . . . They are those special people whose presence or recollections we seek out because experiencing ourselves in relationships to them is a *positive personally-enhancing force in our lives*" (emphasis added). Pearson identifies thirteen types of support people can provide for each other: admiration, satisfaction, love, physical intimacy, companionship, encouragement, acceptance, comfort, example, guidance, help, knowledge, and honesty.

Counselors can use this or a similar list to help clients think about the kinds of support they need and the resources available for meeting their needs. A major task for counselors is to teach clients how to access needed support. When young, people may acquire these supports with relative ease. Sometimes, as with school friends or co-workers, they accompany particular roles. Older adults may need to spend increased effort and make this acquisition of support into a conscious, deliberate process. How? One can start by comparing one's own support system with a concrete list such as Pearson's. Such an assessment enables individuals to identify the strengths and "holes" in their system more clearly than does a general discussion of current supports.

After the assessment, the counselor can work with clients to formulate specific plans and goals for increasing supports. These plans may include meeting people, learning about community agencies or religious organizations, joining support groups, and learning to ask for help from those already in the older adult's circle of friends and relations. Asking for help often requires considerable counseling assistance. Many of today's older adults were raised to cherish self-sufficiency above all; asking for help may be seen as a rejection of that value. We have found two concepts to be useful in helping people to overcome that barrier.

First, "cosmic accounting" arises from the need, over a lifetime, to feel in balance with giving and receiving. It assumes that at any one period of life we may be out of balance in either direction. However, unlike our social lives, in which if you have me for dinner, I have to have you for dinner, cosmic accounting takes a longer, more varied view. And the receiver of what I give may not be the giver of what I receive, thus the "cosmic." The expectation that because we cared for our children they should now care for us may not be realistic. The belief that it is all right for me to accept help from my neighbor because I was a frequent volunteer during my younger years or because I was always there to listen to my friend's problems may be. Instead of "If you receive a good turn, pay it back," cosmic accounting encourages "If you receive a good turn, pass it on."

A reframing approach to overcoming the reluctance to take from people we have not given to may be effective. If a friend needs something that you could give fairly easily but does not ask, how do you feel? Most people say hurt, sad, insulted, distressed. If we do not ask our friends for help, we may be hurting or insulting them. The need to give is an important one. We can help our older adult clients recognize that this need does not apply only to them but to those on whom they could lean — their support system.

Second, we can look at an individual's support systems by drawing a circle that represents that person's life space. At the center or hub of the circle, the person's name appears. Radiating out from this hub are a series of lines or spokes that stand for elements in the person's support system. Although people are the primary components of support systems, counselors may also want to help their clients think about the support they get from their belief system, pets, books, the security of a home, and other nonpeople supports. A person in midlife with a job that is significant to her, a multigenerational family, and a variety of group involvements would have a full circle. To help prepare for some likely losses, the counselor can ask the person to "remove" the spouse, perhaps the family home, some couples who are friends, the job and some of the concomitant associations, and then to see how empty the circle looks. Such a confrontation with the future may be quite unsettling for people, so it should be done only after considerable trust has been established and when the counselor and the client will have sufficient time together to discuss ways of preparing for, or compensating for, some of the anticipated losses.

The above discussion focuses on supports that are part of an individual's informal network. In helping older adults and their families think of ways to augment their support systems, it is important to consider links between this informal network and formal community services. Case-management services often help to facilitate such links. Huttman (1985) cites several reasons why the aging network is becoming interested in the informal system of help. First, utilizing the informal system saves money. Second, combining outside services such as respite care or day care with the services provided by family members may make it possible for impaired older people to stay in the community rather than move to an institution. Huttman also notes that older people use hospitals less and recover from hospitalization better if they have strong family support. Healthy older people can also benefit from such links. For example, older people looking for work can benefit from a joint effort of family, friends, and agency-sponsored programs for older workers.

We have talked in this chapter about groups, life review, and support systems as approaches to working with older adults. All have a place within a coordinated program of services for older adults. In the next chapter we look at principles of program development and at a variety of workshops for older adults and their families.

10

Developing Programs and Workshops

If asked to describe their jobs, most counselors probably would say that working with clients, individually or in groups, is their main responsibility. Although that description may or may not be true, most of the training received by counselors revolves around direct contact with clients. Despite this emphasis on direct contact, many adult counselors spend time on programs and workshops intended to enhance the lives of their clients. Therefore, it is important for counselors to know how to develop comprehensive programs and how to design, market, and present workshops. In this chapter we will use the word *program* to refer to an array of services offered by an organization, and the term *workshop* to refer to short-term, topical, structured educational or growth experiences. The program of any given organization, therefore, may include several workshops, along with other activities.

To illustrate the importance of program-development and workshop-design skills, consider the following. A good counselor can be extremely helpful to a widowed or divorced person or a job seeker who comes for counseling. The same counselor can reach many more people by offering a workshop that addresses the needs of widowed or divorced people or older workers; and a workshop adds the bonus of group support. The kinds of workshops that can be developed are endless—from those designed to assist older workers in finding employment to those that help people prepare for or cope with retirement; from support groups for widows to political-action groups committed to seeking social change; and from groups brought together by a common illness or problem to senior travel clubs.

In this chapter we suggest some program-development strategies for counselors to consider. We then move to a discussion of designing, marketing, and conducting workshops and to a description of examples of counseling-related workshops. The final section considers ways of using older people themselves as part of the service-delivery system.

Designing Comprehensive Programs

In a book on adult learning, Brookfield (1986) discusses the pervasiveness of the institutional model of program development, which consists of five stages: "identify needs, define objectives (preferably in behavioral terms), identify learning experiences to meet these objectives, organize learning experiences into a plan with scope and sequence, and evaluate program outcomes in terms of the attainment of the behaviors specified" (p. 204). Such an approach has a great deal to recommend it because it provides a clear framework that can be explained to both sponsoring organizations and funding agencies. If appropriate assessment techniques are built in from the beginning, the evaluator may be able to tell whether the program made a difference in the lives of participants.

Brookfield cautions, however, that the model has a number of limitations. He notes that predetermined objectives leave little room for unanticipated learning or for a renegotiation of program goals as learners become involved in the process. Brookfield's concerns may be of particular importance to those developing counseling-related programs and workshops in which changing needs may emerge as clients learn about themselves and realize their desire to make behavioral changes and take control of their lives. In this situation, program planners need to build in opportunities for serendipitous learning and to allow for program redirection. To permit such flexibility while still providing for accountability, Brookfield argues that program development should include three elements: a clear definition of the activity, a number of general purposes for the activity, and "a set of criteria by which the success of various practitioner efforts can be judged" (p. 289).

For practitioners engaged in setting up a comprehensive program, a plan that identifies specific tasks and a timetable may be extremely helpful. In its trainers' manual, the National Occupational Information Coordinating Committee (NOICC) (1989, p. 17) identifies three major components of program design and suggests that setting up their (career-development) programs requires two years. The component strategies they have identified are included here, as we think they can be adapted by people developing programs in any area.

Stage one. Planning (0–6 months)
    Form committees
    Conduct needs assessment
    Establish program standards
    Initiate evaluation planning
Stage two. Development (7–12 months)
    Direct committees in program development
    Review the current program
    Revise the plan
    Design the evaluation
    Identify staff development needs
Stage three. Implementation (13–24 months)
    Involve committees in program implementation
    Conduct staff development
    Monitor program implementation
    Evaluate and use results for program improvement

In each of the stages, NOICC suggests using committees. Many organizations that provide services to older adults already have advisory boards and committees. When the composition of these boards is sufficiently broad—a mix of consumers (older people and their families) and knowledgeable professionals—the boards can be extremely helpful in all phases of program development.

Ideally an evaluation procedure is built in from the early stages of program development. Stufflebeam and Shinkfield (1985) have devised a process-oriented system, known as CIPP (Context, Input, Process and Product), that helps program developers assess their programs on an ongoing basis. In their view, evaluation should foster improvement, provide accountability, and promote increased understanding of the program. Thus their model, whose components are described below, is useful for formative as well as summative evaluation.

Context evaluation assesses the needs of the target population and is used to set goals and priorities to address those needs, giving careful attention to the environment in which the program will operate. Methods for carrying out a context evaluation include interviewing clients (for example, older people and their families), conducting hearings at which citizens can request services, surveying potential clients, reviewing records (perhaps of attendance at senior centers or of participation in personal-growth workshops), establishing an expert panel or advisory council (of gerontologists, staff members of mental health centers, or leaders in organizations of older adults). Context evaluation can be useful in identifying needs in order to seek funding or plan programs relevant to the target population.

Input evaluation is designed to develop strategies to use in a program. Program developers identify and evaluate possible approaches. In the process some program ideas can be screened in and others screened out. Methods used include reviewing literature, visiting other programs, and consulting experts. This phase of the evaluation process can be useful in developing proposals for submission to funding agencies. It can also provide the rationale for selecting a particular program or approach.

Process evaluation provides ongoing feedback on a developing program so that developers can make necessary modifications. A designated evaluator can get the necessary feedback through observations, interviews with clients and families, questionnaires, or surveys. For example, if a nursing home were to initiate, as part of its program, a workshop for family members of residents, an evaluator might sit in on some of the sessions, interview participants, ask for written feedback, or ask staff members whether they observed any changes in the interaction between family members and residents. Process evaluation encourages program developers to compare the plan with the program goals and helps keep the staff accountable.

Product evaluation is typically conducted at the end of a program or part of a program. It involves collecting and analyzing judgments from a broad range of people touched by the program. It compares attainments and objectives, and may consider the cost of those attainments. If the model program called for alternative approaches to meeting a particular need, product evaluation will investigate which was most effective. For example, a program for older workers may want to compare the job-placement rate and satisfaction of workers who had individual counseling, group counseling, or a combination. Or a counselor may want to assess the comparative effectiveness of an unstructured support group or a lecture/discussion group for widows. Product evaluation is useful in determining whether a program or part of a program is worth continuing or needs modification.

A major value of this approach is that program development, workshop design, and evaluation are intertwined, and evaluation is used in an ongoing manner to improve services. In a less structured way, ongoing needs assessments and program evaluations are done when service providers listen attentively to the concerns expressed by clients. This kind of ongoing evaluation process can also address an ethical issue related to funding. Given a society in which the financial resources available to provide services for older people are far less than the needs warrant, there may be a tendency for programming to follow funding. Thus if the Department of Mental Health announces the availability of money for older persons with mental illness, agencies may scurry to develop programs in that area, even though in the local community preventive programs may be needed more. Programs developed in response to a clear analysis of context are likely to be "right" for that locality.

Designing, Promoting, and Conducting Workshops

A full-scale discussion of the principles of workshop design is beyond the scope of this book. We do, however, want to make a few suggestions and remind counselors that they already have many of the communication skills necessary for conducting effective workshops. Workshop leaders must be able to present information clearly and give examples that make the material relevant for individual participants. They must know how to listen actively to group members, ask clarifying questions to make sure that participants are understanding the material, and promote group interaction. They also must be able to give appropriate feedback in a constructive manner, particularly if participants are practicing skills. Experienced group counselors clearly have these abilities.

To aid counselors in presenting an effective workshop, Loesch (1985) developed a seven-step procedure: Define your goals, profile the participants, profile the setting, design your agenda, prepare your resources, prepare yourself, and practice. For illustrative purposes, his seven steps will be utilized to show how a counselor might prepare and present a workshop on job-seeking skills for older workers.

The first two steps, *defining your goals and profiling the participants,* can be considered together. Let us assume that you have learned that because of layoffs at two large companies, a number of people over fifty in your community are looking for work. In talking with some of the employees who have been laid off, you learn that most of the workers—both blue-collar and white-collar—had assumed they would continue working at the same company until they retired. Some are angry, some are depressed, and almost all are worried about their future. Many of the workers never had to look for a job and lack confidence in their ability to do so. The goals of the workshop, therefore, would be to provide practical information about how to conduct a job search effectively and to boost participants' self-esteem. After talking with representatives of the companies and getting their agreement to help publicize the program—and, you hope, to underwrite its cost—you decide to give the workshop an upbeat title such as "How to Get the Job You Want."

The *setting* is also important. A cheerful room that affords the participants a substantial amount of privacy is best. Because losing a job is a major loss, participants will want a place where they can express their feelings without being observed by others.

Designing the agenda involves selecting the specific information, skills, and kind of support you want to include. To decide on content it is helpful to consult a list of competencies needed by job seekers, such as that contained in Goodman, Hoppin, and Kent (1984). They have identified six major categories: self-awareness/assessment, decision-making ability, ability to plan the job campaign, ability to communicate with employers, interviewing skills, and ability to keep a job. Talking with potential class members will help you assess which competencies they already have and which need to be taught.

In addition to doing this kind of needs assessment, you will want to consider practical factors such as how much time you have. Knowing how much time is available will help you determine, for example, whether to concentrate more on providing emotional support, on practicing interviewing skills, or on discussing ways to handle age discrimination. If all topics seem necessary, you will then want to consider the order in which they are offered. A program should flow logically. For example, participants need to have gathered some data about their previous experiences before they write a resumé. Also, some activities early in the program should build trust among participants as well as between participants and the program leader. Beginning activities should involve limited self-disclosure and provide opportunities for active listening.

In working with people who have lost their jobs, it is essential to provide an opportunity for discussion of emotional reactions. Such a discussion should not be held at the beginning of a program, as sufficient trust may not have been established. However, until people have had an opportunity to express some of their emotional reactions, they may have difficulty concentrating on cognitive material and developing an action plan.

In designing workshops for older adults, as for any other age group, it is helpful to build in variety. Workshop leaders need to achieve a balance between providing information and helping participants personalize the information. It is also important to vary the types of activities so that some are done in a large group and some in pairs or small groups. Because many older people have difficulty in sitting in one place for a prolonged period, such a change of pace has the additional value of encouraging participants to move around.

In *preparing resources,* such as handouts and audiovisual materials, it is important to consider the reading level of the audience. Materials that are difficult to comprehend can be an additional demoralizer for people who are already feeling vulnerable. However, it is important not to talk down or write in such a simplistic manner that you insult the intelligence of participants. In preparing or selecting printed materials for an older audience, counselors need to be sure that they are clear and in large enough type for aging eyes. Audiovisual materials, such as films that demonstrate interviewing skills, can be valuable additions to a workshop but must be carefully screened to be sure they are appropriate for adults. If the characters in the film are all teenagers, it may be difficult for older workers to identify, even if the suggestions made are worthwhile.

Preparing yourself and practicing will add to the smooth running of a workshop. These suggestions can cover everything from making sure that your audiovisual materials and equipment work to timing your presentations so that you leave enough time for questions. Almost all workshop presenters can tell horror stories of bringing the wrong set of slides, having half the slides in upside down, not having an extension cord long enough to reach the plug, or finding that they finished their whole program in half the time they planned or that they had run out of time before they got through half of what they intended to cover. In presenting a workshop, as in leading a counseling group, leaders must constantly decide how much deviation from their agenda is appropriate. Often this decision requires a delicate balancing of the needs of individual members of the group. Generally speaking, we recommend a time agenda from which you give yourself permission to deviate. Although redesigning during the course of a workshop is often necessary, a practice session may alert you to needed changes.

In addition to assessing needs and designing workshops to meet them, individuals and organizations that offer workshops must publicize them. Although counselors may not think of themselves as marketing experts, even the best of workshops is of no value if the targeted clientele does not know about it. C. Appleton (personal communication, 1989) outlines a three-step public relations/marketing campaign that involves planning, presenting, and evaluating. To plan the marketing approach she recommends that presenters briefly describe the workshop and "FAB" it—identify one special *F*eature of it, one *A*dvantage it has over other workshops, and one *B*enefit it will bring to participants. Identifying the target audience determines where to market the program. Over time, organizations need to develop customized mailing lists, have contacts with representatives of print and broadcast media, and locate distribution points for flyers. Information on workshops can be presented through printed material in the form of press releases and flyers or through public-service announcements sent to radio and television stations. Personal contacts—individual conversations, speaking before groups, handwritten letters—are time-consuming but often effective in recruiting. To evaluate the success of your public-relations efforts, it is important to find out how the people who attend your workshop learned about it.

The following section describes various kinds of workshops that may be useful for older adults and their families. You are encouraged to keep some of the principles of designing, marketing, and conducting workshops in mind as you consider how you might develop workshops like these in your community or agency.

Sampling of Workshops and Group Activities

The variety of workshops that can be conducted for older people and their families is almost limitless. In this section we describe a few, classified into areas in which counselors have expertise: personal growth, education, and career development.

Personal-Growth Workshops. Previously we talked of the reluctance of many older people to involve themselves in activities that are labeled *counseling*. Sargent (1980) contends that despite a high incidence of problems "most older people don't and won't ask for help with their emotional problems. They resist. They not only won't ask, but many of them won't accept assistance if and when it is offered. That's where the nontraditional approaches come in. 'Nontraditional' psychotherapy or counseling is a term used to cover many programs and approaches which are therapeutic and which older people can accept" (pp. 1–2). Sargent's concerns about the reluctance of older adults are shared by some counselors and rejected by others. The reality is probably that some older adults are reluctant, while others are not.

Robinson, Smaby, and Donovan (1989) describe several techniques for using interpersonal influence to reduce reluctance in elderly clients and increase clients' perceptions of counselors as trustworthy and effective. Another way for older people to address their emotional needs without the stigma that may be attached to seeking counseling is to sign up for workshops. Dunckley, Lutes, Wooten, and Kooken (1980) state that workshops carry no stigma, provide information to people who do not wish to acknowledge personal problems, are available to family members and service providers as well as to older people themselves, are an efficient means of information dissemination, and are presented as education so participants have no qualms if they are not expected to pay.

Although broad generalizations about what older adults want are clearly inappropriate, it seems clear that nontraditional approaches are easier for some older adults to accept than are traditional approaches. A number of such approaches and workshops are described by contributors to Sargent's book (1980). For example, a course on "creative living" designed for women over fifty consisted of lectures as well as large- and small-group discussions. In personalizing the information given in the lectures, class members analyzed their own values and behavior and received feedback on how they appeared to other group members. One woman, for example, did not understand her difficulty in attracting friends until she received feedback that she appeared cold. "With much positive reinforcement from both leader and class, she made notable progress in expressing herself warmly and attractively to others, which produced greater confidence in herself" (p. 39).

In the same book, Meyer (1980) describes the New Directions Workshop she developed to assist older adults who were having difficulty with the transition to retirement. Participants learned about the goal-setting process and were urged to set and begin working toward personal goals. She deliberately offered the workshop in the arts-and-crafts room of a parks-and-recreation-department building in order to avoid any connotation of psychotherapy or the "social club" image of the nearby senior center.

The Senior Actualization and Growth Explorations (SAGE) groups developed in the San Francisco Bay area differ from many workshops for older adults in that they address body, mind, and spirit. Gay Luce, a principal founder of the groups, has chronicled their development (Luce, 1979) and explains their philosophy, which sees old age as "a time to discover inner richness, for self-development and spiritual growth." Her book contains descriptions and illustrations of physical exercises and artistic activities by group members, along with suggestions for teaching active listening and promoting participation in group sessions.

The Continuum Center of Oakland University in Michigan has developed a number of structured, time-limited workshops designed to enhance older adults' self-esteem and communication skills. These programs, which are facilitated by peer counselors and have names such as Take Charge of Your Own Aging or Personal Growth for Older Adults, meet in senior centers or congregate living facilities. One of the Continuum Center's programs, Growing Older Bolder, is an assertiveness-training program.

Assertiveness training is an important approach to helping older people improve their interpersonal-communication skills and express their feelings directly. Although such training can be helpful to people of any age, Wheeler (1980) thinks its practical, skill orientation is particularly appealing to older adults. Corby (1975) reports that "one group of men and women in a retirement home (average age: 86 years) increased their interpersonal disclosure levels . . . an average of 67 percent after four one-hour assertion training sessions." Assertiveness training can help older people cope with bureaucracies as well as with the significant people in their lives. Such training may be especially helpful for today's older women, many of whom were socialized to assume a passive role in society. Corby warns trainers that many older people confuse the term *assertion* with aggression and recommends the term *effectiveness training*. She also suggests that in residential institutions it may be desirable for counselors to train the staff and have them teach assertiveness to the residents.

In the previously mentioned Growing Older Bolder workshop, most participants are concerned with relationships with family and friends. They ask questions like "How do I ask for help without intruding?" or make statements such as "I want to see my grandchildren more," "My friends complain about their problems all the time and I'm tired of it," "I just can't say no when my daughters ask me to baby sit." At the end of this program, participants typically report increased ability to express themselves to their family and friends. Many are pleasantly surprised at their ability to change behavior "at my age."

Similar workshops aimed at improving family communication can be offered for middle-aged family members. Workshops with titles such as You and Your Aging Parent are springing up all around the country. Typically they include information on physical changes that occur with aging and on community resources, along with training in assertive communication skills. They also offer the opportunity for participants to share their feelings of resentment, guilt, or fatigue and to provide support for each other. The depth of people's feelings in this area was suggested to us when an announcement of a You and Your Aging Parent program brought several telephone calls from people explaining why they were not coming! Some of these workshops use audiovisual aids such as the film *My Mother, My Father* to stimulate discussion. This film, available from Terra Nova Films in Chicago, shows four families who deal in different ways with the problems of caring for frail elderly parents. A facilitator can then lead a discussion that addresses the need for information and support.

Educational Offerings. The variety of educational workshops for
older adults is exceedingly wide, ranging from classes in English as a second language to instruction in play writing, and
from classes aimed at developing computer literacy to a full range
of college offerings through Elderhostel. Participation in education may enhance the lives of older adults in several ways.
It can boost self-esteem, provide mental stimulation, and increase social contacts, all of which contribute to the larger goal
of empowering older people.

The American Society on Aging devoted a special issue
of *Generations* to late-life learning (1987–1988); it highlights the
diversity of possible programming and also tackles philosophi-
cal questions about the value of education for the elderly. In
the introduction to that issue, Moody (1987–1988, p. 5) states
his belief that "the opposition between so-called quality-of-life
concerns—such as adult education—and more pragmatic concerns—such as income and human services—is actually a false
dichotomy" (p. 5). Moody maintains that four kinds of problems provide a rationale for late-life learning: economic problems, including high unemployment among older workers and
the need for retraining; social service problems, including excessive dependence on understaffed social agencies; political problems, such as the lack of empowerment of the elderly in decisions affecting their lives; and existential problems, including
no clear sense of the meaning of lengthened life. He then goes
on to suggest educational undertakings that would address each
of these problems.

In another provocative article in that issue of *Generations,*
Lumsden (1987–1988) cautions against defining learning as participation in formal, institutionally sponsored educational activities. "Learning may involve the mastery of the contents of
an algebra course on a university campus, or it may involve
self-directed instruction in music. Learning may be as involved
as the pursuit of a doctoral degree, or it may be as simple as
remembering the days of the week that the garbage collectors
make their neighborhood rounds" (p. 12).

The balance of the journal issue makes a strong case for
late-life learning in many different arenas and describes a num-

ber of innovative programs. For example, there is a description of educational activities designed to help blind people live independently (Timmerman, 1987–1988) and a report on a senior center that helped older people become "computer-friendly" as they eagerly learn about desktop publishing, spreadsheets, and sophisticated graphics (Fuchs, 1987–1988).

Peterson (1987–1988) reports that higher education institutions have found that age-segregated programs, designed for and offered exclusively to older people, are more popular than programs that simply allow older learners to sit in courses with traditional students. "Elderhostel is probably the best-known educational program for older persons because of its availability in hundreds of colleges and universities and its reputation for highly interesting programs. Through Elderhostel, older learners live in college dormitories, enroll in a series of courses offered during a one- or two-week period, and participate in a number of special site visits, lectures, or cultural programs" (p. 17). Elderhostel is listed in the Resources. At the local level many community education programs, colleges, and universities offer free or reduced tuition to older adults.

Discussions of learning for older adults often trigger concerns about memory loss and continuing ability to learn. This area has been well researched (see, for example, Belsky, 1984; Poon, 1980). Counselors need to know that it is a myth that intelligence decreases with age. In fact, crystallized intelligence, which is a person's ability to use an accumulated body of information to make judgments and solve problems, appears to increase over the life span of healthy people. Major keys to maintaining mental capabilities are staying socially involved, being mentally active ("use it or lose it"), and having a flexible personality.

Because so many older adults are concerned about memory loss, counselors may wish to develop programs or activities to help people improve their memories. Turner Geriatric Clinic at the University of Michigan Hospitals has produced a workbook entitled *Facts and Fiction About Memory* (Wooley, 1983), which includes a number of appropriate activities. Some of the activities in Houston's (1982) book are also relevant. She suggests that recalling past events, particularly childhood memories involving sensory experiences, helps to improve all aspects of memory. In a related vein, those adults who wish to enroll in a structured learning activity may benefit from a workshop in study skills.

Workshops for Older Workers. As indicated in Chapter Six workshops for older workers take many forms. Some are designed to assist job hunters, some to help with retirement planning. Counselors interested in this area can get many programmatic suggestions and resources from the Worker Equity Department of the AARP. Their programs and legislative efforts are designed to foster increased employment in both the public and private sectors; equal access to promotion and training opportunities; increased knowledge by older workers about employment-protection and retirement options; increased services for older workers in transition, such as those entering the job market for the first time, those interested in new careers, and those who find themselves unemployed late in their careers; and elimination of mandatory retirement based on age (AARP, 1986b). In addition to offering resources to older workers, AARP has prepared a program guide entitled *Second Career Opportunities for Older Persons.* Designed for organizations that plan activities that develop and promote jobs for older people, the guide offers suggestions for setting up job fairs, job-placement services, and employment workshops (AARP, 1982).

Peer Counseling

The idea of using older people to deliver mental health services to their peers is an intriguing one that has its supporters and detractors. In our view, peer counseling has much to recommend it, as well as some limitations. In general the term *peer counselor* (or *indigenous helper*) refers to people from the same population as their clients. Peers can share a neighborhood, an ethnic group, a disease, or a problem. In the following discussion, peer counselor refers to helpers who, like their clients, are older adults. However, because the minimum age for peer counselors may be as low as fifty-five, there can be an age difference of thirty or more years between some "peer" counselors and their clients! Although some older adults are professionally trained counselors, peer counselors usually are paraprofessionals.

Advantages. A basic reason for using peer counselors is that their common background with clients makes them able to understand clients' situations and feelings. Sometimes this shared background brings instant credibility. Although most good counselors can relate to people regardless of gender, age, ethnicity, sexual preference, or marital status, it may take a long time to gain the trust of someone who is clearly different. Peer counselors who are age cohorts, even though they may have had different life-styles, have at least lived at the same time. Thus they have experienced the same wars, the same depressions, and are equally appalled at the price of a quart of milk. Peer counselors, who are often perceived as friends rather than therapists, may be less forbidding or offputting to clients than professional counselors. This perception can be crucial for those older people who believe that a need for traditional counseling services is a sign of weakness or illness.

Perhaps the best reason for using peer counselors is that they can be role models for their clients. Effective peer counselors model successful aging not only in their ability to cope with problems and losses but also in their willingness to take on new roles and responsibilities. Clients who are resistant to making changes may have difficulty justifying their behavior to a seventy- or eighty-year-old peer counselor who is launched on a new career. It is much easier to insist that "You can't teach an old dog new tricks" to a thirty-year-old recently out of graduate school. Peer counselors can also use self-disclosure appropriately to maximize their effectiveness as role models.

Peer counseling can benefit more than the clients. Priddy and Knisely (1982) talk of the value that accrues to peer counselors themselves from serving in this capacity. Many years ago Reissman (1965) introduced the term *helper-therapy principle* to describe the value to a person with problems of providing help to others. This observation is consistent with other literature on peer counseling across the life span. From an organizational perspective, peer counseling may be desirable because of a shortage of appropriately trained and interested professionals or because peer counselors may cost less than professionals. A caution here is that effective peer-counseling programs require a lot of training, support, and supervision from professionals. Consequently the differences in cost may be less than anticipated.

Limitations. Concerns about the use of peer counselors are mentioned here not to discourage you but to alert you to problems that may arise. Because of limited training, the skills of paraprofessional or peer counselors are usually less developed than those of professionals. This relative lack of skills can cause problems at two extremes. Peer counselors may get in over their heads and try to deal with problems beyond their level of competence. (For this reason, among others, professional supervision is essential.) At the other extreme, people may be reluctant to use the skills they do have. Professionals often need to encourage peer counselors who have more skills than self-confidence.

The ability of peer counselors to share their own experiences was listed above as an advantage, but it has a down side as well. Because of a similarity in background and a strong desire to help clients, many peer counselors are prone to giving advice. Supervisors may need to stress the importance of listening before problem solving as well as the value of encouraging clients to make their own decisions.

Peer counselors may also have difficulty in not personalizing anger expressed by their clients. Older adults, like people of any age who are experiencing frustrations, may lash out in anger at anyone who is around them. Peer counselors, trained to help people discuss their feelings, may thus be at risk of being targeted with the anger. Appropriate warnings and support from supervisors are, therefore, important.

Providing Support. In an early review of the literature on using paraprofessionals in education and the helping professions, Matheny and Oslin (1970) concluded that the success of programs depends on proper selection, adequate training, clear

definition of roles, and successful interactions between super-
vising professionals and paraprofessionals. Their conclusions are
still valid. Professional counselors who work with paraprofessionals are likely to have four major responsibilities, each of
which is discussed briefly here.

Recruitment can be accomplished in several ways, each of
which has advantages and disadvantages. A broad-based approach such as a newspaper announcement may yield a large
pool of people, but they will require careful screening. Asking
paid or unpaid staff of an organization to become peer counselors means they will be knowledgeable about the organization
but unfamiliar with counseling. People recruited from the client
population will be familiar with the programs and the value of
peer counseling but may find it difficult to change from being
helped to being the helper.

Selection is always difficult because it involves accepting
some people and rejecting others. It helps to have clear criteria
and to consider the mental health and attitude of applicants as
well as their potential for skill development. An orientation session for people considering peer-counseling training may provide an opportunity for both trainers and potential trainees to
make an informed decision about the suitability of the training. Despite clear criteria and procedures, it may become necessary to deselect someone who initially seemed appropriate. If
it becomes clear during or after the training that a trainee will
not be an effective peer counselor, the trainer has the responsibility to explain the problem and to suggest alternative opportunities.

Training for peer counselors should be skill-oriented. A
number of systematic models exist, Carkhuff (1969), Egan (1986),
Ivey (1974), and Kagan (1984) being among the best known.
Our experience as trainers underlines the importance of having
people practice specific skills and continually evaluate themselves
as they practice. Trainers need to utilize feedback skills that
emphasize positives — what trainees are doing "right" — at the
same time as they demonstrate how to improve.

Supervision and support must be provided on an ongoing
basis. Peer counselors need lots of opportunities to practice skills,

receive constructive feedback, and take part in inservice training. When peer counselors work in group programs, they can meet with a professional staff member prior to and after each session. Additional supervision and support can be offered if the professional occasionally joins a group in order to observe the peer counselor in action and model effective responses. Such sitting in can be tricky as the professional does not want to take over the group and diminish the self-confidence or power of the peer counselor. Rather the goal is to enhance both the skill and security of the peer counselors so they in turn can be effective with their counselees.

In this chapter we have talked about designing programs and presenting workshops that may enhance the lives of older people. Another way in which counselors seek to achieve that end is through advocacy, the subject of the final chapter.

11

Advocating for
Individuals and Groups

Throughout this book we have stressed the importance of identifying and meeting clients' needs through a variety of services. Sometimes counselors can help older people make changes in their own behavior or connect them with available resources. At other times counselors can work to influence organizations, legislation, and policies that have an impact on the lives of older people. Most people who are attracted to the field of counseling have a desire to help other people, and advocacy is another important tool counselors can use to provide such help.

Schlossberg et al. (1978, p. 142) observe that "there are some conditions that counselors cannot change in their role as counselors or program developers. But there is a third type of intervention . . . open to the counselor, and that is social action to change basic conditions." They further state that although they deem it inappropriate for counselors to impose their own values on clients, "it is entirely appropriate that counselors act on their own values in the larger arena of society, that they work in whatever way they can to bring about needed change. Indeed, it may be not only appropriate but morally imperative that they do so." In a similar vein, Atkinson (1980, p. 89) contends that "counselors who fail to recognize the external source of their elderly clients' problems and who continue to focus on changing their clients' behavior will be failing to meet their clients' needs."

In Atkinson's (1980) view, social-change counseling requires consciousness-raising activities at three levels. He recommends that counselors must first raise their own awareness of conditions that affect older adults. They can then begin to arouse the awareness of the general public (the second level) and of older people themselves (the third level). Older people may be more difficult to arouse than would be expected because, according to Atkinson, "many elderly persons, because of a strongly ingrained value of independence and a desire not to be a burden to anyone, bear incredibly oppressive conditions without complaint. Frequently they blame themselves for their plight when societal forces are actually to blame. The result of this self-blame is a loss of self esteem" (p. 90). Addressing a similar point, Betances (1988) says that a major task of counselors is to teach people who are discriminated against by mainstream society to "reject rejection." For many older people who have bought into age bias, this may be a hard lesson to learn.

In simple terms, advocacy is taking a stand for what you believe or being passionate in your quest for compassion and justice. Sometimes counselors may need to make waves by openly disagreeing with existing organizational or governmental policy. A basic goal of all the counseling-related activities described in this book is that of empowering older people. This chapter, therefore, begins with a discussion of advocacy and empowerment. As they strive to be change agents, counselors work at two different levels. Some of their efforts are directed toward the interests of their clients or client groups. Other activities, at the societal level, are directed toward the well-being of all older adults or significant subgroups of the older population. The chapter continues, then, with two sections that correspond to those two levels.

Empowering Older People

In working as advocates, counselors have a basic goal — to enhance the self-esteem of their older clients. In Chapter Five we underlined the fact that people feel good about themselves and in control of their lives when they believe that what they do makes a difference. Therefore, in their advocacy role counselors need to decide not only what they should do for their clients but also what they can help clients learn to do for themselves. Allowing clients to help themselves is a good idea both when counselors are working on behalf of clients and when they are operating at the societal level. In many cases, a joint approach may be most effective. For example, if a woman in need of home health care has strong preferences as to which aide the agency sends but is not stating her preferences, the counselor may wish to call the agency on the client's behalf *and* work with the individual to help her realize she is entitled to make choices and does not need to accept anyone the agency sends. In other situations where clients are intimidated by bureaucrats or professionals, the counselor may want to practice assertive techniques with the clients *and* call the organization. Similarly, if special bus service is discontinued, the counselor may contact the transportation service directly *and* encourage affected persons to launch a letter-writing campaign.

Miller (1981) cautions gerontologists against taking over for older people in their political efforts. He states that "as long as older people are treated as a group who need someone else to advocate for them or to think through policy alternatives for them, they will continue to be powerless" (p. 14). Miller believes that older people need "autonomous, self funded, democratic, powerful organizations in which they can discuss, debate, decide and act on their decisions" (p. 9). Moody (1987–1988) also argues passionately for empowerment when he urges the aging network to adopt a "human development strategy" rather than a "service strategy." In his view the service strategy defines older people strictly as clients in need of help rather than human beings with the potential for learning how to be self-sufficient.

An example of a dual approach is reported by Minkler (1983), who describes a project in which graduate students helped to mobilize groups of older adults to act on their own behalf. The Tenderloin Senior Outreach Project grew out of efforts by students from the University of California at Berkeley to address the interrelated problems of poor health, social isolation, and powerlessness among older people living in single-room

occupancy hotels in inner-city San Francisco. To begin the
project, graduate students offered blood-pressure screening once
a week in the lobby of one of the hotels. They used these occasions to meet residents and facilitate interaction. As trust developed, students encouraged the residents to meet regularly.
Although residents at first seemed to attend these meetings simply to drink coffee and talk with students, they gradually began
to show real interest in one another. Minkler cites a poignant
story of one group member with a drinking problem who was
hospitalized with severe diabetes. After a visit from another
group member, he remarked, "That was the first time since I
was a child that anyone visited me in the hospital. I had no idea
that anyone in this hotel cared, and I'm going to cut down on
my drinking."

As the initial discussion group became popular, residents
of other hotels expressed interest in such a group. When group
discussions indicated that crime was the worst problem, students
encouraged residents to create a crime project and develop an
interhotel coalition. Over time the project expanded as community members worked for the establishment of minimarkets
and "safehouses." Minkler cites another example of a resident
who periodically checked himself into the state mental hospital
for reality orientation. After two years of intensive involvement
with the project, he did not return to the hospital. When asked
why, he explained that he had become so involved in various
organizations, he did not have time for reality! In Minkler's view,
the project led to "gradual empowerment of the elderly as individuals and as a community."

With individuals who are less a part of organized society, counselors may need to take a more active role, at least
in the early stages of projects. For example, Cohen, Teresi,
Holmes, and Roth (1988) write of the need for localized medical services for older homeless men and of the importance of
local "flophouses" and "slop joints" in the support system of these
men. Contact with policy makers may be the appropriate avenue for counselors advocating on behalf of the needs of such
isolated individuals.

Working on Behalf of Older Clients

In working with an individual client, advocacy often takes the form of running interference for that person, typically as part of the referral process. Operationally it means a counselor does not just give clients the names of agencies that might be helpful. Rather the counselor makes sure the agency provides the recommended service, alerts staff members that the client will be contacting them, and informs them of any particular needs or concerns the client may have.

Navigating Bureaucracies. Older clients may benefit from special assistance in dealing with many situations and agencies. Such assistance can be extremely valuable to the older person who is fearful of persons in authority or does not know how to apply for, or follow up on, payments for Social Security, Medicare, Medicaid, or other benefits. For example, many older people, particularly widows who may have had no experience with family financial management, have difficulty with income-tax forms and often fail to take advantage of benefits to which they are entitled. To address that problem, many senior centers and other organizations conduct tax clinics or provide volunteer accountants who help taxpayers prepare their returns. Counselors knowledgeable about such services can make appropriate referrals. The process of helping older adults with such practical concerns may build trust and open the door for dealing with emotional problems as well.

Older people who are involved in an accident or are victimized by a crime may have similar difficulties in dealing with the police department or even getting to the precinct headquarters to file a report. Advocacy in such situations could involve accompanying an older person to the police department or interceding on the person's behalf to get someone to go to the house to take a report or a deposition. Dealing with the criminal-justice system can present additional problems for people in certain ethnic or minority groups. For some, the relationship of their community to the police has been an adversarial one, fraught with ill feeling. As older adults who may now need help, they may find changing their view of the police from enemy to possible protector difficult. Such a change in perspective may require counselor-assisted reframing. An additional problem arises for those older people who do not speak English. Particularly in states that have passed "English as an official language" laws, translators may not be provided by the police or courts, yet their presence may be critical if non-English speakers are to understand the proceedings. Again, counselors may wish to intervene to help their clients get this service.

Sometimes in their advocacy role counselors see the need for a particular service and find a way to provide it. Such is the story of the Adult Day Care Center in Ada, Oklahoma (B. Shelton, personal communication, January 1990). Shelton, a counselor educator at the state university in Ada who is an expert in the field of gerontological counseling, received a call from the retired executive director of the Chamber of Commerce seeking help for a former member who had developed Alzheimer's disease. Several members had been helping this man and his wife, but they found it more than they could handle. Shelton and the former executive director discussed the value of day care and decided to set up a community meeting to assess the need for, and feasibility of, establishing such a center. They advertised in the paper to attract people who might use the service, invited state representatives and representatives of the aging network to attend. Fortunately, the state representative from Ada chaired the House Appropriations Committee.

The human service people and the business people worked well together. The business people knew how to get incorporated but not what a day-care center was. Shelton knew what day-care centers could do but not how to get an organization incorporated. So while Shelton and the director of the local Area Agency on Aging wrote the proposal and contacted ministers and other community people to locate clients for the center, the businesspeople handled the legal paperwork. The head of the Department of Human Services explained standards for day care, and the state representative promised some funding. Once building-code problems were solved, the center opened with twenty clients.

This story illustrates how counselors can act on behalf of a group of older adults and the value of coalition building. In this case, the Alzheimer's patient had some influential friends who knew how to use their network to get to a knowledgeable counselor and also knew how to make things happen. A major challenge for counselors is to assist less-powerful people in articulating their needs and pursuing them with equal fervor.

Advocating with Public and Private Institutions. Public institutions such as libraries or schools may become more responsive to the needs of their older constituents than they now are if counselors or other service providers make them aware of these needs and urge them to institute appropriate services. In many states, colleges and community-education departments of local school districts offer free or reduced tuition to persons over a certain age. Many libraries have an outreach staff member who takes books to the homes of people who cannot come to the library. Counselors who know about the availability of these services in their local communities can tell their clients about them. In addition, counselors can recommend such services to local schools, libraries, or other organizations.

Counselors who are attuned to the sensory losses and physical changes experienced by many older people can serve as advocates by encouraging retail establishments to be sensitive to special needs. For example, grocery stores may need to be alerted to the desire of many older customers for small portions of food and to the difficulty many older people have in reading price and nutritional information through plastic wrapping. Clothing stores may put chairs in their fitting rooms if someone explains their importance. Such amenities make sense from the business point of view as well as from a humanitarian standpoint. Grandparents are likely to accompany their grandchildren to the clothing store — checkbook in hand — if they have a place to sit down!

Working at the Societal Level

Advocating for the aging, as for any other group, involves a number of widely different activities. Some can be done by counselors individually; some are better done through professional associations or special interest groups. Whether acting "in role" as a staff member of a particular organization or as a private citizen, gerontological counselors have special knowledge of the problems of older people and good interpersonal skills that enable them to express their concerns. Both are important for people who wish to function as change agents.

If we follow Atkinson's (1980) recommendations, cited at the beginning of this chapter, counselors will begin the advocacy process by getting personally involved. For some counselors that may mean developing contacts with the aging network, possibly by attending meetings of local Area Agencies on Aging, listening to or testifying at legislative hearings on the needs of older persons, or seeking appointment to the boards of organizations that provide services to the elderly. It may mean joining advocacy organizations such as AARP, the Gray Panthers, or the Older Women's League. These three groups are briefly described here, but there are many others at the local, state, and national level.

Role of Organizations of Older Adults. AARP is the largest organization of older persons, indeed the largest membership organization in the United States. It is a nonprofit, nonpartisan organization with over twenty-seven million members. In addition to serving its members by lobbying at the federal and state levels, AARP offers a large variety of educational and community-service programs and direct membership benefits ranging from low-cost prescriptions to exotic foreign trips. AARP uses volunteers extensively in staffing its own programs (for example, programs to facilitate retirement planning) and also operates a volunteer talent bank — "a computerized volunteer-to-position referral project designed to provide AARP members and others who are age 50 or older with appropriate volunteer opportunities" (AARP, 1987a).

The Gray Panthers, founded by long-time activist Maggie Kuhn, advocates a variety of social issues and forms coalitions with many other peace and social-change groups. Its subtitle "age and youth in action" highlights the group's orientation, which is not exclusively the special interests of older adults.

The Older Women's League (OWL) says in describing its agenda that OWL works to "forge a link between the women's movement and aging activism" (Older Women's League, undated). This agenda states that the three major objectives of OWL are access to health care insurance, Social Security, and pension rights. "The common threads of these three issues are: recognition of the value of women's work—paid or unpaid—focus upon the economic plight of women in later years, and attack upon inequities inherent in public policy. Equal treatment of unequals is not equality."

In addition to working with a national organization such as those described above, advocacy may also mean joining a media watch, monitoring ways in which older people are portrayed in newspapers, on radio or television, and then sending appropriate kudos or complaints. To give one example of such a group, the Michigan Media Project, which describes itself as a "nonprofit advocacy group," is concerned with the image of women portrayed in the media. In addition to monitoring print and broadcast media, members of the group have developed a slide presentation entitled "What's Wrong with Wrinkles?" The promotional literature for the program (Michigan Media Project, undated) asks, "Does being a woman mean being young, sexy and available? That's what the media tells us everyday. What's wrong with this? It's repetitive and demeaning and ignores the value of maturity. Worse, yet, it gives the television viewer, often our own kids, false standards by which to measure women's validity in society." Group members travel with the slide presentation to various groups to present their point of view and enlist cooperation.

Counselors can expose themselves and others to this kind of program in different ways. They may invite a member of an advocacy organization to address their professional organization or community group. Advocacy groups are frequently eager to send representatives to community meetings, and counselors knowledgeable about both groups can serve as liaisons. Counselors may also join the organizations and become personally active.

All such advocacy organizations publish newsletters that inform readers about significant issues before federal and state legislatures and urge member involvement. The success of such urging was underlined in a report from a member of the board of AARP. Writing in an AARP newsletter, Ostrander (1985, p. 3) said, "Last spring, when I voiced AARP's opposition to the proposed $50 billion cuts in Social Security, Medicare and Medicaid before the House Ways and Means Committee, we were able to show your support with 80 bags of mail from AARP members. In response to AARP alerts on the fairness issue in trimming the budget to reduce our federal deficit, 130,000 AARP members signed petitions in less than six weeks. . . . Your federal and state legislators may be alerted to issues when we speak on behalf of AARP, but they *act* when they hear from you, their constituents." *Hot Flash,* a newsletter for midlife and older women published by the School of Allied Health Professions of the State University of New York, is another example of a publication that alerts counselors to the needs of older women and ways to advocate on behalf of their interests.

At the community level, counselors may also become involved with ombudsman services, which, in the aging field, are most commonly associated with nursing homes. Litwin (1985) describes several different models of ombudsman services in this country, all designed to improve services for patients and to protect patients' rights. Some ombudsmen are salaried professionals; others are citizen volunteers who act as patient advocates. Sometimes these two groups work well together; at other times their relationship is adversarial.

The need for such programs stems from an increase in (or an increased awareness of) abuse of the institutionalized aged. J. S. Kayser-Jones (cited in Litwin, 1985) identified four major categories of nursing-home abuse: infantilization, when residents are treated like irresponsible, dependent minors; depersonalization, when residents are treated mechanically; dehumanization, when residents do not receive compassionate treatment and adequate privacy; and victimization, including verbal intimidation, excessive sedation, and punitive restraints as well as thefts of possessions. Such abuses are clearly inappropriate and need to be identified and publicized.

An advocacy organization, Citizens for Better Care, exists in many communities to take such actions, and counselors are advised to contact it. We also think it is important for counselors to promote good publicity for well-run nursing homes, staffed by compassionate and well-trained people. The bad press that nursing homes often get makes it difficult for many older persons to tolerate the thought of being involved with any long-term-care institution. It may also lead to considerable agony on the part of caregivers, who sometimes keep relatives at home longer than is good for the relatives or themselves.

Political Role of Counselors and Their Organizations. At another level, counselors individually or collectively may want to interact with the political system. Such interaction is easier for counselors who are familiar with the aging network and with local, state, and national legislators and executive-branch employees than for those who are not. For example, the Older Americans Act mandates public hearings as part of the planning process for state and local services. Counselors can encourage older persons to testify at these hearings and also testify themselves, making a case for services they deem necessary.

Counselors can also contact elected officials at all levels. Sometimes this contact is one-on-one, from a counselor to an official; at other times such action is taken by officers or representatives of professional associations. Such action is consistent with the mission of some professional associations. For example, the president of the American Association for Counseling and Development (AACD) declared that the theme for her year as president was "Global Visions: Celebrating Diversity, Creating Community." In explaining that theme, she said that having global visions "means [en]visioning the kind of society we want to help create and then developing the innovative techniques, programs and interventions to help achieve it. . . . Celebrating diversity means we are committed to valuing difference and working toward greater inclusiveness of those who have been outside the opportunity structure. . . . [And in] creating community we need to identify what we as counselors and human development professionals can uniquely do to empower people to not only develop their own potential but . . . benefit society" (Hansen, 1989).

Both AACD and the American Psychological Association (APA) have divisions, called Adult Development and Aging, for members who are interested in counseling older adults. (APA's group is also designated Division 20.) AACD, APA, and the National Association of Social Workers, as well as several of the gerontological associations, have lobbyists who represent their interests at the national level.

Many such professional organizations also have government-relations committees that work closely with their lobbyists. Within AACD, for example, the mission of the Government Relations Committee is "to identify and initiate proactive and reactive positions on public policy issues confronting professional counselors, human development professionals, and those whom we serve. This mission encompasses the responsibilities to articulate these positions and provide skills training to AACD members so as to advocate legislative, executive, and judicial positions at the local, state and national level" (*Update,* 1988). Because this committee is interested in life-span needs and services, it has frequently sought passage of legislation that would provide funding for mental health services to older adults. The committee encourages members to contact their legislators on a wide range of human service needs. For example, the committee chair has exhorted members to action and made a case for the advocacy efforts of professionals. "There are two things you can give your legislator without spending more than a postage stamp or a telephone call. One is information. Remember, you are the authority in the counseling profession. The other is recognition. Whenever your legislator does something on your behalf, helps your local or state organization, advances your issues and concerns, show him or her your appreciation. AND LET THE WORLD KNOW ABOUT IT!" (Hebl, 1989).

The breadth of such activities was illustrated in a report submitted by the chair of the Government Relations Committee of the Association for Adult Development and Aging (AADA) to the leaders of the organization (Bodily, 1989). In half a year he had sent advocacy letters to senators and representatives requesting money for comprehensive guidance and counseling through reauthorization of the Perkins Act, which supports vocational education, and had sought support for funding of counseling in AIDS demonstration projects. He had held interviews on Capitol Hill with staff members of several senators and representatives regarding the Bipartisan Commission on Comprehensive Health Care and expressed AADA interest in long-term care, catastrophic coverage, family leave, security and portability of pensions, and health care for workers. He also wrote articles for newsletters of several counseling organizations summarizing legislative concerns and requesting members to contact their representatives.

Coalitions: Older People and Counselors Working Together. Professional associations of counselors and gerontologists often work with organizations of older persons. Coalitions have been helpful in such endeavors as getting hospice care covered by medical insurance, seeking regulations to protect patients in nursing homes, requiring certification or licensure for some categories of professionals and types of facilities. The Advocates Senior Alert Process (ASAP) is a joint project of fourteen professional associations and organizations of older people. In an invitation to participate in the work of ASAP, organization leaders explained that "ASAP involves a trade. Participants receive at no charge information on issues such as health, income security and the Older Americans Act programs. In return we ask for your commitment to act on these important issues" (Advocates Senior Alert Process, 1988).

In order to be successful in influencing legislation, counselors need to work at building such coalitions. Using older people themselves as an important part of this effort can be crucial. Older people know what they need. In addition, older people's efforts (such as annual Senior Power days held in some state capitals) are often newsworthy. Furthermore, the process of acting on their own behalf may help older people enhance their self-esteem and develop a sense of group pride.

In setting up such coalitions, and perhaps as a first step in carrying out the strategies proposed throughout this book, counselors need to confront their own age bias. They may think about how they respond when someone says, "You don't look that old." It is hard not to say thank you, but accepting it as a compliment is an example of ageism. Another social dilemma may be how, or whether, to react if you hear an ageist remark. Although racism and sexism are still rampant in this country, many Americans have become sensitive about making, or listening to, racist or sexist remarks. This sensitivity does not often occur with ageist remarks, as jokes about the foibles of older people abound. As with any minority group older people may enjoy telling such stories on themselves, but resent them being told by outsiders.

Ethical Issues

Deciding whether and when to confront ageist remarks is one kind of ethical issue; it illustrates that ethical dilemmas are not just esoteric questions, they affect daily practices. Other practical ethical questions involving older people include is it "fair" for older people to be allowed to go to the head of the line at the polling place? Should only frail older people be allowed to? If so, who decides who is frail? Should the same rules apply at the grocery store? If so, how does this policy affect the younger person who needs to get in and out of the store quickly to get to work or to pick up a child from the day-care center?

On a broad level, there are ethical questions such as how do we allocate financial and medical resources? Stated crudely the questions are: Who gets, who pays, and who decides? For example, which is more important — prevention or treatment for serious illnesses? Are living wills legal? Who should get specialized medical care? Does a seventy-year-old have as much right to an organ transplant as a seventeen-year-old? Regarding finances, should family members have to "spend down" in order for their relatives to be eligible for benefits? Should caregivers have to leave their jobs in order to provide care for frail relatives? Can we as a nation afford to help provide catastrophic health care coverage? (Can we afford not to?) If so, who should bear the costs? What kinds of regulatory mechanisms do we need to be sure that people have appropriate medigap insurance but are not overinsured with duplicative policies?

Ethical questions such as these are being widely discussed in professional as well as lay publications across the country. To cite two examples, the American Society on Aging devoted a special issue of its journal to ethics and aging (1985), and the Association for Adult Development and Aging (1989) prepared a special issue of its newsletter on ethical issues. Both these publications pose questions such as those raised above. Such questions reaffirm the idea stated throughout this book that gerontological counselors are faced with many difficult and challenging decisions.

Concluding Thoughts

If we may be permitted a personal note in ending this book, we want to express pleasure that you are interested in the growing field of counseling older adults. We find it a fascinating area and hope that you enjoy the challenges and reap some of the many rewards. We have covered theories and demographics, basic issues facing older people and their families, and techniques to employ in working with these groups. We chose to end the book with a chapter about the role of counselors as change agents. It includes some examples of projects designed to heighten the self-esteem and power of older adults through community action. It also talks of strategies that counselors can use to interact with the political system in order to enhance the lives of older adults. It is a fitting way to conclude in that such enhancement is the goal of the entire book.

Resources

Selected Organizations in the Aging Network

Administration on Aging
U.S. Department of Health
and Human Services
330 Independence Avenue,
S.W., North Building
Washington, DC 20201

American Association for
Adult and Continuing
Education
1201 16th Street, N.W.,
Suite 230
Washington, DC 20036

American Association for
Counseling and
Development
5999 Stevenson Avenue
Alexandria, VA 22304

American Association of
Homes for the Aging
1050 17th Street, N.W.
Washington, DC 20036

American Association of
Retired Persons
1909 K Street, N.W.
Washington, DC 20049

American Geriatrics Society
10 Columbus Circle
New York, NY 10019

American Psychological
Association
Division on Adult Develop-
ment and Aging
1200 17th Street, N.W.
Washington, DC 20036

American Society on Aging
833 Market Street, Suite 516
San Francisco, CA 94103

American Speech and
Hearing Association
1801 Rockville Place
Rockville, MD 20852

Association for Gerontology
in Higher Education
600 Maryland Avenue,
S.W., West Wing 204
Washington, DC 20024

Center for the Study of the
Mental Health of the Aging
Division on Special Mental
Health Programs
National Institute of Mental
Health
Rockville, MD 20857

Elderhostel
80 Boylston Street, Suite 400
Boston, MA 02116

Gerontological Society of
America
1275 K Street, N.W., Suite 350
Washington, DC 20005-1275

Grandparents Rights
Organization
555 S. Woodward, Suite 1600
Birmingham, MI 48009

Gray Panthers
3635 Chestnut Street
Philadelphia, PA 19104

Legal Counsel for the Elderly
1909 K Street, N.W.
Washington, DC 20049

Legal Services for the
Elderly Poor
132 W. 43rd Street, 3rd
Floor
New York, NY 10036

National Association for
Humanistic Gerontology
Claremont Office Park
41 Tunnel Road
Berkeley, CA 94705

National Association for
Spanish-Speaking Elderly
1801 K Street, N.W., Suite 1021
Washington, DC 20006

National Association of Area
Agencies on Aging
600 Maryland Avenue,
S.W., Suite 208
Washington, DC 20024

National Association of
Home Health Agencies
426 C Street, N.E.
Washington, DC 20002

National Association of State
Units on Aging
2033 K Street, N.W., Suite 304
Washington, DC 20006

National Caucus and Center
on Black Aged
1424 K Street, N.W.
Washington, DC 20005

National Council of Senior
  Citizens
1511 K Street, N.W.
Washington, DC 20005

National Council on Aging
600 Maryland Avenue,
  S.W., West Wing 100
Washington, DC 20024

National Homecaring Council
519 C Street, N.E.
Washington, DC 20002

National Indian Council on
  Aging, Inc.
P.O. Box 2088
Albuquerque, NM 87103

National Institute on Aging
9000 Rockville Pike,
  Building 31, Room 5C-36
Bethesda, MD 20014

National Interfaith Coalition
  on Aging, Inc.
298 South Hull Street
Athens, GA 30603

National Organization for
  Women
Task Force on Older Women
1401 New York Avenue,
  N.W., Suite 800
Washington, DC 20005

National Senior Citizens
  Law Center
2025 M Street, N.W., Suite 400
Washington, DC 20036

Older Women's League
730 11th Street, N.W.,
  Suite 300
Washington, DC 20001

Urban Elderly Coalition
600 Maryland Avenue,
  S.W., West Wing 204
Washington, DC 20024

U.S. Department of Labor
Employment and Training
  Administration
Office of Special Targeted
  Programs
Division of Older Worker
  Programs
200 Constitution Avenue,
  N.W., Room North 4641
Washington, DC 20210

U.S. House of
  Representatives
Select Committee on Aging
Room 712, HOB Annex 1
Washington, DC 20515

U.S. Senate
Special Committee on Aging
Room 5D-G33, Dirksen
  Office Building
Washington, DC 20510

References

Aday, R. H. (1984–1985). Belief in afterlife and death anxiety: Correlates and comparisons. *Omega, 15,* 7–75.

Advocates Senior Alert Process. (1988). [Unpublished introductory letter]. (Available from 1334 G St., N.W., Washington, DC)

American Association for Counseling and Development (undated). *What is counseling and human development?* Alexandria, VA: Author.

American Association of Retired Persons. (1982). *Second career opportunities for older persons: A program guide.* Washington, DC: Author.

American Association of Retired Persons. (1986a). *Managing a changing work force.* Washington, DC: Author.

American Association of Retired Persons. (1986b). *Workers 45 + : Today and tomorrow.* Washington, DC: Author.

American Association of Retired Persons. (1987a). *AARP Volunteer Talent Bank: A volunteer referral resource for organizations nationwide.* Washington, DC: Author.

American Associates of Retired Persons. (1987b). *A checklist of concerns/resources for caregivers.* Washington, DC: Author.

American Association of Retired Persons. (1988a). *How to recruit older workers.* Washington, DC: Author.

American Association of Retired Persons. (1988b). *How to train older workers.* Washington, DC: Author.

American Association of Retired Persons. (1988c, January/ February). *Working Age, 3*(4).

American Association of Retired Persons & Administration on Aging, U.S. Department of Health and Human Services. (1988). *A profile of older Americans.* Washington, DC: Author.

American Health Care Association. (undated). *Here's help! Death and dying.* Washington, DC: Author.

American Society for Personnel Administration. (1988, July 15). *Resource EXTRA.*

American Society on Aging. (1985, Winter). Ethics and aging [Special issue]. *Generations.*

American Society on Aging. (1987–1988, Winter). Late-life learning [Special issue]. *Generations, 12*(2).

Association for Adult Development and Aging. (1989). Ethical issues in adult development and aging. [Special issue]. *Newsletter.* (American Association for Counseling and Development, Alexandria, VA).

Atchley, R. C. (1980). *The social forces in later life* (3rd ed.). Belmont, CA: Wadsworth.

Atchley, R. C. (1985). *Social forces and aging.* Belmont, CA: Wadsworth.

Atchley, R. C. (1988, June/July). Finding meaning in the leisure of retirement. *Aging Connection,* p. 12.

Atkinson, D. R. (1980). The elderly, oppression, and social-change counseling. *Counseling and Values, 24,* 86–96.

Beck, A. T., Ward, C., Mendelsohn, M., Mock, J., & Erbaugh, J. (1961). An inventory for measuring depression. *Archives of General Psychiatry, 4,* 53–63.

Belsky, J. K. (1984). *The psychology of aging: Theory, research and practice.* Monterey, CA: Brooks/Cole.

Berne, E. (1964). *Games people play.* New York: Grove Press.

Betances, S. (1988, November 6). *Strengthening inter-cultural linkages through effective counseling.* Speech to the Michigan Association for Counseling and Development, Detroit.

Bird, C. (1988). The freedom road. *Modern Maturity, 31*(3), 43.

(Published by the American Association of Retired Persons.)

Bodily, J. (1989). [Unpublished report to leaders of the Association for Adult Development and Aging]. American Association for Counseling and Development, Alexandria, VA.

Brammer, L. M. (1988). *The helping relationship: Process and skills* (4th ed.). Englewood Cliffs, NJ: Prentice-Hall.

Brandon, N. (1969). *Psychology of self esteem.* New York: Bantam Books.

Brans, J. (1987). *Mother I have something to tell you.* New York: Doubleday.

Brine, J. M. (1979). Psycho-social aspects of aging: An overview. In M. L. Ganikos (Ed.), *Counseling the aged: A training syllabus for educators* (pp. 63–81). Falls Church, VA: American Personnel and Guidance Association.

Brink, T. L., Yesavage, J. A., Lum, O., Heersma, P., Adey, M., & Rose, T. L. (1982). Screening test for geriatric depression. *Clinical Gerontologist, 1,* 37–43.

Brody, E. M. (1985). Parent care as a normative family stress. *Gerontologist, 25,* 19–29.

Brookfield, S. D. (1986). *Understanding and facilitating adult learning: A comprehensive analysis of principles and effective practices.* San Francisco: Jossey-Bass.

Brown, R. (1988). [Materials distributed at workshop, Oakland University, Rochester, MI].

Burnside, I. (1984). *Working with the elderly: Group process and techniques* (2nd ed.). Belmont, CA: Wadsworth.

Buros, O. K. (Ed.). (1989). *The tenth mental measurement yearbook.* Highland Park, NJ: Gryphon Press.

Butler, R. L. (1975). *Why survive? Being old in America.* New York: Harper & Row.

Butler, R. L., & Lewis, M. I. (1983). *Aging and mental health* (rev. ed.). St. Louis, MO: Mosby.

Caine, L. (1974). *Widow.* New York: Morrow.

Caplan, G. (1974). *Support systems and community mental health: Lectures on concept development.* New York: Behavioral Publications.

Capuzzi, D., Gross, D., & Friel, S. E. (1990). Recent trends in group work with elders. *Generations, 14*(1), 43–48.

222   References

Carkhuff, R. R. (1969). *Helping and human relations: Vol. 1. Selection and training.* New York: Holt, Rinehart & Winston.

Cherlin, C., & Furstenberg, F. F. (1986). Grandparents and family crisis. *Generations, 10*(4), 26–29.

Clark, M., & Anderson, B. (1967). *Culture and aging.* Springfield, IL: Thomas.

Cohen, C. I., Teresi, J., Holmes, D., & Roth, E. (1988). Survival strategies of older homeless men. *Gerontologist, 28,* 58–65.

Cohen, G. D. (1984). Counseling interventions for the late 20th century elderly. *Counseling Psychologist, 12,* 97–99.

Cohler, B. J. (1982). Personal narrative and life course. In P. Baltes & O. Brim (Eds.), *Life-span development and behavior* (Vol. 4) (pp. 206–241). Orlando, FL: Academic Press.

Corby, N. (1975). Assertive training with aged populations. *Counseling Psychologist, 6*(4), 69–74.

Corey, M. S., & Corey, G. (1987). *Groups: Process and practice* (3rd ed.). Monterey, CA: Brooks/Cole.

Crystal, J., & Bolles, R. (1974). *Where do I go from here with my life?* New York: Seabury.

Crystal, S. (1988, Spring). Work and retirement in the twenty-first century. *Public Policy Generations,* pp. 60–64.

Daitch, M. C., & Lerner, S. (1984). *Report on group apartments for the elderly and prospectus for the future.* Unpublished report, Jewish Family Service, Southfield, MI.

Dunckley, R. S., Lutes, C. J., Wooten, J. N., & Kooken, R. A. (1980). Therapy approaches with rural elders. In S. S. Sargent (Ed.), *Nontraditional therapy and counseling with the aging* (pp. 74–99). New York: Springer.

Ebersole, P. and Hess, P. (1990). *Toward healthy aging.* (3rd ed.). St. Louis: C. V. Mosby.

Edinberg, M. A. (1985). *Mental health practice with the elderly.* Englewood Cliffs, NJ: Prentice-Hall.

Edwards, P. B. (1979). *Leisure counseling techniques: Individual and group counseling step by step.* Los Angeles: University Publishers.

Egan, G. (1986). *The skilled helper: A systematic approach to effective helping* (3rd ed.). Monterey, CA: Brooks/Cole.

England, R. (1987, March). Greener era for gray America. *Insight,* pp. 8–11.

Erikson, E. (1950). *Childhood and society.* New York: Norton.

Florsheim, M. J., & Herr, J. J. (1990). Family counseling with elders. *Generations, 14*(1), 40–42.

Fry, P. S. (1984). Development of a geriatric scale for counseling and intervention with the depressed elderly. *Journal of Counseling Psychology, 32,* 322–331.

Fuchs, B. (1987–1988, Winter). Teaching elders to be computer-friendly. *Generations, 12*(2), 57.

Gadow, S. A. (1987). Death and age: A natural connection. *Generations, 11*(3), 15–18.

Gallagher, D., Thompson, L. W., & Levy, S. M. (1980). Clinical psychological assessment of older adults. In L. W. Poon (Ed.), *Aging in the 1980s: Psychological issues* (pp. 19–40). Washington, DC: American Psychological Association.

Gamses, D. (1988, March 11). [Speech given at the Aging of the Workforce Conference, Detroit, MI].

Ganikos, M. (Ed.). (1979). *Counseling the older adult: A training syllabus for educators.* Falls Church, VA: American Personnel and Guidance Association.

Ganote, S. (1990). Counseling in longterm-care settings. *Generations, 14*(1), 31–34.

Garfinkel, R. (1975). The reluctant therapist. *Gerontologist, 15,* 136–137.

Gazda, G. (1971). *Group counseling: A developmental approach.* Newton, MA: Allyn & Bacon.

Genevay, B. (1990). The aging-family consultation. *Generations, 14*(1), 58–60.

George, L. K. (1986). Life satisfaction in later life. *Generations, 10*(3), pp. 5–8.

George, R. L., & Dustin, D. (1988). *Group counseling theory and practice.* Englewood Cliffs, NJ: Prentice-Hall.

Gilford, R. (1986). Marriages in later life. *Generations, 10*(4), 16–20.

Gold, D. T. (1988, June/July). Sibling bond intensifies in late life. *Aging Connection,* p. 4.

Goodman, J., & Hoppin, J. M. (1990). *Opening doors: A practical guide for job hunting.* Rochester, MI: Oakland University, Continuum Center.

Goodman, J., Hoppin, J. M., & Kent, R. (1984). *Opening doors: A practical guide for job hunting* [leader guide]. Rochester, MI: Oakland University, Continuum Center.

Goodman, J., & Waters, E. B. (1985). Conflict or support: Work and family in middle and old age. *Journal of Career Development, 12*(1), 92–98.

Gruen, W. (1964). Adult personality: An empirical study of Erikson's theory of ego development. In B. Neugarten (Ed.), *Personality in middle and late life: Empirical studies* (pp. 1–14). New York: Atherton.

Gurland, B. J. (1980). The assessment of the mental health status of older adults. In J. E. Birren & R. B. Sloane (Eds.), *Handbook of mental health and aging* (pp. 671–700). Englewood Cliffs, NJ: Prentice-Hall.

Gwyther, L. (1986). Family therapy with older adults. *Generations, 10*(3), 42–45.

Hagestad, G. O. (1984). The continuous bond: A dynamic multigenerational perspective on parent-child relations between adults. In M. Perlmutter (Ed.), *Parent-child interaction and parent-child relations in child development* (pp. 129–158). Hillsdale, NJ: Erlbaum.

Hagestad, G. O. (1986). Dimensions of time and the family. *American Behavioral Scientist, 29*(6), 679–694.

Hagestad, G. O. (1987). Able elderly in the family context: Changes, chances, and challenges. *Gerontologist, 27*(4), 417–422.

Hagestad, G. O. (1988). *Aging and the family.* Keynote address at a conference on mental health and aging, Oakland University, Rochester, MI.

Hagestad, G. O., & Burton, L. M. (1986). Grandparenthood, life context, and family development. *American Behavioral Scientist, 29*(4), 471–484.

Hansen, S. (1990). *AACD theme for 1990: Global visions — Celebrating diversity, creating community.* Unpublished manuscript, American Association for Counseling and Development, Alexandria, VA.

Harris & Assoc. (1981). *A national poll conducted for the National Council on Aging, Inc.* (Available from 600 Maryland Ave., S.W., Wing 100, Washington, DC 20024)

Harvill, R., West, J., Jacobs, E. D., & Masson, R. L. (1985). Systematic group leader training: Evaluating the effectiveness of the approach. *Journal for Specialists in Group Work, 10*(1), 2–13.

Havighurst, R. J. (1952). *Developmental tasks and education*. New York: McKay.

Hayes, R. L., & Burke, M. J. (1987). Community-based prevention for elderly victims of crime and violence. *Journal of Mental Health Counseling, 9*(4), 210–219.

Hayhow, P. (1983). [Workshop on elder abuse presented at a conference on promoting mental health in the later years, Oakland University, Rochester, MI].

Hebl, H. (1989). Share the action: You can and you should. *Update*. (Newsletter of the Government Relations Committee, American Association for Counseling and Development)

Heikkinen, C. A. (1981). Loss resolution for growth. *Personnel and Guidance Journal, 59,* 327–331.

Henderson, S. R. (1978). *Facing life through death* (2nd ed.). Staunton, VA: Full Circle Counseling.

Hospice of Southeastern Michigan. (undated). Crossroads Building, 16250 Northland Drive, Suite 212, Southfield, MI, 48075.

Houston, J. (1982). *The possible human*. Los Angeles: Tarcher.

Howard, J. (1978). *Families*. New York: Simon & Schuster.

Huttman, E. D. (1985). *Social services for the elderly*. New York: Free Press.

Ivey, A. E. (1974). *Microcounseling: Innovations in interviewing training*. Springfield, IL: Thomas.

Jacobs, G. (1989). *Involving men in caregiver support groups: A practical guide*. Bryn Mawr, PA: Bryn Mawr College, Graduate School of Social Work and Social Research.

Jamerino, M. H. (1987). [Presentation at conference of Michigan Funeral Directors, Oakland University, Rochester, MI].

Johnson, C. L., and Catalano, D. J. (1981). Childless elderly and their family supports. *Gerontologist, 21,* 6, 610–618.

Johnson, R. (1982). Assessing retirement maturity. *Measurement and Evaluation in Counseling and Development, 15*(3), 115–121.

Jones, W. (1986, January). *Coping with life's losses*. Keynote address to a conference on mental health and aging, Oakland University, Rochester, MI.

Kagan, N. I. (1984). Interpersonal process recall: Basic methods and recent research. In D. Larson (Ed.), *Teaching psychological skills: Models for giving psychology away* (pp. 230–243). Monterey, CA: Brooks/Cole.

Kalish, R. A. (1985). *Death, grief, and caring relationships* (2nd ed.). Monterey, CA: Brooks/Cole.

Kane, R. A. (1985). Assessing the elderly client. In A. Monk (Ed.), *Handbook of gerontological services* (pp. 43–69). New York: Van Nostrand Reinhold.

Kapes, J. T., & Mastie, M. M. (1988). *A counselor's guide to career assessment instruments* (2nd ed.). Alexandria, VA: National Career Development Association.

Kastenbaum, R. T. (1964). The reluctant therapist. In R. T. Kastenbaum (Ed.), *New thoughts on old age* (pp. 139–145). New York: Springer.

Kastenbaum, R. T., & Aisenberg, R. (1972). *The psychology of death.* New York: Springer.

Katz, S., Ford, A. B., Moskowitz, R. W., Jackson, B. A., & Jaffee, M. W. (1963). Studies of illness in the aged. The index of independence in ADL: A standardized measure of biological and psychosocial function. *Journal of the American Medical Association, 185,* 914–919.

Kaufman, S. R. (1986). *The ageless self: Sources of meaning in late life.* Madison: University of Wisconsin Press.

Kieffer, J. A. (1986). Kicking the premature retirement habit. *Journal of Career Development, 13*(2), 39–51.

Kiyak, A., Liang, J., & Kahana, E. (1976). *Methodological inquiry into the schedule of recent life events.* Paper presented at the meeting of the American Psychological Association, New York.

Knight, B. (1986). *Psychotherapy with older adults.* Newbury Park, CA: Sage.

Kosberg, J. I. (1985). Assistance to crime and abuse victims. In A. Monk (Ed.), *Handbook of gerontological services* (pp. 365–382). New York: Van Nostrand Reinhold.

Kottler, J. A., & Brown, R. W. (1985). *Introduction to therapeutic counseling.* Monterey, CA: Brooks/Cole.

Kovar, M. G., & LaCroix, A. Z. (1987, May). Aging in the eighties, ability to perform work-related activities. *Advancedata,*

136, 1–12. (Published by the Public Health Service, U.S. Department of Health and Human Services, Rockville, MD)

Kübler-Ross, E. (1969). *On death and dying.* New York: Macmillan.

Lasoski, M. C., & Thelen, M. H. (1987). Attitudes of older and middle-aged persons toward mental health intervention. *Gerontologist, 27,* 288–292.

Lawton, M. P. (1975). The Philadelphia Geriatric Center Morale Scale: A revision. *Journal of Gerontology, 30,* 85–89.

Lawton, M. P., & Brody, E. M. (1969). Assessment of older people: Self-maintaining and instrumental activities of daily living. *Gerontologist, 9,* 179–188.

Lawton, M. P., Moss, M., Fulcomer, M., & Kleban, J. (1982). A research and service oriented multilevel assessment instrument. *Journal of Gerontology, 37,* 91–99.

Lazarus, L. W. (1988). *Meeting the challenge of providing services.* Speech presented at the Mental Health Strategy: Partnerships for the 1990's Conference, sponsored by the Michigan Department of Mental Health, Lansing, MI.

Lee, G. R., & Shehan, C. L. (1989). Retirement and marital satisfaction. *Journal of Gerontology: Social Sciences, 44*(6), S226–S230.

Lindeman, B. (1987, July). Nana, I can't visit you. *50 Plus,* p. 4.

Lipman, A. (1986). Homosexual relationships. *Generations, 10*(4), 51–55.

Litwin, H. (1985). Ombudsman services. In A. Monk (Ed.), *Handbook of gerontological services* (pp. 514–530). New York: Van Nostrand Reinhold.

Loesch, L. C. (1985). *Guidelines for conducting workshops.* Unpublished manuscript prepared for Continuing Education in Aging for Professional Counselors, a project of the American Association for Counseling and Development.

Lowenthal, E. (1984). [Speech given at Oakland University, Rochester, MI]. (Tapes available through Video Publishing House, Inc., 1011 East Touhy, Suite 580, Des Plaines, IL 60018, 1-800-824-8889)

Luce, G. G. (1979). *Your second life: Vitality and growth in middle and later years.* New York: Delacorte.

Luft, J. (1963). *Group processes: An introduction to group dynamics.* Palo Alto, CA: National Press Books.

Lumsden, D. B. (1987–1988, Winter). How adults learn. *Generations, 12*(2), 10–15.

Mace, N. L., & Rabins, P. V. (1981). *The 36-hour-day: A family guide to caring for persons with Alzheimer's disease, related dementing illnesses, and memory loss in later life.* Baltimore, MD: Johns Hopkins University Press.

Maclay, E. (1977). *Green winter: Celebrations of old age.* New York: Reader's Digest Press.

Maloney, R. J. (1985). *How to cure low self-esteem.* Birmingham, MI: Awareness Press.

Markides, K. S., & Mindel, C. H. (1987). *Aging and ethnicity.* Newbury Park, CA: Sage.

Maslow, A. (1954). *Motivations and personality.* New York: Harper & Row.

Matheny, K. B., & Oslin, Y. (1970). *Utilization of paraprofessionals in education and the helping professions: A review of the literature.* Paper presented at the annual meeting of the American Educational Research Association, Minneapolis.

McDaniels, C. (1982). *Leisure: Integrating a neglected component in life planning.* Columbus, OH: National Center for Research in Vocational Education.

McDowell, C. F. (1978). *Leisure Well-Being Inventory.* Eugene, OR: Leisure Lifestyle Consultants.

McHolland, J. D. (1972). *Human potential seminar: Trainer's workbook.* Evanston, IL: Kendall College Press.

McKay, M., & Fanning, P. (1987). *Self esteem.* Oakland, CA: New Harbinger.

McKechnie, G. E. (1974). *The Leisure Activities Blank manual.* Palo Alto, CA: Consulting Psychologists Press.

Merrill, F. (1988). *Job search manual for mature workers.* Los Angeles: Council on Careers for Older Americans.

Meyer, G. R. (1980). The New Directions Workshop for senior citizens. In S. S. Sargent (Ed.), *Nontraditional therapy and counseling with the aging* (pp. 55–73). New York: Springer.

Michigan Media Project. (undated). *What's wrong with wrinkles?* (Slide presentation available from 23645 Samoset Trail, Southfield, MI)

Miller, A. (1949). *Death of a salesman.* New York: Viking Penguin.

Miller, M. (1981). The helped and the helpers: A critical view. *Generations,* *6*(2), 14–16.

Minkler, M. (1983, November 20). *Building supportive networks in a "gray ghetto": The Tenderloin Senior Outreach Project.* Paper presented at the annual meeting of the Gerontological Society of America, San Francisco.

Monk, A. (Ed.). (1985). *Handbook of gerontological services.* New York: Van Nostrand Reinhold.

Moody, H. R. (1987–1988, Winter). [Introduction.] *Generations,* *12*(2), 5–9.

Mor, V. (1987). Hospice. *Generations,* *11*(3), 19–21.

Myers, J. E. (1988). *Infusing gerontological counseling into counselor preparation: Curriculum guide.* Alexandria, VA: American Association for Counseling and Development.

Myers, J. E. (1989). *Adult children and aging parents.* Alexandria, VA: American Association for Counseling and Development.

Myers, J. E. (unpublished, undated). *Needed response to the greying of our labor force: Employment, retirement, or life-career counseling?*

Myers, J. E., & Salmon, H. E. (1984). Counseling programs for older persons: Status, shortcomings, and potentialities. *Counseling Psychologist,* *12,* 39–54.

Napier, R. W., & Gershenfeld, M. K. (1985). *Groups: Theory and experience.* Boston: Houghton Mifflin.

National Alliance of Business. (1985). *New directions for an aging workforce: An analysis of issues and options for business.* Washington, DC: Author.

National Council on the Aging. (undated). *Senior community service project: Employing older workers for needed community services.* Washington, DC: Author.

National Occupational Information Coordinating Committee. (1989). *The national career development guidelines* (Trainer's manual). Washington, DC: Author.

Neugarten, B. L. (1979). Time, age, and the life cycle. *American Journal of Psychiatry,* *136*(7), 887–894.

Neugarten, B. L., Havighurst, R. J., & Tobin, S. S. (1961). The measurement of life satisfaction. *Journal of Gerontology,* *16,* 134–143.

Newman, M., & Berkowitz, B. (1971). *How to be your own best friend.* New York: Ballantine.

Norton, L., & Courlander, M. (1982). Fear of crime among the elderly: The role of crime prevention programs. *Gerontologist, 22,* 388–393.

Nussbaum, K. (1988, March 10). [Speech given at the Aging Workforce Conference, Detroit].

Older Women's League. (1986). *Death and dying: Staying in control to the end of our lives.* Washington, DC: Author.

Older Women's League. (undated). *National OWL agenda.* Unpublished manuscript. (Available from 3800 Harrison St., Oakland, CA)

Ostrander, V. (1985). Speaking as one. *Highlights, 3*(5), 3 (Newsletter of the American Association of Retired Persons).

O'Toole, J., Hansot, E., Herman, W., Herick, N., Liebow, E., Lusignan, B., Richman, H., Sheppard, H., Stephansky, B., Wright, J. (1973). *Work in America: Report of a special task force to the Secretary of Health, Education and Welfare.* Cambridge, MA: MIT Press.

Parent care: Resources to assist family caregivers. (1988, January/February). *3*(2). (Published by the University of Kansas, Gerontology Center, Lawrence)

Pearsall, P. (1987). *Superimmunity: Master your emotions and improve your health.* New York: Fawcett.

Pearson, R. E. (1980). *Personal support system survey.* Paper presented at the annual meeting of the American Personnel and Guidance Association, Atlanta.

Perlstein, S. (1985). Transformation: Life review and communal theater. In R. Desch (Ed.), *Twenty-five years of the life review: Theoretical and practical considerations* (pp. 137–148). New York: Haworth Press.

Peterson, D. A. (1987–1988, Winter). The role of higher education in an aging society. *Generations, 12*(2), 16–18.

Pfeiffer, E. (1976). *Multidimensional functional assessment: The OARS methodology.* Durham, NC: Duke University, Center for the Study of Aging and Human Development.

Pifer, A. (1986). Our aging society: An overview of the challenge. In *America's aging workforce: A Traveler's Symposium* pp. 4–12. Houston, TX.

Poggi, R. G., & Berland, D. I. (1985). The therapist's reactions to the elderly. *Gerontologist, 25,* 508–513.

Policy Research Associates. (1988, January/February). *Public Policy and Aging Report, 2*(1).

Poon, L. W. (Ed.). (1980). *Aging in the 1980's: Psychological issues.* Washington, DC: American Psychological Association.

Priddy, J. M., & Knisely, J. S. (1982). Older adults as peer counselors: Considerations in counselor training with the elderly. *Educational Gerontology, 8,* 53–62.

Riessman, F. (1965). The helper-therapy principle. *Social Work, 10*(2), 27–32.

Robison, F. F., Smaby, M. H., & Donovan, G. L. (1989). Influencing reluctant elderly clients to participate in mental health counseling. *Journal of Mental Health Counseling, 11*(3), 259–272.

Rosenberg, M. (1979). *Conceiving the self.* New York: Basic Books.

Rugg, C. D. (1987). Employers face growing dilemma: Retire or rehire older workers? *Mott Exchange, 2*(3), 1–4. (Published by the Charles Stewart Mott Foundation, Flint, MI).

Salamon, M. J., & Conte, V. A. (1981). *The SCLSES and the eight categories of life satisfaction.* Paper presented at the annual meeting of the Gerontological Society of America, Toronto.

Samuelson, R. J. (1988, March 21). The elderly aren't needy. *Newsweek,* p. 69.

Sargent, S. S. (Ed.). (1980). *Nontraditional therapy and counseling with the aging.* New York: Springer.

Savoy, E. (1988, March 11). [Speech given at the Aging Workforce Conference, Detroit].

Schlossberg, N. K. (1984). *Counseling adults in transition: Linking practice with theory.* New York: Springer.

Schlossberg, N. K. (1987). Taking the mystery out of change. *Psychology Today, 21*(5), 74–75.

Schlossberg, N. K. (1990). Training counselors to work with older adults. *Generations, 14*(1), 7–10.

Schlossberg, N. K., Troll, L. E., & Leibowitz, Z. (1978). *Perspectives on adults: Issues and skills.* Monterey, CA: Brooks/Cole.

Schmidt, M. G. (1980). *Personal networks: Assessment, care and repair.* Paper presented at the annual meeting of the Western Gerontological Society, Anaheim, CA.

Shanas, E. (1980, February). Older people and their families: The new pioneers. *Journal of Marriage and the Family,* pp. 9–15.

Shuchter, S. R. (1986). *Dimensions of grief: Adjusting to the death of a spouse.* San Francisco: Jossey-Bass.

Siegel, B. S. (1986). *Love, medicine and miracles: Lessons learned about self healing from a surgeon's experience with exceptional patients.* New York: Harper & Row.

Silverman, P., Mackenzie, D., Pettipas, M., & Wilson, E. (1974). *Helping each other in widowhood.* New York: Health Sciences Publishing.

Simon, J. B., Howe, L. W., & Kirschenbaum, H. (1972). *Values clarification: A handbook of practical strategies for teachers and students.* New York: Hart.

Soumerai, S. B., & Avorn, J. (1983). Perceived health, life satisfaction, and activity in urban elderly: A controlled study of the impact of part-time work. *Journal of Gerontology, 38,* 356–362.

Stark, E. (1987, October). Memory: Age or practice? *Psychology Today,* p. 24.

Stepp, J. (1988, March 10). [Speech given at the Aging Workforce Conference, Detroit].

St. John, A. (1988, March 10). [Speech given at the Aging Workforce Conference, Detroit].

Stone, M. L., & Penman, N. (1988). Designing your retirement: A comprehensive retirement planning workbook. Rochester, MI: Oakland University Continuum Center.

Strimling, A. (1986). Doing talking: The storytelling relationship. *Brookdale Center on Aging Newsletter, 8*(3). (Published by Hunter College, New York)

Stufflebeam, D. L., & Shinkfield, A. J. (1985). *Systematic evaluation.* Boston: Kluwer-Nijhoff.

Sundberg, N. D. (1977). *Assessment of persons.* Englewood Cliffs, NJ: Prentice-Hall.

Temes, R. (1984). *Living with an empty chair.* New York: Irvington.

Timmerman, S. (1987–1988, Winter). Learning to overcome disability. *Generations, 12*(2), 46–49.

Tobin, S. S., & Gustafson, J. D. (1987). What do we do differently with elderly clients? *Journal of Gerontological Social Work, 10* (3/4), 107–121.

Tobin, S. S., & Toseland, R. (1985). Models of services for the elderly. In A. Monk (Ed.), *Handbook of gerontological services* (pp. 549–567). New York: Van Nostrand Reinhold.

Troll, L. E. (1975). *Early and middle adulthood.* Monterey, CA: Brooks/Cole.

Troll, L. E. (1982). *Continuations: Adult development and aging.* Monterey, CA: Brooks/Cole.

Troll, L. E. (1987). *New thoughts on old families.* Presidential address to Division 20, Adult Development and Aging, annual meeting of the American Psychological Association, New York, NY.

Troll, L. E., Miller, S., & Atchley, R. (1979). *Families in later life.* Belmont, CA: Wadsworth.

Update. (1988). (Newsletter of the Government Relations Committee, American Association for Counseling and Development)

U.S. Department of Health and Human Services. (1984). *Older workers: Myths and reality.* Washington, DC: Author.

U.S. Department of Labor, Employment and Training Administration. (1980). *Memo to mature jobseekers.* Washington, DC: Author.

Waters, E. B. (Ed.). (1990). *Generations, 14*(1).

Waters, E. B., & Weaver, A. L. (1981). Specialized techniques to help older people. In J. E. Meyers & M. L. Ganikos (Eds.), *Counseling older persons: Vol. 2. Basic helping skills for service providers* (pp. 107–132). Falls Church, VA: American Personnel and Guidance Association.

Westberg, G. E. (1976). *Good grief.* Philadelphia: Fortress Press.

Wheeler, E. G. (1980). Assertive training groups for the aging. In S. S. Sargent (Ed.), *Nontraditional therapy and counseling with the aging* (pp. 15–29). New York: Springer.

White, K. (1987). Living and dying the Navajo way. *Generations, 11*(3), 44–46.

Wilson, G. T., & Mirenda, J. J. (1975). The Milwaukee leisure counseling model. *Counseling and Values, 20,* 42–46.

Wooley, B. (1983). *Facts and fiction about memory.* Ann Arbor: University of Michigan Hospitals, Turner Geriatric Clinic.

Worden, J. W. (1982). *Grief counseling and grief therapy.* New York: Springer.

Yalom, I. D. (1970). *The theory and practice of group psychotherapy.* New York: Basic Books.

Yankelovich, Skelly, and White, Inc. (1985). *Workers over 50: Old myths, new realities.* Washington, DC: American Association of Retired Persons.

Young, C. I. (1983). *Inscape: A search for meaning.* Rochester, MI: Oakland University, Continuum Center.

Zung, W. (1965). A self-rating depression scale. *Archives of General Psychiatry, 1,* 63–70.

Index

A

AACD. *See* American Association for Counseling and Development
AARP. *See* American Association of Retired Persons
AARP Volunteer Talent Bank, 112
AARP Worker Equity Department, 194
Abuse, 127–128
Acceptance stage of death and dying, 147
Aday, R. H., 142
Addiction-oriented self-help groups, 170
Administration on Aging (AoA), 19, 78, 118–119, 142, 215
Adult children. *See* Children; Family
Adult Day Care Center (Ada, Oklahoma), 204–205
Adult development, theories of, 26–35
Advocacy, 199–213; ethical issues in, 212–213; with public and private institutions, 205; at societal level, 206–212
Advocates Senior Alert Process (ASAP), 211
Age-and-stage theories, 28–31
Aging network, 78–80, 179
AIDS, 139, 145, 211
Aisenberg, R., 120
Alcohol abuse, 15. *See also* Substance abuse

Alliances, forming, 10
Alzheimer's Association, 170
Alzheimer's patients: day care for, 204–205; groups for family members of, 170
American Association for Adult and Continuing Education, 215
American Association for Counseling and Development (AACD), 6, 209, 210, 215
American Association of Homes for the Aging, 215
American Association of Retired Persons (AARP), 19, 101, 103, 104, 105–106, 107, 112, 118–119, 121, 142, 194, 206, 208, 215
American Geriatrics Society, 215
American Health Care Association, 144–145
American Jewish Committee, 173
American Psychological Association (APA), 210, 215
American Society for Personnel Administration, 108
American Society on Aging, 192, 213, 215
American Speech and Hearing Association, 215
Anderson, B., 84
Anger stage of death and dying, 146
Anticipatory-socialization strategy, 9
Appetite, loss of, 137

Appleton, C., 188
Area Agencies on Aging (AAAs), 78–80, 127, 204, 206, 216
Asian Americans, 18, 100–101, 117
Assertiveness training, 190–191
Assessment, 15–16, 47–64; approaches to, 55–60; considerations in, 51–55; framework for, 55–60; meaning of, 47–51
Assessment instruments, 60–64; functioning level, 61–62; life-planning, 62–63; life satisfaction, 63–64
Association for Adult Development and Aging (AADA), 211, 213
Association for Gerontology in Higher Education, 216
Atchley, R. C., 90, 99, 109, 118, 119, 142, 143
Atkinson, D. R., 199–200, 206
Audiovisual materials, 187
Autonomy, 92. See also Control; Independence
Avorn, J., 98

B

Bargaining stage of death and dying, 146
Barriers, identifying and overcoming, 7–10, 65–68
Beck, A. T., 63
Beck Depression Inventory, 63
Belonging needs, 59, 60
Belsky, J. K., 193
Bereavement, 147–152
Berkowitz, B., 84
Berland, D. I., 16–17
Berne, E., 88
Betances, S., 200
Bird, C., 107
Black Americans, 21, 23, 100, 122, 123, 216
Bloch, L., 12
Blue Cross and Blue Shield of Michigan, 154
Bodily, J., 211
Bolles, R., 175
Brammer, L. M., 68–69
Brandon, N., 83
Brans, J., 43
Brine, J. M., 85
Brink, T. L., 63

Brody, E. M., 61, 115, 116, 130
Brookfield, S. D., 181–182
Brothers, 124–125
Brown, R., 6, 69–72, 159, 160, 165
Bureaucracies, 203–205
Burke, M. J., 39
Burnside, I., 131–132, 162, 165
Buros, O. K., 60
Burton, L. M., 122
Butler, R. L., 74, 171–172
By-the-way counseling, 8–10, 153–154

C

Caine, L., 170
Caplan, G., 176–177
Capuzzi, D., 162
Career, 97. See also Work
Career Assessment Inventory, 62
Career choices, 106–107
Carkhuff, R. R., 197
Catalano, D. J., 117
Catharsis, 164
Center for the Study of the Mental Health of the Aging, 216
Centre de Estudios Puertorriquenos of Hunter College, 173
Cherlin, C., 123
Children, 116–117, 120–121. See also Family; Grandchildren
Chinatown Oral History Project, 173
Chinese Americans, 18, 117
Chrysler Corporation, 102
CIPP (Context, Input, Process and Product), 183–184
Citizens for Better Care, 209
Clark, M., 84
Coalitions, 211–212
Cognitive ability, assessment of, 53–54
Cognitive restructuring, 94
Cohen, C. I., 202
Cohen, G. D., 11
Cohler, B. J., 84
Columbia University, 173
Commerce Clearing House, 108
Commonalities, discovering, 162–163
Confrontation, 11–12
Constructive Leisure Activity Survey, 63
Conte, V. A., 63
Context evaluation, in program development, 183

Continuum Center of Oakland University, 190
Control: need for, 74; self-esteem and, 91, 92. *See also* Independence
Corby, N., 190–191
Corey, G., 160
Corey, M. S., 160
Council on Careers for Older Americans, 108
Counseling: by-the-way, 8–10, 153–154; client's knowledge of, 70; effectiveness with older adults, 3–7; group, 90, 94, 131–133, 159–170; peer, 194–198; reasons for seeking, 35–46; reluctance to seek, 7–10, 65–68
Counselors: family and, 126–133; goals of, 6–7, 13; political role of, 209–211; reluctance to work with older adults, 10–17; role of, in group counseling, 166–169; as workshop leaders, 186, 187–188
Countertransference, 16–17
Courlander, M., 39
Crime, 39, 203–204
Crises, as reason for seeking counseling, 35–39
Crisis groups, 170
Crystal, J., 175
Crystal, S., 102

D

Daitch, M. C., 118
Day-care centers, 131, 204–205
Death and dying, 134–155; awareness of, 43; counseling for, 144–152; euphemisms for, 140–141; guilt and, 150–151, 152; stages of, 145–147; as taboo, 140; views of, 72–73, 141–143
Demographics, 17–25; on education, 23–24; family relationships and, 115–116; on health, 24; on income, 20–22; on living arrangements, 22; on population, 18–20; on region of residence, 22–23; on work, 24–25
Denial stage of death and dying, 146
Dependence, 73–74. *See also* Independence
Depression, 52–53, 57, 63–64, 153
Depression stage of death and dying, 146–147

Design: of programs, 181–184; of workshops, 180, 184–187
Despair, 92, 114, 171
Developmental tasks, 30
Discrimination, against older workers, 101, 104
Disenchantment period of retirement, 110
Disengagement, 29
Divorce, 38–39, 139
Donovan, G. L., 189
Driver's license, loss of, 138
Drub abuse, 15. *See also* Substance abuse
Dunckley, R. S., 189
Dustin, D., 161, 162

E

Ebersole, P., 58
Edinberg, M. A., 74, 173
Education, 23–24
Educational workshops, 192–194
Edwards, P. B., 63
Effectiveness training, 191
Egan, G., 5, 69, 73, 197
Elder abuse, 127–128
Elderhostel, 192, 193, 216
Emotional state, assessment of, 52–53
Empathy training, 75
Empowerment, 200–202
Energy levels, 42–43
England, R., 20, 21
Environmental adaptations, 74–76
Erbaugh, J., 63
Erikson, E., 30, 45, 74, 85, 86, 92, 98, 114, 159, 171
Ethics, 16, 212–213

F

Family, 113–133; alternatives to, 117–118; assessment and, 49–50; brothers and sisters as, 124–125; by-the-way counseling of, 10; of choice, 117; counseling and, 10, 126–133; demographics and, 115–116; gay and lesbian relationships as, 125–126; grandparents and grandchildren as, 121–124; husbands and wives as, 118–120; importance of,

113–115; multigenerational, 116–117; overprotectiveness of, 45; parents and children as, 120–121
Family counseling, 131–133
Fanning, P., 83
Fear: of crime, 39; of loss, 134, 138–139
Financial problems, 39, 49–50, 59
Florsheim, M. J., 132
Ford, A. B., 61
Ford Motor Company, 102
Foster care, 118
Freud, S., 98
Friel, S. E., 162
Fry, P. S., 64
Fuchs, B., 193
Fulcomer, M., 62
Funerals, 142, 154–155
Furstenberg, F. F., 123

G

Gadow, S. A., 143
Gallagher, D., 48, 54, 61
Gamses, D., 104
Ganote, S., 10
Garfinkel, R., 10
Gay relationships, 125–126
Gazda, G., 165
Generation gap, 43–44, 122
Generativity, 30, 85, 114
Genevay, B., 132
George, L. K., 86
George, R. L., 161, 162
Geriatric Depression Scale, 63
Geriatric Hopelessness Scale, 63–64
Geriatric Scale of Recent Life Events, 63
Gerontological Society of America, 216
Gershenfeld, M. K., 170
Gilford, R., 119
Goals: in counseling, 6–7, 13; self-esteem and, 91; for workshops, 185
Gold, D. T., 124
Goodman, J., 77, 108, 133, 152, 186
Grandchildren, 116–117, 121–124
Grandparents, 121–124
Grandparents Rights Organization, 216
Gray Panthers, 117, 206, 207, 216
Grief, 134–155; community programs and resources for, 154–155; counseling for, 143–155; stages of, 149. *See also* Death and dying; Loss

Gross, D., 162
Group counseling, 90, 94, 131–133, 159–170; benefits of, 162–165; cautions concerning, 165–166; role of counselor in, 166–169; scheduling of, 160–161; self-help, 169–170
Groups: composition of, 160; starting, 159–162; types of, 160
Growing Older Bolder workshop, 190, 191
Gruen, W., 98–99
Guided imagery, 175–176
Guided life review, 175–176
Guillain-Barré syndrome, 36–37
Guilt, 150–151, 152, 153
Gurland, B. J., 62
Gustafson, J. D., 14–15, 16, 89
Gwyther, L., 132

H

Hagestad, G. O., 19, 114–115, 116, 121, 122
Handouts, 187
Hansen, S., 210
Harris & Associates, 104
Harvill, R., 169
Havighurst, R. J., 29, 63
Hayes, R. L., 39
Hayhow, P., 127
Health, demographic information on, 24
Health and Growing Through Grief program, 154
Health crisis, 35–38
Hearing loss, 137, 138
Hebl, H., 210
Heikkinen, C. A., 150
Helper-therapy principle, 195–196
Henderson, S. R., 146, 147
Herr, J. J., 132
Hess, P., 58
Hierarchy of needs, 57–60
Hispanic Americans, 21, 23, 100, 216
Holmes, D., 202
Homeless people, 202
Home visits, for assessment, 54
Homosexual relationships, 125–126
Honeymoon phase of retirement, 110
Hoppin, J. M., 77, 108, 152, 186
Hospice of Southeastern Michigan, 155

Hospices, 155
Hospitalization, 35–38, 208–209
Hot Flash, 208
Houston, J., 193–194
Howard, J., 113
Howe, L. W., 166
Humor, 12–13
Hunter College, 173–174
Husbands, 118–120, 151
Huttman, E. D., 127, 179

I

Illness: chronic, 40; family and, 121;
    as temporary crisis, 35–38
Imaging, for life reviews, 173, 175–176
Income, 20–22, 100
Incontinence, 127
Independence: importance of, 66–67;
    loss of, 138; self-esteem and, 91
Index of Independence in Activities of
    Daily Living, 61
Indigenous helper, 194–198
Individual differences: awareness of,
    72–73; between younger and older
    adults, 43–44
Individual variability theories, 33–34
Industry, 99
Inferiority, 99
Inheritance, as crisis, 39
Initial interview, 68–72
Input evaluation, in program develop-
    ment, 183
Inspiration, groups as source of, 164–165
Institute on Aging, 104
Institutionalization, 208–209
Instrumental Activities of Daily Living
    Scale, 61
Integrity, 85, 92, 114, 171
Intellectual functioning, assessment of,
    53–54
Internal needs, 44–46
Interpersonal skills, 163
Isolation, 22, 41, 145, 146, 163
Ivey, A. E., 197
I-You activity, 167

J

Jackson, B. A., 61
Jacobs, E. D., 169

Jacobs, G., 131
Jaffee, M. W., 61
Jamerino, M. H., 154
Jewish families, 49–50
Jewish Family Service (JFS), 117–118
Jewish funerals, 142
Job loss, 152–154
Jobs. *See* Work
Job Training Partnership Act (1982),
    108
Johari Window, 88–89
Johnson, C. L., 117
Johnson, R., 62
Jones, W., 148, 150
Journal of Elder Abuse and Neglect, 128
Journal of Gerontological Social Work, 14–15
Justice for Age Discrimination, 104

K

Kagan, N. I., 197
Kahana, E., 63
Kalish, R. A., 140–141, 142
Kane, R. A., 48, 51, 52, 54–55
Kapes, J. T., 60, 62
Kastenbaum, R. T., 10, 120
Katz, S., 61
Kaufman, S. R., 85
Kayser-Jones, J. S., 208
Kent, R., 108, 186
Kieffer, J. A., 103
Kirschenbaum, H., 166
Kiyak, A., 63
Kleban, J., 62
Knight, B., 8, 9
Knisely, J. S., 195
Kooken, R., 189
Kosberg, J. I., 118
Kottler, J. A., 6, 69–72
Kovar, M. G., 105
Kübler-Ross, E., 145–147
Kuhn, M., 117, 207

L

Lacroix, A. Z., 105
Lasoski, M. C., 66, 67
Lawton, M. P., 51, 61, 62
Lazarus, L. W., 10
Learning-from-your-past approach to
    life reviews, 174–175

Lee, G. R., 119
Legal Counsel for the Elderly, 216
Legal Services for the Elderly Poor, 216
Leisure. *See* Retirement
Leisure Activities Blank, 62
Leisure Well-Being Inventory, 62–63
Lerner, S., 118
Lesbian relationships, 125–126
Levy, S. M., 48
Lewis, M. I., 74, 171–172
Liang, J., 63
Libraries, 205
Life-events theories, 31–33
Life expectancy, 18, 19–20, 115–116
Life histories, 51
Life-planning instruments, 62–63
Life reviews, 51, 171–176
Life satisfaction, assessment of, 63–64
Life Satisfaction Index, 63
Life Stories project, 173–174
Lifestyles, between older and younger
    adults, 43–44
Lindeman, B., 123–124
Lipman, A., 125
Litwin, H., 208
Living arrangements, 22, 43–44, 116–
    118
Loesch, L. C., 185
Loneliness, 22, 41, 163
Long-term problems, as reason to seek
    counseling, 40–41
Loss, 134–155; community programs
    and resources for, 154–155; coun-
    seling for, 143–155; death as, 140–
    143, 147–152; fear of, 134, 138–139;
    job, 152–154; less common, 138–
    139; normal age-related, 136–138,
    152–154; sensory, 40, 75, 136–137,
    138, 165, 205
Lowenthal, E., 36
Luce, G. G., 190
Luft, J., 88
Lumsden, D. B., 192
Lutes, C. J., 189

M

McDaniels, C., 63, 97, 99
McDonald's Corporation, 109
McDowell, C. F., 63
Mace, N. L., 170

McHolland, J. D., 168
McKay, M., 83
McKechnie, G. E., 62
Mackenzie, D., 170
Maclay, E., 45
Maloney, R. J., 87
Marital crisis, 38–39
Marital satisfaction, 119
Markides, K. S., 100, 117
Married partners, 118–120, 151
Maslow, A., 44, 57, 59–60
Masson, R. L., 169
Mastery need, 45–46
Mastie, M. M., 60, 62
Matheny, K. B., 196
Meals on Wheels, 131
Medicaid, 24, 203
Medicare, 24, 203
Memorabilia, 173
Memory assessment, 62
Memory problems, 54
Men, demographic information on, 20
Mendelsohn, M., 63
Mental illness, stigma of, 67
Mental Status Questionnaire, 62
Merrill, F., 108
Meyer, G. R., 190
Michigan Media Project, 207
Miller, A., 138
Miller, M., 201
Miller, S., 118
Mindel, C. H., 100, 117
Minkler, M., 201–202
Minority groups: family and, 117; re-
    tirement and, 100–101. *See also* names
    of specific groups
Mirenda, J. J., 63
Mirenda Leisure Interest Finder, 63
Mock, J., 63
Modern Maturity, 107
Moody, H. R., 192, 201
Mor, V., 155
Moskowitz, R. W., 61
Moss, M., 62
Motivation: to seek counseling, 35–46;
    self-esteem and, 83–84
Mourning. *See* Grief
Moving, 41
Multigenerational families, 116–117
Multilevel Assessment Instrument, 62
Myers, J. E., 11, 60, 61, 99, 100

N

Napier, R. W., 170
National Alliance of Business, 98
National Association for Humanistic Gerontology, 216
National Association for Spanish-Speaking Elderly, 216
National Association of Area Agencies on Aging, 216
National Association of Home Health Agencies, 216
National Association of Social Workers, 210
National Association of State Units on Aging, 216
National Caucus and Center on Black Aged, 216
National Council of Senior Citizens, 217
National Council on the Aging, 109, 217
National Homecaring Council, 217
National Indian Council on Aging, Inc., 217
National Institute on Aging, 217
National Interfaith Coalition on Aging, Inc., 217
National Occupational Information Coordinating Committee (NOICC), 182
National Organization for Women, 217
National Senior Citizens Law Center, 217
Native Americans, 100–101, 217
Needs: of dying, 145; hierarchy of, 57–60; internal, 44–46; safety and security, 57
Network, aging, 78–80, 179
Neugarten, B. L., 13–14, 34, 63
New Directions Workshop, 190
Newman, M., 84
Night vision, 40
Non-English speakers, 204
Norton, L., 39
Nursing homes, 208–209
Nussbaum, K., 100

O

Oakland University, 190
Off-time events, 44

Older adults: beliefs about, 4; counselors' reluctance to work with, 10–17; demographics of, 17–25; effectiveness of counseling with, 3–7; overcoming reluctance of, 7–10, 65–68; region of residence of, 22–23
Older Americans Act (1965), 78, 209
Older Americans Research and Service Center Instruments, 62
Older Women's League (OWL), 16, 206, 207, 217
Older workers: career choices of, 106–107; cost of, 104–105; recruitment of, 105–106; stereotypes of, 103–105; training of, 105–106, 108; workshops for, 194
Opening remarks, 69
Operation ABLE, 108–109
Orne, M. T., 9
Oslin, Y., 196
Ostrander, V., 208
O'Toole, J., 97, 98
Overdependence, 73–74
OWL. See Older Women's League

P

Parents, 116–117, 120–121
Pearsall, P., 37, 141
Pearson, R. E., 177
Peer counseling, 194–198
Penman, N., 174
Pensions, 100, 102
Perlstein, S., 174
Permanent self-help groups, 170
Personal-growth workshops, 188–191
Peterson, D. A., 193
Pets, 137
Pettipas, M., 170
Pfeiffer, E., 62
Philadelphia Geriatric Center Morale Scale, 63
Physical attractiveness, 137
Physical condition, assessment of, 52
Physical problems, 35–38, 40, 74–76, 205
Physiology of aging, 14
Pifer, A., 104–105
Planning: group counseling and, 164; life, 62–63; for work and leisure, 97–112

242

Poggi, R. G., 16–17
Policy Research Associates, 21
Political role of counselors, 209–211
Poon, L. W., 193
Population data, 18–20
Positive action, facilitating, 76–80
POSSLQs, 43–44
Poverty, 21–22
Preretirement period, 109–110
Priddy, J. M., 195
Private institutions, advocating with, 205
Problem solving, 76–78
Process evaluation, in program development, 183–184
Product evaluation, in program development, 184
Program design, comprehensive, 181–184
Program development, 180–198; importance of, 180–181; peer counseling, 194–198; workshops, 184–194
Promotion, of workshops, 187–188
Public institutions, advocating with, 205
Publicity, for workshops, 187–188

R

Rabins, P. V., 170
Reframing, 95
Regret, 151
Relationship, therapeutic, 68–76
Religion, 141–142, 145
Reluctance: of counselors to work with older adults, 10–17; of older adults to seek counseling, 7–10, 65–68
Reorientation phase of retirement, 110–111
Residence, region of, 22–23
Resources: assessment of, 55; sharing, 163–164
Retirement: dissatisfaction with, 102–103; early, 44; income during, 99–100; as loss, 136; married partners and, 120; phases of, 109–112; planning for, 97–112; positive attitude toward, 99; psychological meaning of, 42, 98–101
Retirement age, 101–102
Retirement Maturity Index, 62
Ricardo-Campbell, R., 21

Riessman, F., 195
Robinson, F. F., 189
Role change, 37
Rosenberg, M., 84
Roth, E., 202
Rugg, C. D., 109

S

Safety and security needs, 57
St. John, A., 102
Salamon, M. J., 63
Salamon-Conte Life Satisfaction in the Elderly Scale, 63
Salmon, H. E., 11
Samuelson, R. J., 21
Sandwich generation, 116
Sargent, S. S., 162, 188–189
Saroyan, W., 43
Satisfaction: assessment of, 63–64; marital, 119
Savoy, E., 102
Schlossberg, N. K., 6, 13, 26, 32, 35, 37, 44, 47, 99, 110, 199
Schmidt, M. G., 95, 177
School of Allied Health Professions, 208
Schuchter, S. R., 151
Self-acceptance, 87–90
Self-actualization needs, 44–46, 59
Self-care capability, assessment of, 52
Self-concept, 84–85
Self Directed Search, 62
Self-esteem, 83–96; cognitive restructuring and, 94; control and, 92; counseling and, 87–96; goals and, 91; meaning of, 83–86; reframing and, 95; self-acceptance and, 87–90; support systems and, 95–96; threats to, 86–87; values and, 90–91
Self-esteem needs, 57, 59, 60
Self-help groups, 169–170
Self-sufficiency, 66–67
Self-talk, 90
Self-worth, 85
Senior Community Service Project, 109
Senior Actualization and Growth Explorations (SAGE) groups, 190
Sensory losses, 40, 75, 136–137, 138, 165, 205
Services for older adults, 78–80, 154–155

Settings, for workshops, 185
Sexuality, 42
Shanas, E., 116–117
Shehan, C. L., 119
Shelton, B., 204
Shinkfield, A. J., 183
Short Portable Mental Status Exam, 62
Siblings, 124–125
Siegel, B. S., 141
Silverman, P., 170
Simon, J. B., 166, 168
Sisters, 124–125
Smaby, M. H., 189
Social factors, assessment of, 54
Socialization: anticipatory, 9; of older adults, 14
Social Security, 18, 20, 21–22, 101, 102, 203
Social skills, 163
Societal change, advocating, 206–212
Soumerai, S. B., 98
Spouses, 118–120, 151
Stability stage of retirement, 111
Stagnation, 114
Stark, E., 61
State University of New York, 208
Stepp, J., 102, 105
Stereotypes, of older workers, 103–105
Stone, M. L., 174
Strength Acknowledgement exercise, 168–169
Strimling, A., 173–174
Strong Interest Inventory, 62
Stufflebeam, D. L., 183
Substance abuse, 15, 127, 170
Sundberg, N. D., 51, 60
Sunderland, 39
Support systems: analysis of, 176–179; assessment of, 55; defined, 176–177; of homosexuals, 125–126; self-esteem and, 95–96. See also Family

T

Techniques: for working with older people, 65–80; for establishing a relationship, 68–76; for facilitating positive action, 76–80; for identifying and overcoming barriers, 7–10, 65–68
Technology, understanding of, 23–24

Temes, R., 148, 149
Temporary crises, as reason for seeking counseling, 35–39
Tenderloin Senior Outreach Project, 201–202
Teresi, J., 202
Termination phase of retirement, 111
Terra Nova Films, 191
Testing. See Assessment
Thelen, M. H., 66, 67
Theories, of adult development, 26–35
Therapeutic relationship, establishing, 68–76
Therapists. See Counselors
Thompson, L. W., 48
Timmerman, S., 193
Tobin, S. S., 14–15, 16, 63, 79, 89
Toseland, R., 79
Transactional analysis, 88
Transference, 16–17
Transitions: abnormal, 44; as crises, 31–33; normal, 41–44
Transition theories, 31–33
Travelers Corporation, 121
Troll, L. E., 30, 61, 98, 115, 118, 119, 120
Trust, 13, 68–72
Turner Geriatric Clinic, 193
Twenty Things activity, 168

U

United Auto Workers, 101
United Community Services, 80, 112
U.S. Department of Health and Human Services, 103, 215
U.S. Department of Labor, Employment and Training Administration, 107, 217
U.S. House of Representatives, 217
U.S. Senate, 217
University of California, 201–202
University of Michigan Hospitals, 193
Urban Elderly Coalition, 217

V

Values: grandchildren and grandparents and, 122; self-esteem and, 90–91
Variability, individual, 33–34

Varian Associates, 107
Vicarious victimization, 39
Vision problems, 40, 75, 136–137, 138, 165

W

Ward, C., 63
Waters, E. B., 8, 12, 133
Wechsler Memory Scale, 62
Wender, P. H., 9
West, J., 169
Westberg, G. E., 148
Wheeler, E. G., 131, 190
White, B., 8
White, K., 142
Widowhood: demographic information on, 20; grief and, 151; income and, 100; problems of, 142–143; self-help groups for, 155, 164, 170
Widows Together, 155
Wilson, E., 170
Wilson, G. T., 63
Wives, 118–120, 151
Women: career commitment of, 133; Chinese, 18; demographic information on, 20; retirement age of, 101–102; retirement income of, 100; view of death among, 142–143; in work force, 25
Wooley, B., 193

Wooten, J. N., 189
Worden, J. W., 148
Work, 97–112; demographic information on, 24–25; loss of, 152–154; psychological meaning of, 42, 97–101; stereotypes of older workers and, 103–105; training older workers for, 105–106, 108; unique problems of older adults and, 15; women's commitment to, 133. *See also* Older workers; Retirement
Workshops, 184–194; agenda of, 186; using audiovisual aids in, 191; defined, 180; design of, 180, 184–187; educational, 192–194; for older workers, 194; personal-growth, 188–191; promoting, 187–188; setting for, 185
Wrinkled Radical, 117

Y

Yalom, I. D., 162, 164
Yankelovich, Skelly, and White, Inc., 103–104
Young, C. I., 171

Z

Zung, W., 63
Zung Self-Rating Depression Scale, 63

Please remember that this is a library book,
and that it belongs only temporarily to each
person who uses it. Be considerate. Do
not write in this, or any, library book.